The Murder of Tutankhamen

A 3000-YEAR-OLD MURDER MYSTERY

The Murder of Tutankhamen

A 3000-YEAR-OLD MURDER MYSTERY

Bob Brier

Weidenfeld & Nicolson

LONDON

First published in Great Britain in 1998
by Weidenfeld & Nicolson

First published in the USA in 1998 by G. P. Putnam's Sons

A CIP catalogue record for this book is available
from the British Library.

ISBN 0 297 84130 0

Printed and bound in Great Britain by
Butler & Tanner Ltd, Frome and London

Weidenfeld & Nicolson

The Orion Publishing Group Ltd
Orion House
5 Upper Saint Martin's Lane
London WC2H 9EA

Acknowledgments

In Egyptology it is normal to have a team of specialists working on a single project; this book is no exception. When knowledge failed me, which was often, colleagues always were there, ready to help.

On the medical-forensic front I have been doubly fortunate in that many of the experts are close personal friends and I often called on them at strange and inconvenient times. Dr. Gerald Irwin, head of Radiology at Winthrop University Hospital, was the first to suggest that Tutankhamen may have survived for quite a while after receiving a blow to the back of the head, and remained a close consultant throughout the writing of this book. Dr. Michael R. Zimmerman, director of Clinical Laboratories, Maimonides Medical Center, Brooklyn, New York, read an early draft of the manuscript and made important suggestions about the actual cause of Tutankhamen's death following the blow. Dr. Michael Perry, chief of Trauma Radiology, School of Medicine, University of Maryland, also made important suggestions about how to determine if Tutankhamen did indeed linger before death. As always, I have benefited from discussions with Ronald Wade, director of the State Anatomy Board, Maryland. In Egypt, Dr. Fawzi Gabella, head of the Department of Anatomy, Kasr el Einy Hospital, kindly permitted me to examine the two human fetuses discovered in Tutankhamen's tomb. Dr. Nasri Iskander, Curator of Mummies, Egyptian Museum, Cairo, was most helpful in making available to me the mummy of Tutankhamen's grandfather, Amenhotep III. I must also thank my colleagues in the Paleopathology Association who were always willing to discuss the medical aspects of the case.

On the Egyptological front, my colleagues have been equally helpful. Dr. Ali Hassan, former Secretary General of the Supreme Council of Antiquities, permitted me repeated access to closed tombs. Dr. Mohamed Sallah, director of the Egyptian Museum, Cairo, kindly gave permission to examine objects in storage in the museum. In Germany, Dr. Dietrich Wildung, director of the Ägyptisches Museum in Berlin, allowed me to examine and photograph the finger ring indicating that the Vizier, Aye, married Tutankhamen's widow. I will never forget the day when Dr. Hannelore Kischkewitz, curator at the museum, placed the ring in my hand. Thanks are also due to Diana Magee of the Griffith Institute, Ashmolean Museum, Oxford, for supplying a photocopy of Percy Newberry's letter to Howard Carter describing the ring. Closer to home, I would like to thank Dr. Dorothea Arnold, curator of the Egyptian Department, Metropolitan Museum of Art, New York, for granting access to the funerary collars worn at Tutankhamen's burial meal, and for permission to reprint Harry Burton's 1920s photographs of Tutankhamen's mummy. I would also like to thank Dr. Rita Freed, curator, Department of Egyptian and Nubian Art, Museum of Fine Arts, Boston, for the discussions about what daily life at Amarna must have been like.

Special thanks are due the administrators at Long Island University, who made it possible for me to reduce my teaching load and reschedule classes so that I could research this book. My colleagues in the Philosophy Department were both supportive and understanding when their chairman was away, crawling through tombs in Egypt.

I am very appreciative of everyone at The Learning Channel. When I first agreed to make a documentary about the murder of Tutankhamen I must admit, I had misgivings—that they would ask me to say things that I didn't want to, that there would be limitations on what I did say, etc. I was delighted to discover how wrong I was. If anything, when my enthusiasm got the better of me, my director, Peter Spry-Leverton, was there saying, "Now, Bob, are you sure you can say that?" When it became crucial to see the ring in Berlin, or go back to the Egyptian Museum to check an object, The Learning Channel was always agreeable. In the end, I viewed it as private industry supporting research.

In the preparation of the manuscript I have been very fortunate. My wife, Pat Remler, spent many long hours on the computer, improving the manuscript. I may not have always been happy to hear "Brier, this doesn't make sense," but it certainly helped the book. My friend and colleague at the C. W. Post Campus of Long Island University, Dr. Hoyt Hobbs, read many drafts, made essential suggestions—both Egyptological and structural—and was a one-man support team throughout the revising of the manuscript. Also on the editorial front, Elizabeth Himelfarb was always there, ready to do what was needed. Above all, I would like to thank Liza Dawson, my editor at Putnam. I am sure she never knew what she was getting into when she first became involved in *The Murder of Tutankhamen*. It is her unerring vision of what the book should be that has made it as coherent as it is. If this book succeeds in telling the story of Tutankhamen, it is largely due to Liza's efforts.

For P. S.-L.

Tutankhamen and Ankhesenamen
Painting by Winifred Brunton

Contents

Introduction

Pointing to a cranial X ray, Dr. R. G. Harrison, head of the Anatomy Department of the University of Liverpool, was explaining a density on the film. His opinion was that it was

> within normal limits, but in fact it could have been caused by a hemorrhage under the membranes overlaying the brain in this region. And this could have been caused by a blow to the back of the head and this in turn could have been responsible for death.[1]

His patient, the pharaoh Tutankhamen, had been dead for 3,000 years.

Dr. Harrison was part of yet another television special on King Tut, another of the spasms of Tutmania since the discovery of the young king's tomb in 1922. I really wasn't that interested in Tutankhamen. I had seen his treasures in the Egyptian Museum in Cairo, knew the story of the tomb's discovery, and hadn't thought much more about him.

I don't know why I watched television's latest addition to the Tut glut, but as I was about to turn it off, it struck me that Dr. Harrison actually had something novel. On the screen came X rays of Tutankhamen's chest, the long bones of the legs and arms. I was riveted. The X rays contained new forensic evidence about Tutankhamen possibly being murdered. An idea began to percolate, an idea I couldn't dismiss.

There was such a tremendous amount of information to be found in the mummy of Tutankhamen. What if I cast a fresh eye on all of it? The mummy had never been examined with an eye to answering basic questions about a murder victim. Did he die immediately from the blow to the back of his head or did he linger? Was he robust and healthy when he died or had he been ill? What was his last meal? How soon after he ate it did he die? I knew I would probably never be granted permission to examine Tutankhamen's mummy—it was sealed in the Valley of the Kings—and the Supreme Council of Antiquities, Egypt's Antiquities Organization, wasn't about to give permission to remove Tutankhamen for an autopsy. But there were still the X rays, photographs of his internal organs, and the reports of the 1925 examination of the body. There was plenty that could be investigated. The last word on the death of Tutankhamen had not been written.

Dead bodies fascinate me, professionally speaking, of course. My specialty is mummies, with a particular interest is paleopathology—diseases of ancient man. What illnesses afflicted the ancient Egyptian? What were his chances of recovery? How did he cope with his disease? Mummies hold the answers. A modern, high-tech autopsy of an Egyptian mummy can reveal what he ate, when illness struck, and, if we're lucky, the cause of death. Beyond the information gained from mummies, there is an immediacy and intimacy when I look at the face of a mummy that I just don't get with artifacts. I am face-to-face with a person who lived 3,000 years ago.

I remember working with Michael Silva, a third-generation silversmith from Spain. We were trying to figure out exactly how ancient Egyptian craftsmen made their amulets. Using 3,000-year-old terracotta molds, Michael was going to recreate the process and make replicas of the amulets. On the back of one of the molds could be seen the ancient craftsman's thumbprint where it was pressed into the moist clay. Understandably, Michael was moved by this link with ancient humanity he was touching—a ghostly trace left by the man who held that clay 3,000 years ago. In my work, I touch the actual fingers. But other types of Egyptologists are just as passionate about their work, and many have contributed to the evidence I'm going to be presenting here.

We "Mummy People" are called to excavation sites when human remains are found. Wrapped mummies are rare. Far more often, a tomb was looted in antiquity, the mummy ripped apart by robbers searching for jewelry, and its bones scattered by the looters. Mummy People eye the tangle of bones to reconstruct what's left. The density and quality of bones reveal the social status and occupation of a person. For instance, manual labor increases muscle size which causes bone to thicken, so a single arm can tell us if the dead man was a laborer or a man of leisure. Recently I examined the remains of a queen from 4,000 years ago. I had never seen such delicate bones; it was as if she had never lifted her hand and traveled everywhere in her sedan chair. On the other end of the spectrum, the cemetery of the workmen who built the pyramids at Giza held the bodies of men who moved heavy loads. Their spines were severely deformed, especially the lumbar vertebrae which ultimately bore most of the stress. With enough experience and a dollop of imagination, a Mummy Man can discover remarkable things.

My approach to Egyptology has always been an experimental one—a hands-on approach. A couple of years ago I mummified a human cadaver in the ancient Egyptian manner. I was trying to figure out exactly how the ancient embalmers did it. Again, Michael Silva made replicas, this time of ancient bronze and copper tools, so that when I removed the internal organs I would be using the same kind of tools the ancient embalmers used. My colleague in this project was Ronald Wade, director of the Maryland State Anatomy Board. Ron was also a licensed mortician and had been interested in mummification since he was a kid—he mummified a rat for his high school science project. When we began the modern mummification and I made the incision in the deceased's abdomen, Ron and I both had goosebumps. We knew it was the first time in 2,000 years that an Egyptian style mummification had been performed.

As we removed each organ—spleen, stomach, intestines, liver—we knew this was the order in which the ancient embalmers must have removed them. It was almost as if we were watching rather than performing a mummification. Removing the brain through the nasal passage proved to be the most difficult part of the experiment. We really weren't sure we could do it. All we had to guide us were X rays of mummies.

When I presented a slide lecture of what we'd done, one colleague let out a *very* audible gasp. Several others apologized that they were so uncomfortable watching the National Geographic television special on the project that they had to turn it off. Human cadavers, even when mummified, just put some people off.

Consequently, we Mummy People have our own conference, The International Mummy Congress. (I've often thought it should be called "Mummies 'R' Us.") We come from different backgrounds. Many of us have attended medical school, and quite a few are practicing physicians who bring their skills to the study of mummies. Others are physical anthropologists with extensive training in anatomy and physiology.

A few years ago at the Mummy Congress in Cartagena, Colombia, I listened with admiration as a colleague described how she traced trade between ancient Peruvians living on the coast with those living higher up on the Altiplano. It was great detective work based on the principle "you are what you eat." Protein from fish differs from protein from vegetables or terrestrial animals, so by analyzing carbon isotopes from mummies' bones she determined their diet. Naturally the bones of populations that had lived and died on the shore indicated high marine protein, but the inland inhabitants of the Altiplano also showed marine protein, which meant they traded with the shore dwellers for dried fish.[2] If you can figure out dietary habits and trade routes from a mummy's elbow, think what you might learn from a pharaoh like Tutankhamen whose history we know.

This is why I was glued to the television when Dr. Harrison paraded his Tutankhamen X rays. Despite my original lack of interest in Tutankhamen, I now found myself thinking about revisiting the X rays to solve an ancient puzzle. Of course, information from other specialists would be crucial to my investigation, but the key to unlocking the riddle of the cause of death would be the mummy. I just wanted to see if I could figure out how he died; it was to be an academic exercise. At the time I didn't think about murder—or who the murderer might have been.

The past two years have been an adventure. Over dinners at home, and inside several Egyptian tombs, colleagues and I discussed clues, translated hieroglyphs, peered at X rays and photographs of young Tutankhamen and his relatives and argued considerably. When all the facts relating to the boy-king's untimely death were examined, after I'd looked at a frantic letter written by his widow, after I'd held an ancient ring, when I considered the violent, unstable times Tutankhamen ruled in, and examined the forensic evidence with the help of several trauma specialists, murder and intrigue emerged as the best explanation. I must admit, however, that at some point the project ceased to be academic. I was unexpectedly moved as I looked at and handled objects buried with Tutankhamen—the board games he played, the bows he used when hunting in the marshes, the fetuses miscarried by his young bride—a 3,000-year-old death became a personal tragedy. For so many years Tut, in my mind, had been synonymous with treasures and so I'd been aloof from his charms. Somewhere along the way I grew enormously fond of the boy. As the dossier of clues grew, I began to hate the prime suspect. I was delighted to discover that his portraits in the museums in Berlin and Cairo were decidedly sinister. Still, in spite of these clearly nonobjective feelings, I believe my presentation of the facts is undistorted, that murder and political intrigue provide the most reasonable explanation for a tragic event that occurred 3,000 years ago.

What follows is an account of the circumstances that led to Tutankhamen's unexpected death at the age of nineteen, the political and religious turmoil that made it possible and the bold, almost successful attempt to cover it up. It is the story of the life—and death—of Tutankhamen. An army general, high priests, and senior government officials all were involved. It was a unique and fascinating time in Egypt that led a commoner to believe that he could become a king.

Tutankhamen Time Line

Early Dynastic Period
3150–2686 B.C.—Dynasties 0–II
Narmer—First king of Egypt unites Upper and Lower Egypt

The Old Kingdom
2686–2181 B.C.—Dynasties III–VI
Zoser builds the Step Pyramid
Pharaoh Khufu builds the Great Pyramid;
Pharaoh Khephren has the Sphinx carved with his features

The First Intermediate Period
2181–2040 B.C.—Period of anarchy and chaos

Middle Kingdom
2040–1780 B.C.—Dynasty XII
Pharaoh Mentuhotep II restores order to the land

The Second Intermediate Period
1780–1570 B.C.—Period of weak rulers and invasion by the
Hyksos ruling in the north

The New Kingdom
1570–1070 B.C.—Egypt's Golden Age

Dynasty XVIII—1570–1293 B.C.
1570–1546 B.C.—Ahmose I—Hyksos are expelled from Egypt

1551–1386 B.C.—Pharaohs Tuthmosis III, Hatshepsut, and Amenhotep III increase Egypt's wealth and power

1386–1349 B.C.—Amenhotep III (Tutankhamen's grandfather)

1350–1334 B.C.—Amenhotep IV (Akhenaten) (Tutankhamen's father)

1336–1334 B.C.—Smenkare (Akhenaten's son and Tutankhamen's brother?)

1334–1325 B.C.—Tutankhamen

1325–1321 B.C.—Aye

1321–1293 B.C.—Horemheb

Dynasty XIX
1297–1212 B.C.—Ramses the Great—probable pharaoh of the Exodus

The Third Intermediate Period
1069–525 B.C.—The power of the pharaoh weakens

The Late Period
525–332 B.C.—Persian kings rule Egypt

The Graeco Roman Period
332 B.C.—Alexander the Great conquers Darius III, ruler of the Persian Empire

Egypt hails Alexander as a divine being and a savior

50 B.C.—Cleopatra VII becomes queen of Egypt

30 B.C.—Cleopatra VII dies and Egypt becomes the private estate of the Roman Emperor Augustus

The
Murder of
Tutankhamen

I

The King Must Die

Stay away from hostile people,
Keep your heart quiet among fighters.

—The scribe Ani
circa 1400 B.C.

We possess a remarkable amount of evidence about Tutankhamen—
enough to re-create what his last days may have been like. So let's
start with a fictional account, but one that is probably very close to the truth.

Sometime in late autumn, during the eighteenth year of his life,
Tutankhamen went to bed alone. Although peasant husbands and wives
slept in the same room, Egyptian pharaohs lived in separate palaces
from those of their queen and the ladies of the harem. Conjugal visits
were one thing, sleep was another. Tutankhamen reposed in a large
room, sparsely furnished—a few stools, tables, and a single wood bed
with feet shaped like lion's paws. Fish, ducks, and marsh grasses painted
on the room's plastered walls glowed spectrally in the dim light.

In the depths of this night the door slowly, silently opened, just
wide enough for a single man to creep through before closing it behind

him. Somehow he had slipped past the sentries. Had they been told to look the other way? Stealthily the night intruder made his way to Pharaoh's bed, the sound of his steps perhaps obscured by the drip, drip of a water clock. He found the king sleeping on his side, his head supported by an alabaster headrest. From under his clothes the man drew out a heavy object, possibly an Egyptian mace that joined a solid three-inch stone to the end of a substantial two-foot stick. After a single deep breath, he swung the heavy object at Tutankhamen's skull.

Waiting just a moment for the sudden sound in the night to be forgotten, the intruder retraced his steps through the Royal Bedchamber, out the door, and stole through the palace to the safety of night.

The next morning servants discovered the unconscious, but not yet dead, pharaoh and quickly summoned the vizier, Aye, and Tutankhamen's wife, Ankhesenamen. A priest-physician skilled in head injuries was ordered from the temple. The physician has seen many trauma injuries. Blocks of stone sometime fell on workmen during construction; infantrymen received blows to the head. But this was the pharaoh; the physician must be very careful what he does and says. He instructed his assistant to shave Pharaoh's head so a proper diagnosis could be made. As the bronze blade removed the fine dark hair, the surgeon was already thinking about the consequences of treatment—both for the pharaoh and for his own career. If he took decisive action and Tutankhamen died, he could be blamed. Now the head was shaved, revealing one wound, a large, warm swollen mass. It was in an unusual place for such an injury, at the back of the head where the neck joins the skull. The great surgical papyrus did not describe how to treat such an injury.

The blow has caused unconsciousness, but only a slight fracture to the skull. There are no bone fragments that must be removed. Relieved, the surgeon replaces his bronze probe and tweezers in their wooden case. Still, blood is oozing from the pharaoh's nostrils, a sign that the meninges, the skin enclosing the brain, has been damaged. Aye, the prime minister, stands silently next to the bed, calm, weighing what the pharaoh's death will mean to Egypt and himself. Ankhesenamen, frightened, looks to the physician for his prognosis. He has been trained to give one of three responses: 1) "this is an ailment which I will treat," 2) "this is an ailment with which I will contend," and 3) "this is an ailment not to be treated."[1] If he says the ailment can be treated, he implies that the treatment will be successful. If he instead says he will merely contend with it, he implies an uncertain outcome.

The physician quickly evaluates the situation. With no splinters to remove, no bones to set, there was little he could do physically for the king. To say that he will treat the ailment asserts that the king will survive, and of this he is not sure. Should Tutankhamen die, the physician will be blamed. There are only two real alternatives, and given the importance of the patient, it is safer to say that this is an illness not to be treated. Better to hand the fate of the king over to the gods.

The predicament faced by this priest-physician was no different from modern physicians called to treat a famous patient. Doctors in emergency rooms around the world have observed and named it the "famous-patient syndrome." When confronted with a famous patient, medical personnel are afraid to act quickly, to do instinctively what they have been trained to do. Junior staff members defer to senior staff members, discussions take place before actions are taken. Tutankhamen was probably not the first ruler to suffer the consequences of his exalted position, and he was certainly not the last.

Abraham Lincoln may have died because of his fame. After the President was shot in the head, the young surgeon attending him at Ford's Theater did everything right. He examined the entry hole with his finger, determined there was no exit hole, and let the president rest. Then the Surgeon General was summoned, while President Lincoln was removed to a nearby boardinghouse. The Surgeon General was a bureaucrat who had not treated a patient for years, but he immediately took control of Lincoln's treatment. He inserted a probe into the entry hole and slid it in, almost up to Lincoln's eyes. The Surgeon General did not know that the latest medical wisdom, taught in medical schools, was not to probe—the brain is so soft you can't tell if you are following the path of the bullet or causing additional damage. Recent reevaluation of the case suggests that Lincoln might have survived with the bullet lodged in his brain. He was a victim of famous-patient syndrome.

So the surgeon-priest turned to Ankhesenamen and spoke the very words she feared: "This is an ailment not to be treated." As Ankhesenamen sobbed, the surgeon's assistant was instructed to clear the king's nostrils of blood. The pharaoh breathed more easily now, lying peacefully on his low bed. Magician-healers would be called to assist the king.

By afternoon the healers had gathered the ingredients for their poultice: equal parts of berry of coriander, berry of the poppy plant, wormwood, berry of the *sames*-plant, berry of the juniper plant. Mixed with honey, it formed a paste that they spread on the wound and covered with a square of finely woven linen on which had been drawn the Eye-of-Horus symbol. Horus the falcon god had lost his eye in the battle with Seth, but it was magically regenerated by Toth, god of magic. The markings around a falcon's eye became a sign for healing.

For the first few days there was optimism. Tutankhamen briefly regained consciousness and was able to eat. Ankhesenamen brought him chopped figs mixed with eggs because eggs had regenerative properties. The magician-healers placed "flour of egg"—powdered egg shells—in Tutankhamen's wine, so the damaged skull would knit smooth, like an eggshell.[2] Yet, as days became weeks, the pharaoh, drifting in and out of consciousness, weakened. His vision blurred and the pain in his head became almost unbearable, as if something were pressing on every part of his skull. To dull the pain, Ankhesenamen brought more and more of his favorite wine, made from grapes from his own vineyards. When winter came, Tutankhamen lapsed into final unconsciousness and could receive tiny amounts of wine through a straw only with difficulty.

The wailing started with Ankhesenamen, who was with Tutankhamen when he died, spread through the female servants in the palace, then across the river to Thebes, uniting rich and poor in the primal ritual mourning cry that told Osiris, god of the dead, to expect another Westerner. Within a few hours of the shock, Aye began the plans to prepare Tutankhamen's burial.

Our account above of Tutankhamen's death is fiction, but is based on evidence that has survived 3,300 years since his death. We are in an even better position to reconstruct his burial.

The tomb that Tutankhamen had been preparing for himself, next to his grandfather's in the western spur of the Valley of the Kings, was far short of completion when the boy-king died. There was, however, a nearly complete tomb in the main valley that had not been used. Originally intended for a private person, a rare but not unprecedented honor, Aye decided to appropriate this small tomb for his pharaoh. Artists commenced painting appropriate scenes on the walls immediately; there was no time to carve the scenes. As the tomb was being readied, embalmers prepared Tutankhamen's body for eternity.

Mummification was primarily a physical process, but every stage of the embalming was accompanied by religious rituals. The most important step was to remove all moisture from the body as quickly as possible. Bacteria need moisture to destroy tissue; if there is no water, the body will not decay.

Both the brain and the internal organs are extremely moist, so to avoid putrefaction, they had to be removed soon after death. When Tutankhamen's body was brought to the royal embalmers, it was placed on an alabaster mummification table, inclined so that as work proceeded on the body, the fluids would run off into a basin below. The brain was removed by inserting a long wire into the nostril, breaking through the ethmoid bone into the cranium. The wire was then rotated—used as a whisk—to break down the brain tissue into a semi-liquid state that would drain out through the nostrils when the body was turned upside down. The embalmers preserved almost every part of the body so Tutankhamen would be complete when he resurrected in the next world. However, they discarded the brain, unaware of its function. Egyptians believed that you thought with your heart, not your brain, since it is the heart that beats rapidly when someone is excited, not the brain. In the Bible when pharaoh stubbornly refused to let the Israelites go, we are told "pharaoh's heart was hardened."

After Tutankhamen's brain was removed and discarded, an incision was made in the lower left side of his abdomen so the internal organs could be reached. The stomach, liver, intestines, and kidneys were carefully removed and placed in shallow bowls. Later the desiccated organs were deposited in four miniature gold coffins in preparation for the day the king would resurrect in the next world. Only his heart was left in the body, so that he would be able to remember and recite the magic spells that would reanimate his corpse.

Even after the brain and internal organs were removed, considerable moisture still remained locked in the body's soft tissues. To eliminate this, the embalmers covered Tutankhamen's body with natron, a naturally occurring compound of sodium carbonate, sodium bicarbonate, and sodium chloride—basically baking soda and salt. After the body had rested for thirty-five days in natron almost all its water had been leached out. The mummy now weighed less than fifty pounds and was ready for wrapping. As each bandage was applied, a priest wearing the mask of Anubis the jackal, the god of embalming, read magical spells that would ensure Tutankhamen's preservation and resurrection. The priests placed more than one hundred and fifty pieces of jewelry and magical amulets within the linen bandages to ensure the boy-king's immortality.

As the embalmers practiced their art, master craftsmen throughout the land worked to prepare his funerary goods. There were wooden shrines to be carved and gilded, a gold mask and coffins to be fashioned, furniture, linens, clothing, and jewelry to be assembled. Preparation of the ushabtis figures alone was a major undertaking. These hundreds of little servant figurines were expected to magically come alive and serve Tutankhamen in the next world, each one an individual sculpture in wood or stone carved in the likeness of Tutankhamen (fig. 20). The figures were mummiform in shape, the image of Osiris, the god of the dead. Because Egypt was an agrarian society, the work in the next world would be farming, so the ushabtis held agricultural implements in their hands. Tutankhamen had 413 ushabtis, 365 workers, one for each day of the year, 36 overseers—one for each gang of 10 workers—and an additional twelve monthly overseers.[3] There must have been panic in the workshops of Egypt as craftsmen worked in teams through the night to prepare for the burial of the pharaoh.

Maya, the treasurer, commissioned a beautiful miniature wooden sculpture of Tutankhamen on a funerary couch holding a tiny gold crook and flail, so the gods would know he was a great king. Along the side of the sculpture an inscription proclaimed Maya's devotion to his young pharaoh: "Made by the servant who is beneficial to his lord, doing what he says, who does not allow anything to go wrong, whose face is cheerful when he does it with a loving heart as a thing profitable to his lord."[4]

At some point in the preparation of Tutankhamen's funerary goods, time ran out. The seventy days had elapsed, the embalmers' work and all the coffins were complete, but other ritual objects simply couldn't be finished on time. So the tomb of Tutankhamen's brother, Smenkare, was opened and the miniature coffins that held his internal organs were reused for Tutankhamen. Inside each coffin, inscribed in gold, is a prayer from the *Book of the Dead,* a collection of about 200 spells, incantations, prayers, and hymns. The prayers inside refer to Tutankhamen, but beneath his cartouche are traces of the name Smenkare, his brother.

Seventy days after Tutankhamen's death, the funeral procession gathered on the west bank of Thebes to conduct his mummy to its house of eternity. The body was placed on a sled and a wooden shrine draped with garlands was placed over it. Across the top of the shrine two rows of beautifully carved and painted wooden cobras reared up to protect Tutankhamen on his journey to the netherworld. The sled was pulled by the palace officials. Pentu and Usermont, the ministers of Upper and Lower Egypt, wore the distinctive robes of their office, and were joined by ten other officials, all wearing white mourning bands around their heads. As the procession slowly made its way over the barren land toward the Valley of the Kings, the women wailed, tore their garments, and threw sand on their heads in the traditional gestures of mourning. Among them, but feeling very alone, was Ankhesenamen.

When the pallbearers reached the tomb, the procession paused. In the course of wrapping the mummy Tutankhamen's mouth and nose had been covered. Now, before he entered the tomb for eternity, a ceremony was performed to magically open his mouth so Tutankhamen would be able to breathe and say the magical spells of the *Book of the Dead*. The pallbearers, joined by the priests and members of the funeral procession, performed the opening-of-the-mouth ceremony for Tutankhamen.

More a mystery play than a religious ritual, a dozen participants were required for the performance.[5] The officiating priest held a papyrus describing how things should proceed. A small group of the officials played roles of the guards of Horus, who would help Tutankhamen be resurrected like Osiris in the next world. The area in front of the tomb where the play was to be performed was purified with water from four different vases, each representing one of the four corners of the earth. Four burners holding incense were lit, and various gods were invoked. A ritual slaughter was performed, commemorating the battle in which Horus avenged Osiris's death.

In the myth, Seth's conspirators, after dismembering Osiris's corpse, attempted to escape Horus by changing into various animals, but Horus caught them and cut off their heads. Thus, at the opening-of-the-mouth ceremony various animals were ritually killed—two bulls (one for the south and one for the north), gazelles, and ducks. When the bull of the south was slaughtered, one of the legs was cut off and, along with the heart, offered to the mummy. By sympathetic magic, Tutankhamen became Osiris: The sacrificial killing of the animals represented the conspirators who tried but failed to destroy the body of Osiris, and assured that the body of Tutankhamen would remain safe from such an attack. The slaughtered animals provided food for Tutankhamen's long journey.

The high priest touched the mouth of the mummy with the leg of the bull, and then an assistant came forward with a ritual instrument shaped like an adze. Touching the mouth of the mummy with this implement, the priest recited:

Thy mouth was closed, but I have set in order for thee thy mouth and thy teeth. I open for thee thy mouth, I open for thee thy two eyes. I have opened thy mouth with the instrument of Anubis, with the iron implement with which the mouths of the gods were opened. Horus, open the mouth! Horus, open the mouth! Horus hath opened the mouth of the dead, as he in times of old opened the mouth of Osiris with the iron, which came forth from Set, with the iron instrument with which he opened the mouths of the gods. He hath opened thy mouth with it. The deceased shall walk and speak, and his body shall be with the great company of all gods in the Great House of the Aged One in Annu, and he shall receive the ureret crown from Horus, the lord of mankind.[6]

While this ritual was being performed, Tutankhamen's body was resting inside the shrine on the sled, so a statue of Tutankhamen—one of the two life-sized guardian statues almost exactly the height of Tutankhamen—was used instead.

At the conclusion of the ritual, the priest raised the adze and touched it to Tutankhamen's mouth, uttering the spell that would give the young king breath in the next world. *"You are young again, you live again, you are young again, you live again, forever."* He was now ready for immortality.

The pallbearers carried the body of Tutankhamen-Osiris—he was now a Westerner like Osiris—down the thirteen steps leading to the tomb. At the bottom they turned right toward the burial chamber. On their left side they could see three five-foot-high ceremonial beds on which various rituals had been performed for Tutankhamen during the seventy days of mummification. At the corners of the head end of one bed were two beautifully carved hippopotamus heads covered in gold, the second bore the head of a cow with a sun disk between its horns, the third lion heads. These were the gods who controlled whether Tutankhamen could enter the next world. As the pallbearers slowly carried the mummy to the burial chamber, they took quick sideways glances, trying to take it all in—the burial treasures of a king.

Waiting for them in the burial chamber was a rectangular stone sarcophagus containing three coffins, one inside the other like Russian dolls. Their lids lay on the floor. The pharaoh was placed inside the innermost one. While the lector priest recited prayers, unguents were poured on the body to perfume Tutankhamen's way to the next world. Then the lid of the innermost coffin was placed over Tutankhamen, sending him into darkness, the last time anyone would see his face for thirty-three centuries. The lid to the middle coffin was placed on its lower half, and finally the outermost coffin lid was lowered into place. Each coffin bore a likeness of the boy-king. Once the final lid was in position, Ankhesenamen placed a miniature wreath—the "Wreath of Victory"—around the sculpted vulture and cobra protecting her husband's forehead. The tiny wreath commemorated the god Osiris's victory over his enemies. As the wreath was positioned, a priest recited:

> Thy father Atum binds for thee this beautiful wreath of vindication on this thy brow. Live, beloved of the gods, mayest thou live forever.[7]

With that, heavy the heavy stone lid of the sarcophagus was slid into place. The sad party of mourners walked slowly up the steps of the tomb into the blinding sunlight. As soon as the mourners left the tomb, a team of workmen hurried into the burial chamber to assemble the panels of three nested shrines around the sarcophagus, as an overseer watched. When their work was completed, they were replaced by masons who constructed a plaster wall sealing the burial chamber from the rest of the tomb. The statue used for the opening-of-the-mouth ceremony and its twin were placed in front of the wall, guarding their king. The last objects for the tomb—chariots, chests of linen, ebony foot stools—were quickly carried into the antechamber by servants, watched all the while, lest the pharaoh's treasures be stolen from him. Now the antechamber was sealed by the masons, the wet plaster stamped with the seal of the Royal Necropolis, a jackal over nine bound captives, the nine traditional enemies of Egypt. Even in death, Tutankhamen was victorious.

Ankhesenamen's long day was not yet over. A ritual last meal in honor of Tutankhamen's victory over death had to be eaten at the entrance to the tomb. The participants wore brightly colored pectorals made of flowers and beads sewn onto a papyrus collar (fig. 16). Normally the meal was eaten by the family of the deceased, but in this instance Ankhesenamen, Tutankhamen's last living relative, was joined by the palace officials—Pentu, Usermont, Aye, Aye's wife, Tey, and General Horemheb. The servants brought a banquet of sheep, four different kinds of duck, three different kinds of geese, all washed down by considerable quantities of wine poured from an elegant long-necked vase painted with blue lotus petals. But none present were thinking about the meal. They pondered their futures. Who could have known that two of the men eating together would become kings of Egypt, and, within a very short while, one of the two women would be dead.

When the meal was completed, servants ritually broke the dishes, cups, and beautiful wine jar, and placed the fragments, along with the bones of the meat and fowl, inside large storage jars. They then swept the area with brooms and placed the brooms in the jars. The jars were sealed, carried to a nearby pit that had been dug, and buried. The funeral was over.

We actually have the broken dishes, collars, and brooms from the last meal. They are in the Metropolitan Museum of Art in New York. There is indeed a surgical papyrus that instructs physicians whom to treat and whom not. Painted on Tutankhamen's tomb wall are scenes of the funeral procession and the opening-of-the-mouth ceremony. Of course, we have the treasures from Tutankhamen's tomb, but we also have X rays of his skull.

But before we can get to the evidence of his murder, we must first understand what brought him to this moment. We must understand the evolution of Egyptian society, religion and its pharoahs. The next chapter is Egypt 101—a crash course in the history of Egypt that made the murder of a pharaoh possible. Stick with it and you will see the forces develop that bent Egypt until it snapped.

2

Egypt Before Tutankhamen

The wealth of an army is its leader.

—*Instruction of Ankhsheshonq*
circa 300 B.C.

Two thousand years before Tutankhamen was born, three distinct forces were set in motion that would determine the course of Egypt's social organization and which would ultimately lead to his death. Egypt would get its first king, a national military would be established, and a priesthood would develop. Over the centuries these power bases grew strong and rich; they became so essential to Egyptian society that to change any one of them could bring disaster. Thus for centuries and centuries Egypt presented a seemingly static face to the ancient world. Internally Egypt was a wealthy, well-oiled machine, with each of the three powers supporting the others. Tutankhamen had the unfortunate distinction of being alive when there was a dramatic, revolutionary effort to change all three simultaneously. To understand how shockingly different the times Tut grew up in were, we first have to understand how and why the country had enjoyed such an unparalleled period of stability. Before we get to play detective, we have to do our history lessons.

EGYPT BEFORE KINGSHIP

The concept of a pharaoh in many ways defines our notion of ancient Egypt, but of course Egypt did not always have a king. Let's look back to Egypt around 4000 B.C. when the verdant Nile Valley was dotted with small villages stretching for a thousand miles along the Nile. We don't have written records from this period, but there seem to have been two independent political entities, Upper and Lower Egypt, each governed by its own chieftain. All indications are that life along the Nile was safe and satisfying, partly because Egypt was relatively inaccessible to the rest of the world and thus had few marauding enemies to fear and partly because the river provided economic bounty.

Each year the Nile overflowed its banks, depositing fresh rich topsoil on the flat plains that spread to either side of the river, enabling Egypt to grow an abundance and variety of crops. Other countries relied on unpredictable rain that only during certain seasons fell in sufficient quantity to irrigate fields. Even if rainfall were spread perfectly throughout the year, fields would soon be exhausted of nutrients if they were planted more than once a year. Egypt's great good fortune was to have a river that renewed the topsoil annually and flowed in sufficient volume to water the crops. Every year Egypt harvested a variety of crops, while other countries thanked the gods when when they produced one. No wonder the ancient Greek traveler Herodotus called Egypt the "Gift of the Nile."

The annual inundation amazed the Egyptians, who had no explanation for its sudden great growth, nor the fact that its color changed to red and then to green. It was a natural occurrence, of course, but it must have provided the equivalent mystery and pyrotechnics of a Las Vegas magic show. Today we know that torrential spring rains in Ethiopia, far south of Egypt, ran off granite bedrock to swell the Nile. The oversized

Nile rushed north from sub-Saharan Africa, arriving in Egypt almost twenty feet above its normal level. It was red in color from all the runoff soil suspended in the water, but as it overflowed and the soil settled, its color changed to the green of the floating vegetation. The annual show provided by the Nile was surpassed only by the dazzling daily performance put on by the sun. Each day it rose in the east, traveled across a cloudless, jewel-like sky, and descended in a fireball of colors in the west, constant and predictable, like the Nile.

The population of the Nile Valley was probably less than a million. Although Egypt was a vast country, 95 percent of the population lived on the 5 percent of the land that hugs the Nile. The Nile was the heart of the country—even the seasons of the year were determined by the Nile. Our 365-day calendar comes from the Egyptians, but they counted only three seasons: 1) *Inundation,* when the Nile overflowed and flooded the land; 2) *Emergence,* when the waters receded; and 3) *Summer,* the dry season. Each season had four months of thirty days each. At the end of the year, "5 extra days" were added to make 365 days in the year. Inundation was Egypt's most unusual season for it was a time for relaxing—the fields were underwater and little agricultural work could be done. During these weeks, plows and implements were repaired, future crops were discussed, and plans for the future were made. Emergence was the season for planting, in Summer crops were harvested.

The food staple of the farmer was bread and beer, a phrase that became synonymous with "food"—our "meat and potatoes." A common funerary prayer begins, "May the king make an offering to Osiris, Lord of the West. May he give bread and beer, cattle, geese, and oxen and all things good and pure upon which the gods live." The long growing season allowed the Egyptians to raise a variety of crops—the most important being emer (wheat) and onions. Meat was reserved for the upper classes, but the farmers had fish from the Nile and perch was the favorite, but whatever the Egyptians ate, it was accompanied by onions. Year after year Egypt's crops were reassuringly plentiful and inevitably a sense of security arose along the banks of the Nile, a feeling that nature and the world would not present any horrifying surprises.

This feeling was encouraged by Egypt's geographical isolation from her neighbors. To the west of Egypt spread endless miles of desert. In order for ancient peoples to cross, wells had to be dug, provisions stored; in all, tremendous organization and careful planning were required. From Libya, for example, the journey to Egypt would be across more than four hundred miles of arid shale. Six centuries after Tutankhamen, when the mighty Persian king Cambyses sent an army of 20,000 men across this wilderness, they disappeared without a trace.

Egypt is bordered by the Red Sea on the east, backed by one hundred miles of inhospitable sand. (Incidentally, the camel, "the ship of the desert," did not arrive in Egypt until the Roman occupation, more than a thousand years after Tutankhamen.) To the north, hundreds of miles of the Mediterranean formed a third natural barrier, even if it was more psychological than real. Egyptians had developed their navigational skills on the smooth-flowing Nile, and they remained river sailors, not tempted by the lure and dangers of the open sea. The south offered a river-borne ingress into Egypt, for the Nile stretched far below Egypt's southern border. Since the current flows from south to north and the prevailing winds are from north to south, travel in either direction was easy. Going north, sailors floated with the current, steering with oars; for the southward journey they hoisted sails and followed the wind. Boat travel was easy except at Egypt's southern border where huge river boulders create a cataract. Although it was possible to travel south past this barrier, navigation was quite difficult and laborious. The crew had to haul the boats out of the river and drag them around the boulders or use ropes to guide them through the rapids. It was not an easy journey.

In later centuries, Egyptians would wander to other lands and would bring back riches, but it was always clear to them that they were living in paradise, that it existed in this time, in this place, and nowhere else in the world.

KINGSHIP COMES TO EGYPT

Ancient Egyptians revered their pharaoh, not simply as a leader, but as the embodiment of the country itself. Egypt's first pharaoh, Narmer, early in the third millennium B.C., created a nation from two independent states. Ever after, Egyptians referred to their country as "The Two Lands" whose continued unification depended entirely on the pharaoh.

The Narmer Palette, one of the most significant objects in all the priceless collection of Cairo's Egyptian Museum, depicts Narmer's conquest that resulted in the unification of Egypt and celebrates the importance of this achievement.

Nearly three feet high and carved from a slab of stone, the mammoth Narmer Palette introduces Egypt's first pharaoh, King Narmer. From early times Egyptians had used small slate palettes to grind ingredients for eye paints (a little bit of fat, a little pulverized malachite and you had green eye shadow). To commemorate important events, large ceremonial palattes were carved.

On one side of the palette King Narmer is shown wearing the traditional white crown of Upper Egypt as he strikes his enemy, presumably the ruler from the north, whom he grasps by the hair. The other side shows him walking in a procession and wearing the red crown of Lower Egypt (the north). He is now king of both the north and the south, the first king of the First Dynasty. This unification took place around 3200 B.C., nearly 2,000 years before Tutankhamen became King of Upper and Lower Egypt, but when the boy-king ascended to the throne, the concept of kingship was virtually unchanged since the time of King Narmer. Egypt would for the next 3,000 years be ruled by kings with absolute power, who were accepted as gods on earth and personally responsible for Egypt's well-being. Each pharaoh was pope, president, king, and commander-in-chief—all in one.

Soon after Narmer unified the northern and southern territories, the country's isolationism ended; Egypt became an aggressive international force led by the pharaoh. Egyptian armies ventured outside the borders of Egypt in search of lands to conquer and of gold to claim.

RISE OF THE MILITARY

There are no extant military records from the first few centuries after Narmer, but the origins of Egypt's army are to be found in this period.[1] With a centralized government under a single king the organization of an army was inevitable. A pottery fragment inscribed with Narmer's name found at Tell El-Mayshieh in southern Palestine suggests Narmer may even have ventured outside of Egypt with his army.[2] We do not know how large these early armies were, but excavations have shown that their main weapons were the mace, spear, battle ax, and dagger. Warfare in the ancient world was mostly hand-to-hand combat, soldiers were face-to-face with the enemy they killed. In today's military, generals make decisions at a distance, which are then carried out by the troops on the battlefield. In ancient warfare the generals were in the front lines, leading by example. The military man soon became intimately acquainted with killing.

Egypt could support an army because of the Nile. With the ability to grow more food than a farmer's family could consume, specialization of work developed among the Nile Valley dwellers and so a professional standing army could be maintained. As the army grew bolder, its expeditions moved further and further from Egypt's borders. Seven centuries after Narmer, the pharaoh Sneferu was able to boast that he had subdued the Bedouin tribes and made the Sinai safe for his turquoise miners.

With kingship there also came a desire and ability to focus national attention on huge projects such as irrigation canals. Digging and dredging irrigation canals required the organization of gangs of men working toward a common goal, possible only after central organization and authority were in place. Men could be coordinated to dredge and channel, coaxing flood waters further and further inland. This created more arable land, raising agricultural productivity ever higher.

Central coordination also produced, as a side effect, the beginnings of astronomy. Advance warning before the floods arrived was required to allow the time necessary to refurbish increasingly extensive canal systems. Timing was critical. Fix the old canals too soon and the hot Egyptian sun would turn them to dust blown away by the wind; fix them too late and the floods would arrive before the system was finished. Fortunately, Nile inundations were quite regular, occurring within the same five- or ten-day period each year. Needing to know when that time of year was coming before it happened prompted astronomer priests to observe the heavens and learn how to predict the time of the year from the stars, one of the earliest examples of serious astronomy. Mathematics, too, had to be improved to accurately measure fields whose boundaries were washed away each year by the Nile.

So fundamental were the pharaohs to Egyptian society that ancient Egyptians reckoned their history, not as a sequence of events, but as a series of reigns of kings during which events occurred. Instead of numbering years consecutively—as our 1999 follows 1998—when a new king was crowned, a new calendar began with day 1, year 1 of the reign of King X. If one king died, the next king started another calendar: day 1, year 1, King Y. This has proven a great help to modern Egyptologists in determining the length of each pharaoh's reign. But it also shows that ancient Egyptians saw no unity, even of time, without their pharaoh.

In addition to placing all central authority solely with their pharaoh, they viewed him as a god necessary for their safety. The pharaoh's protection is described in one of the oldest myths of Egypt. The story tells how the god Re once appeared on Earth in human form to rule as the original pharaoh. During his reign the country flourished as a kind of Eden, without want, suffering, or disease. Re's subjects lived such carefree lives that they gradually forgot to pay him homage and respect for the paradise he created. This angered Re, who created a blood-thirsty demon in the form of the lioness Sekhmet and loosed her on his errant subjects to teach them a lesson they would not soon forget. When she wantonly slaughtered hundreds of people, the frightened survivors became respectful again. But crazed by all the blood, Sekhmet nonetheless continued killing, despite Re's order that she stop. Re called all the gods together to agree to a scheme to save humnanity. Sending some to produce vast quantities of beer and others for red dye to color it, he ordered that the mixture be spread over the ground. When Sekhmet arrived the next day to begin her round of slaying, she saw the beer and, thinking it was blood, drank until she fell, intoxicated, into a deep sleep. Thus did Re, the pharaoh's prototype, save humanity. In time, however, Re grew weak and returned to the netherworld, sending his son Horus, the falcon, to rule in his place.

To his subjects, pharaoh was Horus incarnate, and each ruler took as one of his names "The Horus so-and-so." Through his father Re, Pharaoh preserved the human race, but he also had the power to destroy it. The message was understood by every subject—only by obeying and honoring Pharaoh would unimaginable evils be kept at bay. As long as Egyptians believed that, it would be hard to imagine anyone lifting a hand against a pharaoh.

THE AGE OF THE PYRAMIDS

The pyramids are the ultimate testament to just how important the concept of kingship was in ancient Egypt. Five hundred years after Narmer's unification of Egypt, the pharaoh was stronger and more powerful than any other ruler on earth. Understood to be a living god, the pharaoh required a resting place for eternity that had to be a monument worthy of a god. When the pharaoh's days on earth were over, his mummy was placed in his pyramid till the time he would ascend to the heavens. Built more than a thousand years before Tutankhamen, the pyramids reflected the role of kingship in Egypt, a role Tutankhamen would have to assume as a boy.

As a kid, I watched Charlton Heston on television and wondered about the slaves hauling huge blocks while a cruel overseer whipped them mercilessly. I always wondered why all the slaves didn't jump the overseer; they certainly had him outnumbered. The answer is that such a scene never happened. The pyramids were built with free labor, paid for by the pharaoh. When Menachem Begin, the Prime Minister of Israel, visited Egypt, he mentioned that his ancestors built the pyramids. He had it all wrong. Not only were they not built by slaves, the pyramids were completed more than a thousand years before Moses and the Israelites were in Egypt. The pyramids were built at the beginning of Egypt's long history; they were ancient by the time of Tutankhamen. Even as a young nation, Egypt was very sure of itself. Think about what was involved in pyramid building.

There are more than seventy pyramids in Egypt, and to construct something like the Great Pyramid at Giza thousands of laborers had to be coordinated in teams that worked for twenty years on one structure. Quarrymen cut and shaped 2½ million blocks of limestone, each weighing an average of five tons. Transportation men floated the blocks across the Nile from the quarry to Giza. When the blocks were off-loaded from the barges they were pulled on wooden sleds by gangs of workers to their final position in the pyramid. All of this was without the use of the wheel, which would sink into the sand under heavy loads. To build the Great Pyramid, a new block was put into place an average of every three minutes, day, and night, for twenty years. Today, it is difficult to imagine a single building project of such enormity continuing for twenty years. Only a society of great wealth and stability led by an absolute ruler could sustain such a project. The pharaoh's word was law; so it was said, so it was done.

With a divine king and a strong military, two of the three forces that would lead to Tutankhamen's death were in motion. It is now time to talk about the third force, religion. No other people have ever been so focused on religion and have had such concern with life after death as the ancient Egyptians. This too may result from Egypt's unique geography.

During prehistoric times Egyptians were buried in sandpits in the desert, cultivated land being too precious to use for cemeteries. This was fortunate, since the moisture and high mineral content of the soil would have destroyed cadavers. On the other hand, simple desert burials, with no coffins enclosing the deceased, allowed hot, dry sand to quickly dehydrate bodies. Without moisture bacteria do not act on soft tissue, so Egypt's dead were naturally preserved.

Because these graves were shallow, occasionally the sand would blow away, revealing a dead body that had retained its flesh and hair—a still recognizable individual. Whether such events gave rise to the idea of eternal life or whether they merely reinforced an existing religious belief in life after death, we will probably never know, but what is clear is that their own eyes told the ancient Egyptians that a dead person did not vanish from existence altogether.

Soon after Narmer, Egyptian burials grew more complex. Shallow pits became brick-lined tombs; bodies were covered with animal skins and placed upon woven mats. As time passed, the brick structures became more elaborate depending on the social status and wealth of the deceased. The woven mats were extended to cover the whole body like a crude coffin. But these early funerary practices threatened the natural preservative process. All these changes removed the bodies from the natural drying process in the hot sand. The longer body fluids are retained the more its soft tissue decomposes. Ironically, the tombs intended to preserve the bodies led to their destruction, forcing the Egyptians to devise means of artificially preserving the dead—mummification.

Egyptian religion required mummification. Contrary to what many modern occultists claim, the ancient Egyptians did not believe in reincarnation—the idea that a soul returns to earth after a person dies to inhabit a different body, and that this cycle of birth, death, and rebirth is repeated many times. Mummification would not have been necessary had the Egyptians been reincarnationists; because the soul of the deceased could inhabit a new body, it wouldn't need the old one. The ancient Egyptians believed in *resurrection*—the belief that people exist just once, and that their earthly bodies would reanimate, would get up and go again, in the afterworld. It was a belief that would dominate Egyptian society for thousands of years and remain virtually intact for centuries after Tutankhamen.

To understand the nuts and bolts of the ancient religion and the belief in life after death, you have to understand Egypt's oldest myth: the story of Isis and Osiris. Isis and Osiris were both brother and sister and husband and wife. Osiris brought civilization to Egypt, introducing farming and cattle-raising, thus freeing the early inhabitants of the Nile Valley from misery. Then Osiris left Egypt to bring civilization to the rest of the world, leaving Isis, the powerful goddess of magic, to keep their evil brother Seth in check.

Upon Osiris's return, Seth obtained his brother's exact bodily measurements by trickery, and constructed a wooden chest to fit him precisely. During a banquet Seth offered the magnificent chest as a gift to whoever could fit into it, but guest after guest tried and failed. Of course it fit Osiris, but as soon as he settled inside the chest, Seth sealed the chest, poured molten lead over it and threw the chest into the Nile where Osiris died. A violent storm subsequently carried the chest to Byblos, in Lebanon, where it washed up in the branches of a tree. In time the tree grew to extraordinary size, its trunk enveloping both the chest and Osiris inside it. In the course of building his palace, the king of Byblos cut down the tree for one of the pillars

As soon as Isis learned what had happened to her husband (don't ask how, it's a *very* long story), she set out to recover his body. Enlisting the aid of the queen of Byblos, Isis had the pillar cut open so she could recover the body and bring it back to Egypt for proper burial. When the body was returned to Egypt, Seth discovered it, hacked it into fourteen pieces, and scattered them throughout Egypt. Isis eventually recovered every piece, except one, the phallus, which had been thrown into the Nile and eaten by fish. She reassembled her deceased husband, fashioned an artificial phallus for him. Transforming herself into a bird, she hovered over Osiris's body, and brought him back to life by reciting magical words. And shortly thereafter, their son Horus, the falcon-headed god, was born. (Yes, this is the same Horus as in the Re myth; the Egyptians didn't seem to notice or care that he had two fathers.)

Almost all of Egypt's funerary beliefs are derived from this myth. Isis's search for all the pieces of her deceased husband's body and the fashioning of an artificial phallus emphasize the importance of an intact body. Isis hovered over a *complete* body. Osiris retains the same body he had inhabited while alive. Finally, and most important, she speaks the proper words and he is resurrected. Mummification thus becomes essential to immortality; the body must be preserved for the afterlife and the proper rituals performed. The chest that exactly fit Osiris was the precursor of the anthropoid coffin, shaped like the deceased and intended to protect his body.

Myths furnish insights into the nature of society, and the Isis and Osiris myth not only tells us about immortality but also suggests that there is justice in the world. In the story's final twist, Horus the falcon god fights an elemental battle to avenge the death of his father, and defeats his uncle Seth.

It is not surprising that the world's first concept of justice comes out of Egypt. To have justice, there must be a sense of order, a belief that there are rules governing behavior. This sense of order permeates every aspect of Egyptian society. The Egyptian believed that when he died he would be called upon to appear in the Hall of the Double Truth, a court presided over by the gods of Egypt. There he would make his pleas as to why he should be admitted to the next world. If found worthy, he was declared "true of voice." In a second judging his heart would be placed on one side of a balance scale and on the other side a feather, the hieroglyphic symbol for the Egyptian word "maat"—truth, divine order. If the scales balanced and his heart was as light as the feather, uncluttered with evil deeds, he could proceed to the netherworld. If his heart was found to be heavy with evil, it was thrown to a creature with the body of a crocodile and the head of a hippopotamus who was called the "devourer of hearts." Once the creature ate your heart you ceased to exist. When western legal systems adopted a symbol of justice, it was the balance scale of the Egyptians. In the myth of Osiris, Seth who represents evil poses a constant threat to divine order because he was not killed in the battle, he was merely defeated. So Egypt had to remain ever vigilant;

evil emanating from Seth was always lurking, waiting to upset "maat," divine order.

Ultimately it was the pharaoh's responsibility to establish and maintain divine order in the land, and once each year the king sailed up the Nile on his royal barge and took part in a kind of mystery play that ensured that good would triumph over evil throughout the land. The play, based on the myth of Osiris, is the oldest written drama in the world. Inscribed on the walls of the Horus Temple at Edfu in the south of Egypt, it is called "The Triumph of Horus." Pharaoh played the part of Horus.

THE PRIESTHOOD

As Egypt grew, the pharaoh, occupied with the administration of a growing government, could no longer journey to each temple to make the necessary offerings and recite prayers pleasing to the gods, and there were plenty of them. Each town had its patron deity—Sobek, the crocodile god; Thoth, the Ibis-headed god; Horus, the falcon god. Hundreds of Egyptian gods in temples up and down the Nile competed with each other for prominence in the hierarchy.

Someone was needed who could stand in for the pharaoh at the shrines of the gods, who could make offerings, recite the prayers that ensured the sun a successful journey through the night. Thus, early in Egypt's history, a group of men were selected to recite the words and perform the rituals in place of the king. These were the priests of Egypt. They performed an important religious function, but the priests did not contribute to the nation's economy. The priests were a luxury, and a sign of Egypt's prosperity. These substitutes for the pharaoh set the pattern of the priesthood for thousands of years.

Because the priests were merely acting as representatives of the pharaoh, they were not required to hold deep religious convictions. Their duty was to perform a task, to place the proper offerings upon the altar, utter the appropriate prayers in the prescribed manner, to honor and please the god, so the god would in turn favor Egypt with prosperity. Priests were not required to be devoted to the god they served and this was not unusual in the ancient world. In the Old Testament there is little said about what the followers of Yahweh must believe. One had to follow the law, but none of the Ten Commandments says that you must believe. It was not until Christianity that there was an emphasis on what was "in your heart." So when we think of the priests of Egypt we should not think of purely spiritual servants of the gods. These were men who could be ruthless, who were capable of evil, and in a large bureaucracy there was plenty of opportunity.

The role of high priest in a temple was usually hereditary; we have autobiographies from priests who say they held the same position as their fathers and grandfathers—Prophet of the god Min, First Priest of Amun, etc. With such a huge priesthood, there were plenty of opportunities for capable and ambitious men to rise to the top. The high priest of each temple controlled the temple's fields, orchards and cattle—it was an administrative position that led to great personal wealth and power. Along with the position of high priest came estates, servants, gifts, bribes, and all the trappings of nobility. Beneath the high priest were the second and third prophets of the god, and beneath them were endless ranks and casts of priests, a hierarchy that would rival any modern corporation.

The different branches of the priesthood were fiercely competitive, each claiming priority for their god, seeking the pharaoh's special patronage and the rewards that it would bring. At Memphis, near modern Cairo, the patron god, Ptah, who created the universe was proclaimed to be the foremost of all the gods. But every city claimed its patron deity was the foremost. Thrusting your patron god to the forefront didn't just earn you theological brownie points; it was a struggle for wealth and status, something the priests of ancient Egypt knew very well.

One could succeed in the priesthood by merit and often scribes rose through the ranks to high office. Each temple had its own hierarchy of priests, each group performing specific duties, each holding special privileges. The temple scribes kept careful records of the gifts bestowed on the temple by the pharaoh, and they recorded the yield of the temples' lands, inventoried the storerooms—the grain, wine, linen, and gold. They copied sacred prayers on papyrus scrolls so the lector priests who read the prayers would have clear copies. Other scribes were temple librarians, organizing the papyrus scrolls so they could be easily located and consulted. Besides the religious texts, the temples kept medical texts for the priest physicians and books of dream interpretations to be consulted by those who wanted to know what their dreams meant.

The "stolists" were priests who attended the statues of the gods. They followed a precise routine of devotion to maintain the god's continuing good will. Each day at the prescribed time the stolist priests entered the "holy of holies"—the innermost sacred room in the temple, withdrew the statue of the god from its shrine, and performed the morning rituals. The "god" was anointed with fragrant oils, placated with incense, presented with the choicest foods, then wrapped in pure white linen, and replaced in the holy shrine. As the doors were closed and bolted, prayers and incantations were chanted.

Many of the priests holding lesser positions were married, had families, and held jobs outside the temple. They were carpenters, teachers, and scribes who would, at regular intervals, serve thirty days in their temple, a kind of religious national guard, and then return to secular life.

When pharaohs conquered foreign lands and returned with gold and captives, they donated a portion of the tribute to the temples, to thank the gods for looking upon them with favor in battle, and to ensure their continued goodwill. Foreign captives became a sizable source of manpower and maintained the temples, as well as the fields and orchards owned by the temples. Pharaohs often gave large tracts of land to the temples so the cattle and produce could provide a continuing annuity. As each succeeding pharaoh tried to surpass his predecessor's generosity, temples grew incredibly wealthy and the priests numbered in the tens of thousands. In the years just before the birth of Tutankhamen, the priesthood of Egypt had swollen to the largest bureaucracy the world had ever known, a powerful force, second only to the pharaoh.

It is interesting that although pharaohs conquered foreign lands, Egypt never became a true empire. The gods of Egypt were the gods of only Egypt, the pharaoh was king of Upper and Lower Egypt, not of the world. Life on the banks of the Nile was too good to want to live elsewhere—to colonize and live in foreign lands. If you died on foreign soil, far from the Egyptian embalmers, your body might not be mummified and all chance of immortality would be lost. Better to live in Egypt. So when the pharaoh rode out with the army each year to conquer his neighbors, the troops always returned home to Egypt. For the Egyptians, the center of the universe was Egypt, and at the center of Egypt was the pharaoh.

Much of our understanding of ancient Egypt comes from the ancient Egyptians' belief in life after death. Because they believed you could literally take it with you, tombs were filled with furniture, food, clothing, even games to amuse themselves in the next world. There were items of luxury, practicality, and whimsy. It was as if they were packing for a trip to a place they had never visited and weren't sure what to bring, so they brought everything. Tombs are windows into daily life in ancient Egypt. Their contents weren't carefully arranged like mini-apartments; objects were piled on top of each other and crammed into every small space. On top of a bed might be the toiletry objects of the lady of the house—her favorite scents and oils still in delicate alabaster jars, her eyepaint in slender ceramic tubes. Next to this might be stacks of fine linens, clothing, and food, breads, and sweets of all kinds, and wine jars of a favorite vintage sealed for eternity, joints of meat, roast ducks—it was the ultimate picnic. This is how we know what the Egyptians ate and drank at banquets, what they wore, and what kind of furniture they had. Sometimes, the scenes painted on the tomb walls are just as revealing.

Every ancient Egyptian wanted immortality and the chance of attaining it was directly tied to his wealth and status. The kind of tomb you prepared for your afterlife depended on what you could afford. The beautifully painted tombs that we see in art books were prepared for Egypt's aristocracy. The nobility invested as much as they could afford in their tombs, and sometimes as a special favor, the pharaoh would grant a member of the court a prime location. For most Egyptians—the farmers, the craftsmen, and the laborers—there were no beautiful tombs packed with furniture, food and luxuries. When his time came, the common man was wrapped in a sheet, perhaps from his own bed, and placed in a mass burial site for the poor. There, surrounded by hundreds of his deceased neighbors, he awaited resurrection. Since most commoners couldn't write, they left no literature, no records of their hopes and concerns, no stories of their lives. Most of what we know about ancient Egypt comes from the privileged few.

The idea of decorating tomb walls with scenes from daily life was based on a principle of ancient Egyptian magic: if you showed it, it would happen in the next world. Egyptian tomb walls are covered with scenes of the deceased feasting, hunting, fishing, overseeing the work in his fields on his estate. The whole family was almost always portrayed— the wife, kids, and pets—so the deceased would have company in the next world. When I look at the paintings in an Egyptian tomb, I get the feeling they thought the next world was just like this one, only better, maybe with air-conditioning. You never see an unhappy camper on a tomb wall. They may be working in the fields, but they're wearing their finest linen robes.

Sometimes a high official would write his autobiography on his tomb wall, chronicling his accomplishments. Military men often gave vivid accounts of their campaigns, royal scribes related their duties in the palace, and governors listed the territories under their jurisdiction and the taxes they collected for the king. Sometimes the vizier, the equivalent of prime minister, listed his official responsibilities. Each tomb was a miniature world revealing the life of the deceased. Preserved by Egypt's dry climate, the tombs form a three-dimensional encyclopedia of ancient Egypt.

As the custodians of writing, priests were often the keepers of records, an essential part of any bureaucracy, and as Egypt grew, so did the numbers and importance of the record keepers. Because the fertile land along the Nile produced a surplus of crops, the pharaoh collected the excess (the origin of taxes) to pay the army and the priests. When taxes were collected up and down the Nile, accountants were needed to tally the crops grown by each farmer and to record how much was deposited in the pharaoh's granaries. Egypt's booming economy produced an army of bureaucrats, and becoming a scribe was a sure path to upward mobility.

Ancient texts urged the youth of Egypt to learn how to write. *"You won't have to march in the army, your robes will be clean, you won't have to work the fields in the heat of the day, . . ."* Once you could write, you were on your way up. There were all kinds of scribes. Some spent their days listing inventories in temple storerooms and had titles like "Scribe of Amun," others wrote religious texts and were called "Keepers of the Secrets." If you showed ability, you might become a "Royal Scribe" attached to the palace, perhaps answering correspondence, or composing inscriptions to be carved on the temple walls.

As Egypt became prosperous, the country was divided into administrative units called nomes, almost the exact equivalent of our states. There were forty-four nomes, each with a nomarch, or governor, and under him were other officials, the mayors of the towns, overseers of construction, overseers of the scribes, overseers of the stables. All of these officials were selected from the ranks of the scribes. No wonder parents were always urging their children to "Be a scribe." This was the middle class.

There were books that told you how to move quickly up the ranks— *"Don't indulge in drinking beer, lest you utter evil speech." "Study the writings, put them in your heart, then your words will be effective." "Attend to your position, be it high or low; it is not good to press forward, step according to rank."* It was practically a Dale Carnegie course for ancient Egyptians.

What made the whole thing possible was the growing population of farmers. There were no hungry mouths. Each new arrival could be fed, and still there was a surplus. Luxury industries could be supported. Artists were hired to decorate tomb walls, jewelers and craftsmen were paid for their creations, and it was all the gift of the Nile.

By the time Tutankhamen came to power the three major forces of Egyptian society—kingship, the military, and religion—had been in place for centuries and were growing stronger, more demanding, and independent. The pharaoh could not maintain Divine Order without the priesthood and the military. The priests were eager for donations from the pharaoh and for booty from the military. The military, strong in their own right, still asked for the god's favor for successful campaigns, and it was politic to have the support of the priests. It was a delicate balance among them, for each of the three institutions had grown so strong that it was almost unstoppable. But the notion of divine kingship remained central to it all and Egypt without a pharaoh was unthinkable.

Kingship was the foundation of civilization throughout the ancient world. Every great nation had a leader without whom there would be chaos, but Egypt alone perceived its king as divine—the pharaoh was the son of Re, the sun god. Other nations were led by mere mortals; in Egypt a god was at the helm.

Of the 170 or so kings whose reigns were recorded, most followed and upheld the traditional role of kingship. They led the army, built monuments, and made offerings to the gods. Under the pharaoh's guidance, divine order prevailed and Egypt prospered, but the line of succession from Narmer to Tutankhamen was not without its breaks.

There is a tendency to think of Egyptian history as perfectly seamless, but there were times when the fabric of Egypt tore. The point to be made is that when such rare events occurred, the society was so well established that it could right itself again. There may have been brief periods of chaos, but the infrastructure was still there, the land still produced, the priests still had wealth, the concept of kingship was unchanging, and the military was in the wings. For example, the pyramids were built during the Old Kingdom (2686–2181 B.C.), but by 2200 B.C. Egypt had descended into anarchy and the era of pyramid building was over. We are not sure why Egyptian society collapsed; there are few records. One theory is that the last pharaoh of the Old Kingdom lived too long. Pepi II became pharaoh as a child and reigned for more than ninety years, the longest reigning monarch in the history of the world.

Unlike modern England, where the monarch is a figurehead, Egypt's pharaoh actually led the army into battle. As Pepi grew older and older, perhaps he was unable to govern, the army was not maintained, and Egypt grew weak. Egypt was tumbled by its greatest strength, a strong central government built around its king as absolute ruler. If the pharaoh was weak, Egypt suffered. Tutankhamen would learn this lesson firsthand.

For more than a century after Pepi, Egypt was without a true king as local governors fought for supremacy. Even in this period of weakness, Egypt was not invaded. Its natural barriers of sand and water held. Finally a local ruler, like King Narmer, unified the land, and Egypt had its pharaoh. Like a boat righting itself after capsizing, Egypt had returned to exactly the same position that had served it so well. With a single absolute ruler leading a strong military and priesthood, divine order had returned to the land. But we are still eight hundred years away from Tutankhamen's reign, and we have talked only in terms of "political forces," "kingship," and "the priesthood." It would be an oversimplification to view Egypt only as a vast mechanical system, totally determined by the laws of physics. It was also the personalities that made Egypt great. It is time to meet Tutankhamen's family.

3

Tutankhamen's Ancestors
The Glorious Eighteenth Dynasty

Respect the nobles, sustain your people.
Strengthen your borders, your frontier patrols.
It is good to work for the future,
One respects the life of the foresighted.

—King Khety Nebkaure
circa 2150 B.C.

Egypt believed its rightful place in the world order was on top, dominating her neighbors. The history of Egypt can be viewed, in fact, as a series of conquests; it was the natural order of things. To maintain supremacy, the pharaoh repeatedly led the army out of Egypt, smashed some foreign country, then returned home with anything of value that wasn't nailed down. The subdued country was expected to send annual "tribute" or the pharaoh would return. Today we would view this as unprovoked aggression, which it was, but it was also the way of life in the ancient world. No pharaoh ever boasted, "There were no battles in my reign."

Annual invasions were necessary because the Egyptians never colonized. Once they conquered a foreign territory, that was it; they went home and waited for the yearly tribute. But with the army far away in

Egypt, there wasn't much incentive for foreign countries to send tribute, so the pharaoh would ride out with his army again, repeating the cycle. War was the natural order of things in Egypt.

Tuthmosis I, one of the early pharaohs in Tutankhamen's dynasty, is best known for his military exploits, but he is also significant because he is the reason that the pharaohs of the New Kingdom are buried in the Valley of the Kings and not in pyramids. An autobiographical inscription in the tomb of Tuthmosis's Overseer of the Works, Ineni, describes how the first tomb was constructed.

> I inspected the excavation of the cliff-tomb of his majesty, alone, no one seeing, no one hearing . . . It was a work of my heart, my virtue was wisdom; there was not given to me a command by an elder. I shall be praised because of my wisdom after years, by those who shall imitate that which I have done.[1]

Secrecy was indeed crucial if Tuthmosis's body was to be protected. Soon after the collapse of the Old Kingdom the pyramids of Giza were plundered by tomb robbers, and all the bodies destroyed. When the government was finally stabilized, the pharaohs of the Middle Kingdom resumed building pyramids, but a diminished work force and reduced resources resulted in interiors being constructed of mud brick with only a thin stone casing skimming their exterior surfaces. These pyramids were also plundered, so Tuthmosis's secret tomb carved into the cliff of a desolate valley was meant to outsmart tomb robbers. Eight generations later, Tutankhamen would join his august ancestor in this place that became known as the Valley of the Kings. Those generations included some of the greatest monarchs ever to rule Egypt.

Tutankhamen's ancestors, the kings of the Eighteenth Dynasty, elevated the concept of the warrior-pharaoh to heights never before seen. The pharaoh Tuthmosis created an army of thousands of well-trained, well-equipped career soldiers. It was totally unlike the small corps Narmer had organized, and it had an advantage that Narmer couldn't have imagined—the chariot.

Two horses pulled these chariots that carried two men, a driver and an archer. Chariots were constructed from imported wood—elm wheels for its suppleness, and ash as the body because of its strength. The floor was woven from leather thongs and covered with a leather flap, acting as a shock absorber, providing a relatively stable platform from which the archer could shoot his arrows. It was a light body with a lot of engine.

Supporting the charioteers were the infantry. Each soldier carried a leather shield, spear, battle ax, and dagger. The infantry marched fifteen miles a day. By the time Tuthmosis was through with his campaigns Egypt was master of the seven hundred miles between Egypt and the Euphrates river. On the banks of the Euphrates, Tuthmosis erected a stela—a large round topped stone, resembling a giant tombstone, that served as an ancient Egyptian bulletin board. If you wanted to announce something, you carved it on a stela and Tuthmosis proclaimed that this was Egypt's northern territory.

The only surviving child of Tuthmosis and his queen was Princess Hatshepsut. There is no word for "queen" in ancient Egyptian. The phrase we translate as "queen" is actually "king's great wife." Had Hatshepsut been a son, the royal crown would have passed directly to him, but she was a girl and this created a problem. It is not always clear how the successor to the throne was chosen. It wasn't as simple as in England—where the laws of primogeniture decreed that the throne was passed down through the king's eldest son, with specified contingencies for all possibilities. In Egypt, the pharaoh had several wives and could also marry his sisters, so the lines of succession for his children could be rather complex. Overall, the rule known as the "Heiress Theory" covered most cases: whoever married the eldest, most royal daughter became pharaoh.

When Tuthmosis died, his son Tuthmosis II by a minor wife was married to his half sister Hatshepsut, the eldest daughter of the pharaoh and his great wife. Marriage to Hatshepsut established Tuthmosis II's right to the throne. The couple had a successful, uneventful twenty-year reign. When Tuthmosis II died he left two children, a daughter by Hatshepsut, and a young son, Tuthmosis III, by a minor wife. Hatshepsut ruled as regent for the young boy for about seven years. Then, suddenly, one of the most incredible events in Egypt's long history occurred: Hatshepsut changed her royal title from "Queen" to "King" and had herself portrayed in full male royal regalia, complete with a beard. This was unheard of in conservative ancient Egypt. By wearing the false beard and the royal kilt of the pharaoh, Hatshepsut was attempting to stay within the traditional boundaries of Egyptian kingship—she was the king who happened to be a woman. The only reason Hatshepsut pulled it off was that she was a good administrator, and her reign brought prosperity throughout the land. That she chose to be represented as king posed several challenges for the artists and scribes in Hatshepsut's court. Was the pharaoh to be referred to as "his majesty" or "her majesty?" (They did it both ways.)

When Hatshepsut died on the 10th day of the 6th month in the 22nd year of her reign (February 1482 B.C.), Tuthmosis III became sole ruler of Egypt and through his conquests went on to become the greatest military leader Egypt had ever seen. In the sixteen years following Hatshepsut's death, Tuthmosis III led fourteen military campaigns north of Egypt, causing Egyptologists to dub him the "Napoleon of Egypt." In year 33 of his reign, Tuthmosis battled his way to the Euphrates river, defeated the King of Mitanni, and erected his own stele alongside his grandfather's, and another one across the river.

A generation after her death, Tuthmosis had Hatshepsut's name erased from all her monuments in an official attempt to remove any trace of her from the records of Egypt. It was too revolutionary to admit that a king of Egypt had been a woman. This erasure of a pharaoh's name and memory established an ominous precedent. A hundred years later, a similar purge would sweep through Egypt. This time Tutankhamen would be the target.

When Tuthmosis III died after fifty-four years as king, Egypt was the military power feared by all in the Middle East. He was Tutankhamen's great-great-great grandfather. The remaining pharaohs between Tuthmosis III and Tutankhamen maintained the grand tradition of their ancestors. They elevated the Eighteenth Dynasty above all previous and subsequent eras of Egypt's glorious history.

Now Tutankhamen's direct ancestors begin to emerge. Twenty-five years before his birth, Egypt was ruled by his strong-willed, decisive grandfather, Amenhotep III, a man whose probity and strength would echo loudly through the lives of succeeding pharaohs. Secure in his claim to the throne because his father had publicly nominated him as his successor, Amenhotep was able to marry a commoner; his wife did not have to be of pure royal blood to establish his right to rule. To commemorate his marriage to the Lady Tiye, he sent the ancient Egyptian equivalent of a telegram, a carved stone in the shape of a scarab (beetle), a symbol of good luck. On the base of the scarab was the inscription:

> . . . *the king's great wife, Tiye, may she live,*
> *The name of her father is Yuya*
> *The name of her mother is Tuya*
> *She is the wife of a mighty king.*

Anyone reading between the lines would get the message: Tiye is a commoner, but you had better accept her as my wife. All indications are that it was a successful marriage. Statues of the king show Tiye next to him, represented almost equal in size—a great honor to his queen. Royalty was always shown as idealized, but Tiye's portraits often convey a sense of the person. The beautifully sculpted head of Queen Tiye in the Berlin Museum is that of a mature woman with handsome regular features, a strong woman who got whatever she wanted.

Tiye bore the king six children—four daughters, and two sons. The princesses were given important titles. One daughter, Sit-Amun, was called "The King's Wife," which suggests to some Egyptologists that she married her father. Often sisters married their own half brothers, but it was rare for a pharaoh to marry his own daughters. The oldest son, named Tuthmosis after his ancestor, was groomed for the throne by being given the important position of high priest of Memphis, one of the two capitals of Egypt (along with Thebes). This was a shrewd maneuver on the part of Amenhotep III. It was always politic to honor the gods of Egypt, and he now had a loyal family member inside the powerful priesthood. The younger son, Amenhotep, was named for his father, but he was mentioned in no royal inscriptions, is not shown in any statues, and his name appears only on one broken wine jar. Such were the inauspicious beginnings of Tutankhamen's father, a prince who appeared to have no future. We will look closely at this enigmatic figure in the next chapter.

The reign of Amenhotep III was as close as Egypt, or almost any other country, ever got to paradise. Never did precious unguents and oils flow so freely, turquoise, lapis lazuli, and gold adorn more necklaces, or rich, aromatic cedar form more temple doors. Food was abundant and there was peace. Thanks to Amenhotep's predecessors, Egypt now firmly controlled the area from northern Syria to the Fifth Cataract of the Nile (the center of the Sudan). The military rarely had to demonstrate its might by fighting, so firmly had all the earlier invasions driven the lesson home. A steady flow of gold from Nubia (Sudan) and the western desert kept Egypt's economy strong, prompting a foreign king corresponding with Amenhotep III to observe: "Gold is like dust in your country, one has only to pick it up."[2] From Kush, in the south, came elephant tusks, giraffe skins, and ebony wood for palace furniture. From Afghanistan came lapis lazuli to be carved into amulets of the gods, and used as inlays in jewelry. By now foreign traders were regularly plying the Mediterranean. From Crete came exotic jars for palace use; Cyprus contributed copper ingots. Amenhotep had favored the gods, and the gods had favored Egypt. It was good business all around.

Amenhotep and Queen Tiye led a cosmopolitan life, successfully integrating both halves of the country. They traveled frequently between Memphis and Thebes. Memphis, the northern capital, was situated where the Nile began to branch out into the delta fan on its way to the Mediterranean. It was the administrative center of Egypt where the king resided to control the country; it held the national archives and accommodated thousands of bureaucrats. Little remains of Memphis today, because of a rising water table at the site. A colossal statue here, a massive column there, evoke what must once have been the busiest city in the world. Sadly, the office complexes that composed the city were constructed of sun-dried bricks that time and rising water have returned to the mud they came from. The palace suffered the same fate. All the precious documents from the archives disintegrated and rotted away, the fate of wet papyrus. Glorious temples have sunk out of sight into the moist ground.

The 400-mile journey from Memphis south to Thebes took the royal barge about three weeks, sailing against the current. The boat was a huge lumbering craft, probably two hundred feet long, built for comfort on river voyages. Along the way Amenhotep stopped to perform rituals in the temples, events that would be remembered by generations of priests who would fondly recall their brush with a living god.

If Memphis was like Washington, filled with records and preoccupied with business, then Thebes was like Paris, wealthy, glamorous, and alluring. Thebes was a city of edifices built for the glory of gods, not of functional office buildings. With every military conquest, Amenhotep's ancestors had heaped large portions of their plunder on Thebes's temples in gratitude for their success. Coffers overflowed with gold, storehouses burst with endless bolts of white linen—the priestly cloth—and produce arrived in endless streams from thousands of acres of donated farmland. The priests were rich and on their way to becoming independent—their land produced wheat, cattle, vegetables, everything they needed plus a surplus that could be sold.

So when the royal barge finally docked at Thebes, Amenhotep and Tiye would have been met by a thriving, prosperous priesthood. Homer called the city "Hundred-Gated Thebes" because of the countless huge pylons that formed the entrances to temple upon temple. And indeed Thebes had temples to many gods, but the reason for the city's importance was the patron deity Amun, the "hidden one." To this god Egyptians attributed the resurrection of their country from the anarchy and foreign domination that followed the Old Kingdom. By Amenhotep's time almost a thousand years of pharaohs had taken Amun as their special patron and pledged donations for his support, making Thebes more splendid with every gift. Amun had eclipsed even the old god Re, incorporating that former preeminent god in one of his titles, Amun-Re. Represented as a man with a tall crown surmounted by two ostrich plumes, Amun was married to the goddess Mut. With their son Khonsu, they formed the trinity, the holy family of Thebes.

Amenhotep's own name meant "Amun is pleased." He proceeded to outdo every other pharaoh in ensuring that god's continued satisfaction. Perhaps urged on by the priests, Tutankhamen's grandfather embarked on the most massive building ever to honor the patron god of Thebes and himself. He seems also to have had genuine beliefs of his own. After all, he named his oldest son Tuthmosis, "Toth is born," in honor of Toth, the god of writing. His second son was named for Amun, as was Amenhotep himself, and his eldest daughter was named for that god as well.

The pharaoh began his homage to Amun at the great temple of Karnak, the largest religious structure ever built. It was not really a single cathedral but a complex of temples and shrines sprawling across acres of land in no particular order. Like Topsy, it just grew as over the centuries each pharaoh dedicated his particular monument to the gods. When Amenhotep began his addition to the Great Temple of Amun at Karnak, the pylons of Tuthmosis I and his daughter Hatshepsut were still standing. People still marveled at Tuthmosis's obelisks, the first to be erected in Karnak Temple.

First, Amenhotep constructed a pair of grand entrance pylons (the Third Pylon) in front of all the other buildings at Karnak, so that these largest, most magnificent gates would be the first anyone would see. Their cornices were brightly painted and festooned with colorful pennants that flew from sixty feet high; shining electrum (a gold-silver alloy) covered poles. The imposing structure was dedicated to Amun.

A mile and a half from Karnak, in central Thebes, stood another temple of great importance. Once each year, shaven-headed priests bore the weighty gold statue of Amun to a special divine barque while others carried the statue of his wife Mut to her ship to form a convoy that sailed to this temple. Priests in their finest white robes joined important dignitaries adorned in silver and gold to trail the vessels in a procession called the "Beautiful Festival of the Harem," the most festive, most important holiday of Thebes. The celebration re-created the wedding of the two gods and of the conjugal bliss that followed. It took place in the "Harem of the South," a smallish temple used just once each year. Amenhotep directed his architects to replace the old temple with a beautifully proportioned, more imposing substitute. They produced a colonnade hall of seven pairs of majestic lotus columns leading into an open court. Two sides of the court were flanked with a double row of papyrus-bud columns roofed by slabs of stone, creating a shady spot beside an open yard prefaced by a forest of columns. Past the court, at the far end of the temple, a double sanctuary was constructed—the holy of holies—that housed the gold statues of Amun and Mut. Amenhotep had outdone himself in this tribute to the great god. It was the largest temple ever built by a single pharaoh.

Amenhotep took such interest in these projects that he built a palace across the river, where open land was still available, so he could reside in comfort, near enough to oversee the construction. Only a few walls of this palace have survived, since such buildings were intended for the lifetime of just one pharaoh and were constructed of impermanent mud bricks. Enough remains, however, to show it was a splendid affair. Floors were brightly painted with scenes from nature, walls with colorful decorative borders. Rather than a single large building, it was a compound with a separate building for the king and his staff, another for the queen and her court, another to serve as the kitchen, and still others to house the palace guard. In addition, there was a large auditorium, or festival hall, in which Amenhotep celebrated special jubilees celebrating his long rule. Life must have been sybaritic here. It seems that, despite proximity to the Nile, Amenhotep constructed an artificial lake behind the palace large enough for Queen Tiye to sail her barge.

As time passed, Amenhotep's personality mingled more and more with the glory of the city. He ordered a pair of the largest statues ever carved of himself, seated in seventy-feet-high majesty, to lead the way to a new temple dedicated to his memory. Nothing of this temple survives today, but the massive seated statues of Amenhotep still gaze eternally toward Thebes. These are the famed colossi of Memnon that amazed visitors in antiquity. The unparalleled building spree of Amenhotep must have energized the city to an unprecedented frenzy. He provided steady work for thousands of workers quarrying, cutting, dressing, and transporting tons of stone. Hundreds of artists carved and painted scenes on gleaming new temples and the luxurious palace. Riches flowed into Thebes as never before. A magic grew about Thebes that captured the hearts of poets. "She is called 'The City,'" says a late New Kingdom hymn in her praise; "all others are under her shadow, to magnify themselves through her."[3]

Soon the banks of the Nile were dominated by magnificent architecture, presenting a rich facade that hid a less than perfect interior. The houses and shops of the mortals sprawled in confusion behind the temples, forming a maze of dirty, narrow winding streets. It was a noisy city filled with the sounds of horses, penned ducks and pigs, and people busy at their work and at surviving. Although they resided in the greatest city in Egypt, life remained hard for the common people. Clouds of dust hung over their houses from the continuous cutting and polishing of stone for all the construction. Overpoweringly pungent odors emanated from all the animals and crowded conditions, and flies, lice, and fleas were ever-present.

Despite its face of splendor and energy, or maybe because of it, Thebes began to question itself. Many in the upper class believed that the priesthood of Amun had become too rich, too materialistic, and too powerful. Although the king and the nobles of the city continued to pay tribute to Amun, as time passed, some of the faithful added an interest in other cults. Amenhotep led the way when he took the new title, "Dazzling Sun Disk of All the Land." It became popular at the court to contemplate the nature of the sun-disk, the Aten, an interest not confined to the king alone, for Queen Tiye named her pleasure boat *The Aten Gleams*. People in the highest places were thinking about religion now, instead of merely going through the old motions. This profoundly affected the mind of Amenhotep's ignored second son, who would ascend the throne before long.

For his final resting place, Amenhotep selected an isolated wadi west of the Valley of the Kings that had never been used before. Why he chose not to be buried near his august ancestors of the Eighteenth Dynasty we will never know. Amenhotep III had a mind of his own.

Then tragedy struck the elderly king and his wife—their eldest son, Tuthmosis, the high priest Ptah, died. This was the son groomed to succeed his father. Their grief must have been intense, compounded by the fact that all of Amenhotep's plans for the future, for Egypt after his own passing, died with his boy. Now there was the real question of who would succeed the pharaoh. There was the second son, named Amenhotep for his father, but there probably was a reason he had been so rarely mentioned. He may have been afflicted with some very strange disease. No doubt there were other contenders for the throne, perhaps sons by Pharaoh's minor wives, some of whom were princesses of foreign countries, but only one was Tiye's child. She must have schemed successfully in his behalf, because, with all his problems, he became the heir and more. In what seems a surprising move, the aging king appointed his younger son, Amenhotep, to be coregent, which meant that they would rule together. There could be no controversy as to who ruled Egypt when the king died. The question is why did Amenhotep III, the energetic and powerful ruler, agree to share his power?

The answer can perhaps be found in Amenhotep III's mummy, which was discovered in 1898 under strange circumstances by a very nervous Egyptologist. Victor Loret, a Frenchman, served for a short time as head of the Egyptian Antiquities Service. High-strung and unsuited for his high administrative position, Loret managed to antagonize both European and Egyptian authorities, and consequently lasted only two years. He had barely time to undertake the first systematic excavation in the Valley of the Kings, discovering the robbed tombs of Tuthmosis I and Tuthmosis III, Egypt's Napoleon. He also found the tomb of Amenhotep II, in which lay the answer to our question.

This, too, was a plundered tomb. Broken bits of blue ceramic and wooden funerary objects with Amenhotep II's name littered the entrance passage when Loret uncovered it. Crawling through the passageway, Loret came to a square shaft, or "well," designed to catch water so that the burial chamber would remain dry during the rare cloudbursts that occurred in the Valley of the Kings. Placing a ladder across the well, Loret crossed into a square-pillared antechamber and saw broken funerary boats, models of what the pharaoh would need in the next world, gilded images of the king, and broken ushabti servant statues that were supposed to come to life in the next world and perform any tasks needed. It was now late into the night, Loret was tired, and with only his candle to illuminate the scene, his imagination started to take over. Then the candlelight fell on something for which he was not prepared.

> I went forward (between two columns) with my candle and, horrible sight, a body lay there upon the boat, all black and hideous, its grimacing face turned towards me and looking at me, its long brown hair in sparse bunches around its head. I did not dream for an instant that this was just an unwrapped mummy. The legs and arms seemed to be bound. A hole exposing the sternum, there was an opening in the skull. Was this a victim of human sacrifice? Was this a thief murdered by his accomplices in a bloody division of the loot, or perhaps killed by soldiers or police interrupting the pillaging of the tomb?[4]

What Loret had seen was the mummy of a prince, disturbed so soon after his burial that the oils and resins used in embalming were still liquid. The robbers had placed the body in one of the model boats, where the oils solidified and glued the mummy to it. Regaining his composure, Loret continued his descent, eventually arriving at a burial chamber containing a lidless stone sarcophagus. Peering over the top, Loret saw a coffin with a garland of flowers at its head and a wreath at its foot. He had found the mummy of Amenhotep II.

Loret's long evening was not over. Examining the four side chambers off the burial chambers he found statues of the pharaoh, vases for the seven sacred oils the king would need, meat and fruits to sustain him in the next world, and wooden models of boats for his journey to the netherworld. It was in one of these side chambers that Loret received his next shock:

We passed to the rooms to the right. In the first one we entered, an unusually strange sight met our eyes: three bodies lay side by side at the back in the left corner, their feet pointing toward the door. The right half of the room was filled with little coffins with mummiform covers and funerary statues of bitumen (resin-painted) wood. These statues were contained in the coffins that the thieves had opened and rejected after having searched in vain for treasures.

We approached the cadavers. The first seemed to be that of a woman. A thick veil covered her forehead and left eye. Her broken arm had been replaced at her side, her hands in the air. Ragged and torn cloth hardly covered her body. Abundant black curled hair spread over the limestone floor on each side of her head. The face was admirably conserved and had a noble and majestic gravity.

The second mummy in the middle was that of a child of about fifteen years. It was naked with the hands joined on the abdomen. First of all the head appeared totally bald, but on closer examination one saw that the head had been shaved except an area on the right temple from which grew a magnificent tress of black hair. This was the coiffure of the royal princes (called the Horus lock). I thought immediately of the royal prince Webensennu, this so far unknown son of Amenophis II, whose funerary statue I had noticed in the great hall, and whose canopic fragments I was to find later. The face of the young prince was laughing and mischievous, it did not at all evoke the idea of death.

The last corpse nearest the wall seemed to be that of a man. His head was shaved but a wig lay on the ground not far from him. The face of this person displayed something horrible and something droll at the same time. The mouth was running obliquely from one side nearly to the middle of the cheek, with a pad of linen whose two ends hung from the corner of the lips. The half-closed eyes had a strange expression, he could have died choking on a gag but he looked like a young playful cat with a piece of cloth. Death which had respected the severe beauty of the woman and the impish grace of the boy had turned in derision and amused itself with the countenance of the man.

These three corpses, like the one in the boat, had their skulls pierced with a large hole and the breast of each one was opened.[5] The condition of the three mummies in the side chamber and the one in the boat was caused by methodical tomb robbers. In their search for jewelry, they had hacked at the wrappings on the heads first, quickly stripping the outer linen; they then hacked at the chest searching for more jewelry, damaging the royal bodies.

Loret had no idea of the identities of the four mummies, and his judgment was certainly confused that night. The third mummy in the side chamber that he described as a man is clearly that of a young woman. To this day the identities of most of these bodies remain uncertain. One identification was made almost a century later and required both modern technology and a find in Tutankhamen's tomb, but more about that later. The four mummies that so moved Loret were not the only ones he found that night. One of the side chambers had been sealed with limestone blocks, with only a small opening near the ceiling. Loret climbed to the top and with his flickering candle was barely able to make out nine coffins, neatly arranged—six against the wall and three in front of them. That was all he could see, and he realized that the wall would have to be taken down before the coffins could be studied. But first the tomb had to be cleared.

Loret mapped the tomb, superimposing a grid to record the positions of more than 2,000 objects. Only after all this was he finally able to examine the nine coffins behind the wall. Loret had discovered the mummies of eight kings of Egypt and an unidentified woman. These mummies had been rescued from their plundered tombs by a Twenty-first Dynasty king in order to protect them from further desecration. Written on the bandages of the mummy of Seti II was the sad story of how the convention of kings came to be held in the tomb of Amenhotep II. On the sixth day of the fourth month of winter, in the twelfth year of the reign of Pinedjem I, the king had collected despoiled royal bodies, rewrapped them, and placed them in the tomb of Amenhotep II for safekeeping, where they remained until Loret's discovery.[6] Among the mummies was Tutankhamen's grandfather, Amenhotep III.

The mummy of Amenhotep III along with the others was taken by boat to Cairo where it remained till it was unwrapped on September 23, 1905.[7] The mummy of the father provided the clue as to why his son, Amenhotep IV, became co-pharaoh with his father. The king was fat and in very poor health when he died.

When I examined the mummy in the Egyptian Museum in Cairo, it was clear that Amenhotep must have been in great pain toward the end of his life. He suffered from horrible abscesses on his right lower incisors and his upper right canine. I could tell that he had lost the incisors some time before death as the sockets had filled in with new bone growth. Dental disease was common in ancient Egypt for kings and commoners alike, not from eating too much sugar as it is today, but from their daily bread. All grains in Egypt were stone-ground, which meant that along with your bread, you ate a considerable portion of sand and grit. Years of eating Egyptian bread wore down the teeth, exposing them to decay. Skilled as the Egyptian physicians were, they did not practice dentistry.

With the severe deterioration of his teeth, Amenhotep III must have been in constant pain. He may have been sedated with wine or even the new wonder drug of the Eighteenth Dynasty imported from Cyprus—opium. Cypriot physicians collected the sap that oozed from slits in the poppy's capsule, then dried the sticky mass for easy application. Applied directly to a wound or tooth, it may have had about the same effect as a modern-day injection.[8] Amenhotep would have found it difficult to carry out the affairs of state as his health deteriorated and may have been so sedated that he was in no condition to make decisions. Under these circumstances it would have been easy for the determined Queen Tiye to convince her husband to share the duties so difficult for him in his pained state with their son, Amenhotep IV. As coregent, her son was assured the throne when the old king died.

When the young king finally came to power after his father's death, one of the first changes he seems to have made was to approve a new technique for the mummification of his father. The embalmers injected tree resin and salts under the skin of the arms, legs, and neck to fill them out and to give the body a more lifelike appearance. It was a small break with tradition but one that foretold dramatic changes to come.

THE HANDWRITING ON THE WALL— WHAT THE TEMPLES TELL US

Temple walls are a crucial source of information for Egyptologists. They provided huge surfaces for pharaohs to boast of their deeds, and, because the walls were made of stone, they have survived. If a king wanted to announce how much land he dedicated to the temple, it was carved on the wall. When a pharaoh returned from a victorious military campaign, the triumph was recorded in full detail for all to see and marvel at the bravery of their pharaoh. There were glorious scenes of the pharaoh charging into battle in his war chariot, killing his enemy with arrows, and returning victorious with bound captives. Invariably, at the end of the panorama, are the scribes, counting piles of severed human hands—the Egyptian method of tallying the number of enemies killed. Actually two versions of the story were carved on the walls, one in words and one in pictures. When Napoleon invaded Egypt in 1798, hieroglyphic writing hadn't been decoded yet so they couldn't read the inscriptions. Because so many of the scenes were of battles, they assumed that temples were palaces. They couldn't imagine putting such violent scenes in a place of worship. But to the ancient Egyptian it was all connected. Conquering foreign territories was part of the divine order, something assisted by the gods. Every war was a holy war. If Napoleon's men could have read the inscriptions, they would have realized that these were temples and they could have read the dates of the battles, numbers killed, and even the names of the king's horses.

If you can read a temple wall you can learn a lot about Egyptian history. The wall paintings in the tombs of the nobles and the funerary objects found inside them have given us rich details about the people's daily lives. It's in the temples, however, where we find the official party line history of Egypt, but because most of the official records and temples from the northern capital, Memphis, have sunk into the mud, what records we do have really only give Egypt's southern party line.

Thebes rarely saw rain or high humidity so the temples and tombs are well preserved, the papyri they housed still legible. During the reign of Amenhotep III and his Eighteenth Dynasty ancestors, the information from Thebes is rich with detail. We have Amenhotep's temples and we have his tomb, but suddenly the records break off with the king's death.

The first clues as to what happened after Amenhotep died came from inside the walls of Karnak Temple. By the turn of this century, some of Karnak's great pillars had fallen, its huge gateways were crumbling, and major restoration was needed. In 1926, French Egyptologist Henri Chevrier began reconstructing the second pylon at Karnak (built by the pharaoh Horemheb). The crumbling pylon had to be completely dismantled and each block numbered for reassembly like a huge Lego project. As the blocks were being taken down Chevrier discovered, inside the pylon, blocks from the mysterious time right after Amenhotep III's reign.

The Amarna Talatat

The blocks found at Karnak Temple became known as "talatat," from the Arabic word *talata* meaning "three," because the blocks measured three handspans wide. These newly found blocks were decorated with the cartouches (oval shapes encircling royal names) of Amenhotep IV. They were from an entrance gate at Karnak built by Amenhotep III just before he died and completed by Amenhotep IV after his father's death. A picture began to emerge: Amenhotep IV ruled for a time with his father, and when the old king died, it looked as though his son completed his father's pylon in the usual Egyptian style.

As more talatat were uncovered it was noted that they were actually decorated in two different styles. Some were traditional, others came from a temple built by Amenhotep IV and on these the art changed. He and his wife and children are shown as grotesque and deformed. There were scenes of the pharaoh worshipping the solar disk, its long rays terminating in hands holding an ankh, the symbol of life, extending toward the pharaoh. Such scenes had never been seen before. The excavators realized that Amenhotep IV had built a temple to the sun disk, the Aten, in Karnak Temple, which was ancient Egypt's equivalent of the Vatican. A previously obscure god was being thrust into prominence inside the national church. As more and more blocks were discovered, it became clear that this was more than a new style of art; it was a full-blown religious revolution. On many blocks the faces of the king and queen had been hacked out, the hands at the ends of the Aten sun disk had been slashed. Amenhotep IV may have started a new religion, but clearly at some point it was rejected.

The Reconstruction of the Talatat

Over the years, more than 40,000 blocks were found and kept in large storehouses for the day when sense could be made of them. Far too many blocks were missing to reconstruct the temples from which they came, but in 1965 Ray Winfield Smith, an American businessman, conceived of a plan to re-create on paper what couldn't be put together in stone.[9]

His idea was to photograph every single talatat—not just those in Egypt, but even blocks that had over the years found their way into museums and private collections around the world. Every block was photographed on the same scale, creating pieces for a giant jigsaw puzzle. Then, with the aid of a computer, the temples could be reconstructed on paper.

A detailed description of each block listing all significant features was entered into the computer. If a piece had the head of a pharaoh that was broken off at the neck, that was recorded so the computer could search through the thousands of talatat for the blocks that had the body of a king beginning at mid-neck. When the computer found blocks that were possible joins, the photos were located and fitted together to see if there was a match. As the six-year project continued, it became clear that the talatat came from not one but several different temples built by Amenhotep IV during the early years of his reign.

Chevrier also found colossal statues of Amenhotep IV that once stood in front of his temple called *Gem-Pa-Aten—"The Aten is Found."* One of the statues, sculpted in the nude, shows the king almost as a hermaphrodite with wide hips and breasts but no genitalia. One can only wonder what the people of Thebes thought of these statues of their king. There is not a single contemporary account of how the man in the street felt about his new pharaoh.

Probably there was general acceptance in the beginning; after all, the new king buried his father, the revered Amenhotep III, completed his father's gateway at Karnak, and then began building his own temple, just as expected. Perhaps even the unusual representations of the royal family were quietly endured, but there must have been murmuring in the street when the bizarre statues of the king were matched by even stranger representations of Amenhotep IV inside the temple.

The main decoration of the temple was a depiction of the *Sed* festival, traditionally celebrated when a pharaoh had ruled for thirty years.[10] Amenhotep IV celebrated his *Sed* festival only four years or so after he became pharaoh. During a traditional *Sed* festival, just as Narmer had done centuries before, the pharaoh wore the white crown of Upper Egypt and the red crown of Lower Egypt to assert his dominion over the Two Lands. He would demonstrate his strength and vigor by running a racecourse and shooting arrows. Then the king would visit the shrines that housed the statues of the gods from different localities that had been assembled for the festival. But Amenhotep's was no ordinary *Sed* festival. There were no statues of Amun, Osiris, Ptah, Isis, and the other gods. All the shrines held statues of Amenhotep IV. All the familiar gods of Egypt had been banished in one broad sweep!

Now a young man in his early twenties, Amenhotep IV married Nefertiti. Little is known about her background before the marriage, but her looks alone made her a remarkable woman. Nefertiti was the king's great wife and the queen who would be remembered into the twenty-first century both as an icon for femininity and beauty and as a symbol of Egypt. Nefertiti's reputation as a great beauty is based primarily on a single statue, the famous "Nefertiti Bust," now in a Berlin museum. Her regular features, long graceful neck, and wide-set eyes are classic. I suspect that it is an accurate likeness of the Queen.

But this is not the way the queen was shown on Akhenaten's new temples at Karnak. Nefertiti, Akhenaten, and their two daughters all appear to be deformed with wide hips and elongated heads. Most peculiar of all was Akhenaten himself, shown with an elongated jaw, thin neck, spindly arms, fullness of breasts, sagging abdomen, and bulging thighs; the people of Egypt had never seen anything like this—neither had the Egyptologists.

In the fifth year of his reign Amenhotep IV changed his name to Akhenaten, "it is beneficial to Aten," which is the name the world knows him by today. We will talk about the importance of his name change later in the chapter. Akhenaten (Amenhotep IV) is the most discussed pharaoh in Egyptology and the discussion invariably turns to what he looked like. Some investigators believe he may actually have been normal, that the physical distortions were merely an artistic convention portraying the pharaoh as both male and female—he was everything. Others are convinced that he was grossly deformed and that it became an artistic convention to portray the members of the royal family with the same deformities as the king, something like the situation in seventeenth-century Spain, when the king of Castile lisped and all the courtiers affected a lisp.

Early investigators looking for the cause of the deformity offered a medical diagnosis. It was suggested that Akhenaten suffered from Froelich's syndrome, a malfunction of the pituitary gland that causes symptoms matching the unusual physical features in the Akhenaten portrayals. But the entire royal family was shown with the same unusual physical shapes. All the princesses are depicted with elongated heads, and Nefertiti is often indistinguishable from Akhenaten. Could every member of the royal family have been afflicted with Froelich's syndrome? Surely not.

One problem with the Froelich's syndrome explanation is that it always causes undeveloped genitalia and sterility in males. Akhenaten and Nefertiti eventually had six daughters. The symptoms of Froelich's syndrome so clearly match Akhenaten's appearance, however, that some Egyptologists believe Akhenaten did not father the six daughters. Yet, if the six princesses are not Akhenaten's children, why do they have his unusual physical characteristics?

I have always been convinced that there was something physically wrong with Akhenaten, but that it wasn't Froelich's syndrome, because there are all these children. Recently, a suggestion has been put forward that seems far more likely—Marfan's syndrome. This illness was first diagnosed in 1896 by Antoine Marfan, a French pediatrician who was examining a five-year-old girl with long thin fingers and toes, and a curved spine. As the symptoms were recognized by other physicians it was noted that they were often accompanied by eye problems, elongated faces, and deformed rib cages. Because the various symptoms tend to accompany one another, they constitute a "syndrome." Many of the features of Marfan's syndrome can be seen in Akhenaten and members of the royal family. For example, the thin slanted eyes in the colossal statues of Akhenaten (fig. 1) could easily be the result of Marfan's syndrome. About half of those suffering from Marfan's have the lenses of their eyes dislocated—off-center—which gives an unusual appearance.[11]

Akhenaten and the entire royal family are shown with extremely long fingers and toes, spindly arms, narrow chests—the precise symptoms of Marfan's syndrome. But could they all have had the same condition? Was it contagious?

Although the syndrome was identified in the nineteenth century it wasn't until the middle of this century that the cause was understood to be genetic. The condition results from a mutant gene that controls the development of the body's connective tissue. All the symptoms associated with Marfan's syndrome are caused by defective fibrillin, a protein responsible for holding our muscles and bones together.[12] Although not contagious, Marfan's syndrome is passed on genetically. Our bodies have between fifty thousand and one hundred thousand different genes, the basic unit of heredity. Genes usually come in pairs, one from each parent, and they are the cause of Marfan's syndrome. If the DNA in your body mutates in the gene that controls fibrillin, you will be the first in your family to have the syndrome. You can also inherit it from a parent who has the gene.

Of the many statues of Akhenaten's parents, Amenhotep III and Queen Tiye, not one shows any sign of Marfan's syndrome. Akhenaten was apparently the first person in his family to exhibit any of the characteristic features of Marfan's syndrome, so his condition was probably the result of a mutant gene. About 25 percent of Marfan's sufferers acquire the syndrome by a gene mutation.

The trait is dominant, which means that only one parent need be afflicted for the children to inherit the defective gene. Each child of a Marfan parent has a 50 percent chance of inheriting the Marfan gene. Thus, the six daughters of Akhenaten each had a 50 percent chance of having the Marfan gene passed on to them. This may explain the appearance of the Amarna princesses, long fingers (the medical term is *arachnodactyly*—"spider fingers"), and thin spindly arms and legs. Some of the daughters may have inherited the gene, and this could explain the curious depiction of the royal family.

If Akhenaten did, indeed, suffer from Marfan's syndrome, it still leaves the question: why did he permit the court sculptors to show his physical characteristics? For more than a thousand years pharaohs had been portrayed as young, well muscled, and perfect, no matter what they looked like. Akhenaten could have stayed with the traditional art style and been portrayed slim and well muscled like his ancestors before him. He chose not to and the entire royal family followed suit. Why?

I think the answer is a psychological one. But how do you confirm a psychological theory about someone who has been dead for 3,000 years? I thought that if I talked to people with Marfan's syndrome I might see how it affected their lives. How did they feel growing up different? Did they feel left out? Were they shunned? A geneticist colleague[13] working on Marfan's syndrome suggested I talk to a New York chapter of people with the syndrome. I called the organizer of the group, Julie Kurnitz, to see if I could attend their meeting and try out my theory on them. I would give a brief slide lecture about Akhenaten and ask for the group's reactions.

Most of the people who attended the meeting were women, many would blend in with any crowd; their physical characteristics were not extreme. But some could have been sisters of Akhenaten. Julie has classic Marfan features; she is tall with an elongated chin, narrow eyes, long thin arms, fingers, and toes, unusual features but not freakish. If anything, Julie is a handsome woman. Even before talking with the group, I revised my view of Akhenaten: he wasn't a freak. You can look different without looking freakish. None of the women in the group had physical features that were shocking.

Julie introduced me to the group and I began talking about Akhenaten and showing slides. After the second slide, I began to hear a lot of "Yups," and "Wows." As I continued with slides of the elongated hands and feet of the royal family, there were even more exclamations—"Marfan toes!" They had found a kinsman from ancient Egypt. After my talk I asked if any of the women had been treated differently when they were growing up, felt left out, had been shunned. And if so, how they had reacted. One woman said as a child she was always told to stand in the back to hide her long hands when a family photo was taken. Another young woman with close-cut hair and wire-rimmed glasses told a similar story and then provided the insight I was looking for. She said she rebelled and did everything she could to accentuate her appearance, wore capes and strange clothing and bizarre makeup. Who knows what she would have done had she been king of Egypt. The group understood

Akhenaten, it seemed perfectly reasonable for him to have colossal statues, to validate himself, to assert himself. It would have been a great catharsis after having been shunned and ignored for so long.

They were a group of wonderfully open people eager to share their experiences. When it became obvious that I was an Akhenaten fan, they removed their shoes and compared their feet with the pictures I had of the king's feet. Julie tried to extend her extremely long fingers into the position of the Amarna hands with the fingertips turning slightly upward. It was a very touching experience to meet with this group and at the end they asked for copies of the slides I had shown. Akhenaten will become a poster boy for the Marfan Association in their effort to reach out to others with the disorder. He never knew what made him different.

THE MOVE TO AKHETATEN—AMARNA

If Akhenaten was reacting to his lonely childhood, he went at it full steam. He placed a proclamation on the temple wall declaring his rejection of the gods of Egypt, saying that the old gods ceased to exist, and that a single new god had been embraced. In the early stages of the change, the new god took the form of the traditional sun god, Re-Horakty—"Re the Horizon Horus," appearing as a falcon-headed man wearing a royal kilt. This version first appeared on the southern gate at Karnak, which was completed by Akhenaten. But the "Re-Horakty" form of the god did not last long. In the third year of Akhenaten's reign the falcon-headed god was replaced by a disk, the Aten. The sun disk was an ancient symbol in Egypt—the word "aten" means "disk"—which first appeared a thousand years earlier during the Old Kingdom. The sun god is a central theme in Egyptian religion. The word for sun was "re," which was the same as the word for sun god, although they were not written the same way in hieroglyphs. The role of the sun god changed over the centuries, rising and ebbing in importance. Re was the patron deity of the northern city Heliopolis—literally "sun city." Although Amun, Mut, and Khonsu were the patron gods of Thebes, interest in the sun cult was growing. Amenhotep III, for example, was called "the Sun King." Still, the Aten, an aspect of the sun, was a minor god. But Akhenaten changed that. Inscriptions found on the Karnak blocks showed that in the fifth year of his reign Amenhotep IV changed his name to Akhenaten, "it is beneficial to Aten."

Names held a special significance in ancient Egypt. Often Egyptian children were given two names at birth—one known only to the mother, another for public use. The "real" name was the one only the mother knew, so if someone attempted a magical spell using the commonly known name it wouldn't work. Isis, the goddess of magic, was called "She who knows all the names"—no one was beyond her magic. Akhenaten's name change was not just the whim of an adolescent, it was a statement about things to come.

At about the same time he changed his name, Akhenaten announced that he would move his capital from Thebes to a remote site in Middle Egypt. It was here in an isolated city that Tutankhamen would be born. Akhenaten's revolution had evolved over a period of four or five years, what seems like an instant in Egyptian history, but there was plenty of time for tensions to develop. The strange depictions of the king and his family hurt no one; even the elevation of the new god Aten to a place of prominence at Thebes might have been acceptable to some, but when Akhenaten declared the Aten the sole god of Egypt, the battle lines were drawn. It meant that no longer would royal donations of gold, linen, wine, grain, cattle, captives, and land enrich the temples of Amun, Mut, Khonsu, and all the other gods up and down the Nile. Akhenaten was a god against the gods.

If the priesthood of Amun had been weak and unsupported, the temples would have closed, perhaps eventually to be replaced by priests of the new religion. But the powerful priesthood at Thebes had its own lands, its own revenues, and didn't require Akhenaten's patronage for survival. The priests must have been furious. The pharaoh had decreed their gods were false, had withdrawn support of the temples, and was abandoning them. The tension between Akhenaten's court and the tens of thousands of priests must have been incredible. The release valve was Akhenaten's decision to leave Thebes. But who would stay, and who would accompany him?

What must it have been like at Thebes at the time of the big move? The older people probably clung to their gods and said, "Let him go . . ." Thebes was prosperous, life was good for the upper classes who had no desire to leave the comforts of their homes. Officials like Ramose, the mayor of Thebes, stayed behind. His dilemma is reflected on the walls of his tomb in the Valley of the Nobles near Thebes. Ramose had completed two walls of his tomb, showing him with his beautiful wife and family in the traditional art style. Everyone wears his finest garments, every curl of his wig is in place, everyone is perfect— just the way he wanted to be for eternity. Then Akhenaten changed the style of art. Caught in the middle and desperate to be politically correct, Ramose completed his tomb decoration in the new style, featuring Akhenaten with his misshapen body preaching to his followers, and showing Akhenaten and Nefertiti in their "Window of Appearances" giving an audience. Ramose was also careful to show himself wearing gold collars—his reward for switching to the new god—or was it a bribe for seeming to do so? Ramose died before his tomb was completed. The funeral procession that buried him was quickly painted on the wall. Ramose had one foot in the old religion and one in the new. I wonder what he thought would happen to him in the next world?

This was the first religious revolution in recorded history and it must have been an exhilarating time for the followers of the Aten. There may have been some who had been wronged by the priests, who were unhappy with their lives, or who simply wanted to be part of the great adventure. When I think about Akhenaten's move to Amarna, I am re-minded of the communes of the 1960s. Their members were rarely the overachievers of society, they were often the ones who hadn't quite found their niche. Unhappy with society, they were "dropping out," hoping to make a better life. What's amazing about Akhenaten's "cult" is that its leader was the king of Egypt. They were all dropping out with the pharaoh!

So when Akhenaten left Thebes to start his utopian community, I don't think many of the Theban establishment followed him. They would have had to give up too much. The names of the nobles of Amarna are not ones known at Thebes. The boats full of people that traveled to Amarna must have been like the pilgrims who came to America. They were not aristocracy, they were simple people hoping to better their lives. Hundreds of craftsmen were need to build an entire city; they were probably offered incentives to follow the king on his holy quest.

There are no records of what the trip was like. Boat travel was usually reserved for the upper classes, the poor rode donkeys. But since the pharaoh was their leader, perhaps everyone went by boat. Sailing north with the Nile current, the one-hundred-fifty-mile trip would have taken a week, and the convoy of boats must have been buzzing with excitement about their wonderful new city presided over by a single god. There must have been a joyous feeling of optimism. Life will be good. We can do anything, the pharaoh is our leader.

4

Amarna—The Holy City

I am your son who serves you, who exalts your name;
Your power, your strength, are in my heart.
You are the living Aten whose image endures.

—Akhenaten
circa 1340 B.C.

When Akhenaten and his pilgrims landed at the site of their new city, they were met only by barren desert. The modern name for the site is Tell el Amarna, Amarna for short, named for the bedouin tribe inhabiting the site when excavators arrived centuries later. No one lived there when Akhenaten selected this spot for a new capital. He had chosen virgin territory, unsullied by shrines and temples for other gods, like Joseph Smith leading the Mormons into the unknown Utah desert. Probably a few thousand hearty people made the initial exodus, setting up tents and temporary shelters to watch a city rise before their eyes. The logistics of organizing and feeding them must have been complex. The tent city would have been coordinated like a military camp, with a quartermaster in charge of supplies. Crops could not be planted immediately, for there were no fields or irrigation canals; fortunately, plenty of fish and birds were available. First, they must have built a brewery and bakery to produce the two staples of the Egyptian diet. They would have been positioned next to each other because both depended on the same vital ingredient—yeast.

The workmen were the real heroes of the new city. While the stone masons freed blocks from quarries with bronze chisels and wooden mallets, brickmen formed the millions of bricks needed to build an entire city. Brickmaking was a simple matter. Nile ooze was placed in a rectangular wooden mold; the mold could then be removed to leave the future brick to dry in the burning Egyptian sun. Artists and craftsmen worked frantically to decorate the new houses and government buildings as courses of bricks rose higher and higher. Probably they sent word back to their friends in Thebes to come and join them, for there was plenty of work. There was no time to waste. Brightly colored ceramic tiles and inlays in the shapes of rosettes and flowers needed firing in pottery kilns to lend accents to painted murals on the walls.

The two essential building materials in ancient Egypt were readily available at Amarna: stone and Nile mud. Temples in ancient Egypt were built of stone blocks because they had to last for eternity. Houses, however, even the royal palaces, were built with a core of mud brick plastered then painted over. There must have been a constant haze over the city from the dust and sand stirred up by all the construction as the stone blocks were cut and dragged from the quarries to the temple sites. Living on a construction site, however, must have fascinated the city's children as they watched in awe as a new temple materialized. When the walls reached six feet or so, mud brick ramps had to be added so blocks could be hauled on sleds to the top. Five or six major buildings went up simultaneously, providing continuous excitement. In the early days at Amarna, every child probably dreamed of growing up to be an architect. It is curious that with all the building activity in Amarna and in the rest of Egypt, not a single architectural papyrus has ever been discovered. There is no written record that tells us how to build a pyramid, design a temple or, even, build a wall. It may be that they once existed and have all perished, but I don't think so. I suspect that such information was a trade secret, passed down from father architect to son. We have plenty of literary and religious papyri, but not one on any of the trades.

The plan of the city was dictated by the geography formed by the Nile on the west and by abrupt cliffs on the east. Space for the main city lay between these borders, a crescent about three miles wide by eight miles long. A "Royal Road" ran north and south, splitting the length of town. At more than 125 feet wide, it composed perhaps the greatest thoroughfare in the ancient world. Designed originally for grand chariot processions of the royal family, it came to serve as a commuter road along which administrators rode on donkeys from homes in the suburbs to their central city offices.

Running from east to west, two dried river beds, on which nothing was built for fear of flash floods, divided the city into three sections: the central city and the north and the south suburbs. The complete city sprawled—seventeen miles north to south—including suburbs at each end, each with bright new workshops, temples, and homes. Beyond the northern suburb a village was set aside for the workmen, crammed with tiny houses. The estates of the rich and famous of Amarna were mansions that followed similar designs. A large entrance hall supported by slender wooden columns brightly painted with lotus motifs led into a large living room dominated by four massive columns. Bedrooms, bathrooms, and guest rooms ran off from this communal room. Behind the main house were servants' quarters, granaries, storerooms, kitchens and stables. All these grand houses were built quickly at the same time—an ancient, upper-class housing development.

The central city, called "Island Exalted in Jubilees," was the administrative heart of the new capital. Here the foreign office filed correspondence between Akhenaten and the rulers of Asia in a building known as the "Place of Pharaoh's Dispatches." Also, Akhenaten stored all the old correspondence from his father's reign: letters and trade agreements between Amenhotep III and his foreign emissaries. Someone had thought to bring the files with him when they moved. Near the Records Bureau was the police station with dormitories, training grounds, and stables for the police cars of the day—chariots. Even in a theocratic city there would be thieves to apprehend, marital spats to resolve and, as soon as they were constructed, tombs containing great wealth to protect. Nearby was the university, known as the "Per-ankh," "house of life," where future priests were educated. But a new curriculum was taught, most likely designed by Akhenaten himself. Young priests in training were no longer called upon to recite the myth of Isis and Osiris or chant the "Hymn to Re" until they were committed to memory, since all these gods had ceased to exist. A new liturgy of prayers and hymns had been written by Akhenaten, who, it seems, not only provided the revelations for the new religion, he composed its hymnal.

What an exciting time it was for the initiates of the Aten. This was radical theology. No country had ever reduced its pantheon to a single, all-powerful deity. Here was a heady, powerful concept whose details would have to be developed. With their leader, the pharaoh, they expected to do so, then they would change the world. The students were supervised by Meri-Re, the high priest of the Aten. Since his name means "Beloved of Re," perhaps he was a minor priest from Thebes who had switched his allegiance to Akhenaten's new theology early on and accompanied him to Amarna in the first wave of pilgrims.

Dominating the central city was the royal residence, perhaps the largest in the ancient world at this date. It was a huge, rambling, elaborate maze of audience halls, open courts, private apartments, nurseries, kitchens, and huge storage rooms. Fronted by three terraced gardens of exotic plants, the palace faced the Nile to benefit from its cool breezes. Most unusually, the compound straddled the main road, with an overpass—an innovation in architecture—joining the east to the west wings. This overpass became the most notable feature of the palace and of the city. It was called the "Window of Appearances," for it was here that Akhenaten and Nefertiti made an appearance, often accompanied by the princesses, to give audience to assembled dignitaries in the road below.[1] From this window, too, they handed out collars of massive rings of gold as rewards to the faithful. Religion has its own strong attractions, but a few ounces of gold must have amplified those attractions considerably.

A private temple, "Castle of the Aten," near the palace provided a sanctuary where the royal family worshipped privately and were rejuvenated by the Aten's rays. For ordinary citizens a great swathe of a city temple soon rose to challenge even the unparalleled Karnak in area. Measuring almost two hundred yards in length by fifty wide, nothing like it had ever been seen. Egyptian temples were, for the most part, dark mysterious places, roofed over by stone slabs that left only small slits cut in the stone to admit shafts of light into a murky interior. Traditional temples mirrored our railroad flats—one section simply led into the next in line. First came an open court, a large area where the common people could pay their respects to the gods. A ramp at the back of the open court led to a second, more secluded, court covered with a roof. This second chamber was reserved for the nobility. As you moved deeper into the temple, rooms became smaller and more intimate as the floor rose and the roof lowered, creating the atmosphere of a special sacred space. The third section, the "holy of holies," was the precinct of the priests alone who attended the gods. Oracles resided in the "holy of holies," cult statues used for forecasting the future and obtaining divine guidance. Normally, they remained in their shrines of stone, though on special festival days they were carried around the town in portable shrines of gilded wood that resembled the sacred barks of the pharaoh.

Akhenaten swept all this aside in designing his new cathedrals. Since there were no statues of the Aten, and all the old gods had been banished with their idols, there was no need for a "holy of holies." Because the solar disk was the object of all the worship, darkened passageways and even a roof would be entirely out of place. The new temple of the Aten was designed to be an open-air affair, full of light and sun. Essentially, it consisted of a rectangular perimeter wall that defined an open court two football fields in size. Inside was nothing but the sweep of space and rows of offering stands, one for each day of the year, at which the Aten received daily food offerings. Akhenaten's other temples varied only slightly from this design. Some were smaller, more like a kiosk, but all were light, airy, and open to the sky. I think of Akhenaten and his followers as like California sun worshippers, every one with a perpetual tan.

The new temples, however, did retain one architectural feature of Theban temples, probably because it was too dramatic to omit. Massive entrance pylons, like those found at Karnak and Luxor temples, separated the outer precincts from the inner temple. Poles mounted on the pylon's face flew long streamers fluttering in the breeze to symbolize the breath of life.

All this knowledge of Amarna comes from a series of extraordinary excavators who were intrigued by the enigmas of the lost city. John Gardiner Wilkinson, one of the first British Egyptologists, the son of a minister, attended Oxford but left, before obtaining his degree, for a career in the army. While stationed in Italy, Wilkinson learned of the attempts of Egyptologists to decipher hieroglyphs. Excited, he headed straight for Egypt where he remained for twelve years. Like all the pioneers of Egyptology, Wilkinson was self-taught, but his brief military experience prepared him for the spartan regime that was to become his life. After taking up residence in Thebes, Wilkinson first cataloged the tombs in the Valley of the Kings. It was a simple matter. With a can of paint in one hand and a brush in the other, he numbered each one. His numbers remain to this today.

Wilkinson traveled to Amarna in 1824. He found the remains of temples, palaces, tombs, houses, and broad thoroughfares, everything you would expect in an ancient city, but something was askew. The art—the wall paintings, carvings, and sculpture—differed from anything he had ever seen in Egypt. Like their images on the blocks that were found a century later at Karnak, the king and queen were portrayed as deformed. The king had wide hips and obvious breasts, an almost feminine figure. The body of the queen had equally wide hips and obvious breasts, though this was not notable for a woman. However, her neck was impossibly long and her arms were thin and spindly. Pictures of the princesses showed elongations at the backs of their heads. Accompanying these figures was a solar disk with its rays shining down upon the royal family, each ray terminating in a hand that held either an ankh, the symbol of life, or a scepter, the symbol of power. Who were these peculiar people? Wilkinson could not tell; their names had been erased.

Wilkinson couldn't decipher the hieroglyphs on the boundary markers that defined the limits of the city, but he was the first to observe what would later provide a crucial clue to Amarna's fate. The city hadn't merely been abandoned; it had been taken apart.[2] The palaces, temples, and houses had been razed to ground level, so that practically all that remained were their foundations and random blocks of stone. Only the tombs were intact, because they had been cut into mountains and couldn't be dismantled. The decorations on their walls would later provide further clues to the cataclysm at Amarna. Decades of speculation followed, but the first formal excavation of the site didn't take place until half a century later.

The French Archaeological Mission began excavating at Amarna in 1883 to attempt to solve the riddles of the family of royal misfits, their curious art, and the destruction of their city. Something unprecedented had happened here. The site was different from any previously investigated. Most excavations focused on single buildings, like Luxor Temple, or building complexes, like Karnak, but this was an entire city, although not much of it was left. All the French could see were mounds in the sand stretching for miles. It was not clear where they should begin. Because the city had been intentionally dismantled, this was a challenging excavation and there was little hope of finding treasures to bring home.

Nevertheless, the excavation proceeded, clearing the foundations of palaces, temples, and houses from sand. They discovered the suburbs and the wide road running through the city. In the east, where cliffs rose suddenly from the plain, they examined the rock cut tombs—one group to the north and one to the south. These were the tombs of the nobility and high officials of the city. In each, the unusual-looking king and queen and the sun disk were carved on almost every wall. The French were slow to publish their findings, so in 1890 Flinders Petrie, a young British archaeologist eager for answers to the questions raised by this unique site, began his own excavation.

In an era filled with colorful, adventurous Egyptologists, Petrie out-did them all. With a long white beard and ragged clothes, he looked like Charlton Heston's Moses from a Cecil B. DeMille production. Petrie thought nothing of walking sixteen miles to town to pick up the weekly wages for his crew, then walking back to camp.

Even in the early days of excavation there was a brisk market for an-tiquities. One of the problems on all early excavations was theft by the workmen of small objects found as they were digging. If a workman un-covered a fragment of jewelry and hid it in his robes, he could sell it for more than a month's wages. Petrie instituted a system of paying his workers a fair price for the objects they unearthed, when they turned them in, so he was the only excavator who got a fairly complete picture of finds from his site. Still, thievery from the outside remained a prob-lem. Disreputable characters would lurk on the fringes of an excavation to see what they might pilfer under cover of the night. This didn't faze Petrie, who recorded his encounter with a thief:

> One man Quibell held down while I walloped him. He swore that he would go to the Consul; that I had broken his leg; I let him crawl off on hands and knees some way, and then, giving a great shout, ran at him, when he made off like a hare."[3]

These were the wild west days of Egyptology.

Petrie became intrigued by the new art style. For a thousand years the king of Egypt had been depicted as young and vigorous, well muscled, ready to stride into battle. The pharaoh always was victorious. But at Amarna there were no battle scenes, no pharaoh smiting the tra-ditional enemies of Egypt. Even more surprising, there were no scenes of pharaoh making offerings to the gods, indeed, no recognizable gods at all. Instead, Petrie found scenes of the pharaoh and his family in which the king affectionately cradled his children on his lap, tender scenes of the pharaoh kissing a daughter or his wife, and scenes of the pharaoh and his queen worshipping the sun rather than any recognizable Egyptian god. Nothing like these pictures had ever before appeared in 2,000 years of Egyptian art.

This was an incredible departure from centuries of traditional Egyptian art in which not only the subject matter, but even the proportions of the figures and their relative sizes were carefully regulated. When artists began decorating a tomb or temple, the first thing they did was draw a red grid on the wall to guide proportions—two squares for the head, four squares for the shoulders, etc. They almost reduced wall decoration to paint-by-numbers. When it came to Akhenaten, all the old rules of proportion went out the window. The queen often stood just as tall as the pharaoh, his children were drawn in the same scale, even commoners seemed little shorter than their king. Petrie found Amarna art completely absorbing, an artistic breath of fresh air.

The more that was revealed about the mystery family as the excavation continued, the more Petrie became enamored. It seemed as if this pharaoh—whose name was eventually revealed to be Akhenaten—was a religious visionary! After centuries of worshipping a multitude of deities, the pharaoh banished all the others in favor of one god—the solar disk, the Aten. He had introduced monotheism to Egypt. "Living in Truth," the motto adapted by Akhenaten, seemed to Petrie to be the crux of the revolution. Akhenaten must have had a physical deformity, but in keeping with his motto, he permitted, or perhaps insisted, that he be portrayed realistically. The idea carried over to choices of subject, hence the intimate family scenes.

All in all, the art was lovely. In 1891 Petrie unearthed beautifully painted floors in what had once been the palace. Birds flying over marshes with animals cavorting below still glowed in their original, vibrant colors. Petrie copied 250 square feet of floor paintings himself for eventual publication. The floor was so spectacular that Petrie built a wooden walkway for visitors, so they could amble around the paintings without causing damage to them. Concerned that local carpenters might scratch the floors by dragging their materials across them, Petrie performed all the carpentry himself. For years after Petrie closed his excavations, tourists continued to flock to the wonderful paintings. Unfortunately, as there was no pathway from the river, visitors often cut across a farmer's fields and damaged his crops. One night the farmer hacked the pavements to bits.

Petrie was a religious man who saw the beginnings of his own faith in Akhenaten's monotheism. Like many early Egyptologists of similar background, he came to Egypt because it was a part of the Holy Land, the place of the Exodus, to find confirmation for the Bible. Still, aside from the religious aspect, Petrie was not far from the truth. Akhenaten is the first individual whose abstract ideas had a profound effect on his society; the first man in recorded history to speak of a single god. As Petrie put it:

> No king of Egypt, nor of any other part of the world, has ever carried out his honesty of expression so openly. Thus in every line Akhenaten stands out as perhaps the most original thinker that ever lived in Egypt, and one of the greatest idealists of the world. No man appears to have made a greater stride to a new standpoint than he did . . .[4]

Petrie had no formal training in translating hieroglyphs so he couldn't completely understand the inscribed material he found; nonetheless he realized how important the boundary markers for the city were, and hoped to make some sense of their inscriptions. Assigning a letter to each stela, he began assiduously copying their inscriptions, including one of the most inaccessible stelae that required viewing through a telescope![5] When his drawings were later translated by others, the fourteen standing stones Akhenaten had erected to define the area of his new city were told an amazing story.

The stelae, all carved within a four-year period, presented two versions of the same declaration. Akhenaten claimed that the Aten, himself, had led him to the site, and commanded him to build upon the spot where the Aten first manifested himself, where the world had come into existence. The pharaoh had been directed through a mystical vision to build a new city in the wilderness. He named the city Akhetaten—Horizon of the Aten. He assured any reader of the stela that

> His majesty appeared in his great chariot of electrum, like the Aten when he rises in his city horizon . . . Now, it is the Aten, my father, who advised me concerning it, Akhetaten. No official ever advised me concerning it; or people who are in the entire land ever advised me concerning . . . making Akhetaten in this deserted place.[6]

Perhaps, looking across the horizon, Akhenaten saw a line of cliffs broken only by a wadi (valley) and realized the landscape formed the shape of the hieroglyph for horizon [O]. Perhaps this was his sign from the Aten. When I was staying at Amarna a few years ago, I rose early one day and looked out my window to see the sun rising in a notch in the cliffs across the Nile, just like the hieroglyph. I could not help but think, "Akhenaten really did see it."

After describing the buildings he would construct for "his father," the Aten, the stelae closes with a remarkable pledge:

> As for the southern landmark which is upon the eastern mountains of Akhetaten . . . I shall not pass beyond it toward the south, forever and ever . . . As for the middle landmark which is upon the eastern mountains of Akhetaten . . . I shall not pass beyond it toward the east forever and ever . . .[7]

Akhenaten vowed never to leave the city. I wonder if anyone at the time realized the effect that the pharaoh's pledge would have on Egypt. If the king remained in the city forever, he could not fulfill the traditional roles of a pharaoh. He could not lead the army against the enemies of Egypt, nor attend to any matter of state that required him to travel outside of this one city. This meant that the management of the country had passed from the king to civilian functionaries. Resignation of royal power left the more ambitious members of the court scrambling to pick up the pieces. Nor would Akhenaten have the opportunity to connect with the offended, yet still powerful, priests in Thebes and Memphis. The king had taken a throne that provided absolute power, then made the decision to abrogate all responsibility! Akhenaten wasn't just changing the religion, he was changing the role of the king. In tradition-bound Egypt, this was a revolution as stunning as his banishment of the old religion. It seems that Akhenaten's idea of kingship was to shepherd his people in their spiritual lives only.

One day Akhenaten gathered his followers in a worship service at the site of one of the boundary stelae and spoke to those assembled in a sort of "Sermon on the Mount":

> To the great and living Aten . . . ordaining life, vigorously alive, my Father . . . my wall of millions of cubits, my reminder of Eternity, my witness to what is eternal, who proclaims Himself with his two hands, whom no craftsman had devised, who is established in the rising and setting each day ceaselessly . . . He fills the land with His rays and makes everyone to live . . .[8]

This declaration contains an important phrase—"whom no craftsman had devised." The implication is subtle but clear: the Aten, the true god, is intangible and abstract. This announcement signaled the end of all cult statues—mythology and symbolism were gone. No longer would craftsmen sculpt figures of the gods. No longer would there be a familiar image for the faithful to focus on, no more "Books of the Dead" with their vignettes of the denizens of the journey to the netherworld. The new god was as elusive as the sun's rays.

The shift from visual gods to an abstract concept was perhaps the most fundamental change that Akhenaten instituted. Ancient Egyptians were advanced and sophisticated in many areas, but they were not abstract thinkers. They left no philosophical writings, such as would come from the Greeks a thousand years later. Egyptian mathematics was the best in the ancient world, but it was not abstract. They developed some geometry because they needed to resurvey farm boundary lines that were swept away each year when the Nile flooded the fields, but they did not inquire about the nature of space. All their thoughts were directed to specific, concrete needs. Akhenaten, it seems, thought in ways completely new to the Egyptians. When he moved his followers to Amarna, he carried them on a greater mental journey than any of them could imagine.

AKHENATEN THE DREAMER

The fullest explanation of the theology of the new religion comes from a hymn carved on the walls of several tombs at Amarna. The most elaborate version is incorporated in the west wall of the tomb of Aye, a favorite courtier of Akhenaten. All indications are that Akhenaten himself composed it. Although written centuries before the Old Testament, it has a similar tone. In fact, scholars find resemblances to Psalm 104.

Splendid you rise in heaven's lightland,
O living Aten, creator of life!
When you have dawned in eastern lightland,
You fill every land with your beauty.
Your are beauteous, great, radiant,
High over every land;
Your rays embrace the lands,
To the limit of all that you made.
Reign Re, you reach their limits,
You bend them (for) the sons whom you love;
Though you are far, your rays are on earth,
Though one sees you, your strides are unseen . . .

How many are your deeds,
Though hidden from sight,
O Sole God beside whom there is none!
You made the earth as you wished, you alone,
All peoples, herds, and flocks:

All upon earth that walk on legs,
All on high that fly on wings,
The lands of Khor and Kush,
The land of Egypt.
You set up every man in his place,
You supply their needs;
Everyone has his food,
His lifetime is counted.
Their tongues differ in speech,
Their characters likewise;
Their skins are distinct,
For you distinguished the peoples . . .

You are in my heart,
There is no other who knows you,
Only your son, Nefer-khepru-re (Akhenaten), Sole one of Re,
Whom you have taught your ways and might . . .[9]

Poetry shows Akhenaten at his best. The "Hymn to Aten" is one of the great intellectual achievements of the ancient world. By so elegantly stating the essential theological doctrine, this hymn must have been a great inspiration to his followers. Only one god—the Aten—is responsible for creation of the world and that god created the people of all nations, not just the Egyptians. Of course, if the Aten was the god of all people, then the Egyptians were no longer superior. By embracing all the people of the world, Akhenaten had undermined the justification for all of Egypt's previous military campaigns. The world no longer revolved around Egypt; it revolved around the sun.

The "Hymn to the Aten" reveals Akhenaten as a man of sensitivity, an inspired poet, while his speech on the boundary stelae shows a visionary, a mystic. The policies instituted and the changes made during his reign were so radical in their humanism and so divergent from tradition that they could only have been initiated by the pharaoh himself. From temple and tomb walls we discover a man devoted to his family.

From his city we observe the bold planning of a creative mind. From his art we discern his love of beauty, his belief in "living in truth."

Nefertiti, whose name means "the beautiful one has come," is always shown at his side making daily offerings to the Aten. They are together at every official function, affectionately holding hands in public and embracing in their chariot as they drive to the temple. The king refers to Nefertiti as "Sweet of Love" and " in the sound of whose voice the king takes delight." Each boundary stela includes a long preamble extolling the virtues of his beloved queen:

> And the Heiress, Great in the Palace, Fair of Face, Adorned with the Double Plumes, Mistress of Happiness, endowed with Favors, at hearing whose voice the King rejoices, the Chief Wife of the King, his beloved, the Lady of the Two Lands, Neferne-feruaten-Nefertiti (Good like the beauty of Aten—a Beautiful Woman Comes), May she live forever and always.[10]

Devoted to his young daughters, he is often shown holding one or more on his knee, kissing them tenderly. Akhenaten, a champion of family values, emerges from the ruins of Amarna as a man we can like, thoughtful and caring. We understand why Petrie was taken with the man.

It is tempting to look only at this side of Akhenaten, the man who preached love and peace, but there was another, darker side. Akhenaten was also an intolerant elitist. A second look at Amarna art reveals that the Aten shines only on Akhenaten and the royal family, not on the Egyptian people. The common man is never shown receiving the Aten's rays and the symbols of life and power. The Aten was Akhenaten's personal god; everyone else had to make do with secondary light reflected from Akhenaten.

An examination of the records found at Amarna show that the king was also inept and disinterested in ruling the country. The Egypt that he inherited from his father, Amenhotep III, was in its golden age, at the peak of its power. Taxes collected from her foreign territories flowed into Egypt each year, but, after Akhenaten took over, no one minded the store any longer. Revenue was only forthcoming as long as Egypt was strong with an army to enforce the collection of tribute. Akhenaten, unwilling or unable to attend to the affairs of the government, effectively turned over the administration of the country to his aides. Without a strong king at the helm, Egypt's tax revenue and lucrative trade agreements were allowed to lapse. The army received little support. While Akhenaten contemplated the Aten, the affairs of state disintegrated from neglect. He was the flower child of a wealthy man (Amenhotep III) who inherited, but ignored, the family business.

Under Akhenaten's disinterested control, Egypt's power in the Near East declined rapidly. Donald Redford, the Egyptologist who has devoted more than a quarter of a century to unearthing Akhenaten's scattered monuments, believes his findings reveal "one of the most displeasing characteristics of the way of life Akhenaten held up as a model, refined sloth."[11] As Egypt gradually lost its dominant position in the Near East, the residents of Amarna, although isolated, must have sensed that all was not well in the land. The new god, the abstract Aten, had not provided for the country and its people as well as the old gods of Egypt had. In the end, Akhenaten resorted to lavish rewards to keep the faithful true to his cause. Scenes carved on tomb walls show Akhenaten, Nefertiti, and the princesses standing at the palace's "Window of Appearances,"[12] while citizens of Amarna gather in the street below, reaching up to receive necklaces of gold handed down by the royal family. By the end of Akhenaten's reign, the distribution of gold necklaces may have been little more than a bribe to keep the people faithful.

With his control slipping, Akhenaten in a surge of fanaticism dispatched workmen throughout Egypt to chisel out the name of Amun, the Chief god of Thebes, wherever it appeared on monuments. Even the three hieroglyphs signifying "Amun" in his father's name (Amenhotep) were erased.

Akhenaten died in the seventeenth year of his reign, taking his vision of a new world with him. His body was never found; no inscription tells us what caused his death. We only know that a reign that began by preaching peace and beauty ended in a regime of intolerance.

5

Tutankhamen's Parents

God will attack the rebel for the sake of the temple,
He will be overcome for what he has done . . .
He will find no favor on the day of woe.

—King Khety Nebkaure
circa 2150 B.C.

Immediately after Akhenaten's death, messengers were dispatched to announce the news throughout the land. They traveled to Thebes in the south and Memphis in the north. Normally, such an announcement would cause the whole nation to grieve from both sadness and worry because it demonstrated Seth's triumph over Osiris, a disruption of the divine order. Akhenaten's death must have been different, eliciting a variety of emotions in different segments of society. Divine order had already been profoundly disrupted, by Pharaoh himself, during a reign marked by years and years of confusion. At least in private, there must have been great rejoicing among the priests of Amun in Thebes; their prayers had been answered, the pharaoh who chiseled out the name of their god had felt Amun's revenge. In Memphis, priests awaited the day when they could again worship Ptah, creator of the world, as they had for centuries past.

The military establishment, too, must have cheered. Nothing pained them more than to merely stand by watching Egypt's dominance ebb away. It had been decades since they made their last annual campaign to wrest tribute from the territories. First, Amenhotep III had focused all thirty-five years of his reign on building in Thebes, seeking immortality in temples rather than in the battles that tradition dictated. Thirty-five years of parades had been hard to endure, but at least the earlier drubbings of Egypt's vassal states had so cowed them that they remained loyal. It was the last fifteen years that had wrenched the army's collective heart. One by one, Egypt's foreign tributaries had fallen under the power of the hated Hittites or equally despised Mitanni, after plaintive letters from ambassadors for an Egyptian army had fallen on Pharaoh's deaf ears. The soldiers must have rejoiced more than anyone when news reached them of Akhenaten's death—now, their careers might begin again.

The citizens of Amarna would have been agitated by uncertainty and fear. What and where would their place be in a new universe? Their religion, which was the sole reason for Amarna, had been the vision of one man. With the prophet dead, who would take his place? What would become of his city and people? These questions soon would be answered, but first there was a funeral to prepare.

Traditionally, seventy days were required for mummifying a pharaoh and all the accompanying rituals, but along with everything else in his religion, Akhenaten had changed the concept of life after death. The old belief that the next world was a continuation of this one, only better, was too materialistic and worldly for the pharaoh who gave the world its first abstract god. Akhenaten believed the next life would be a shadow existence—the deceased, or at least his spirit, remained in his tomb and awoke each morning when the Aten appeared on the horizon. From broken fragments excavators found in his tomb, we know that Akhenaten was buried with ushabti statues. These traditional netherworld servants, in his case, did not hold farm implements for work in Elysian fields, they held ankhs, the sign of life.[1] We do not know what other new rituals or prayers would have honored Akhenaten's spirit, but I believe that the high priest, Meri-Re, must at least have recited the Hymn to the Aten.

Work began on Akhenaten's tomb when he first moved to Amarna, and continued until the time of his death. The desolate spot he selected for his eternal resting place lay six and one half miles from the city. The first time I traveled the forbidding landscape, I wondered, why here? The only way to reach the tomb is through a valley strewn with boulders, natural obstacles for transporting workers and supplies. Once there, though, I understood why Akhenaten had been drawn to the spot. It has the distinct feeling of the Valley of the Kings in Thebes. Similar white limestone cliffs rise above the valley floor. The plan of the tomb is like those in the Theban valley where Akhenaten saw his father, Amenhotep III, laid to rest. Perhaps Akhenaten, still suffering from childhood rejection, was seeking his father's acceptance at the end.

The royal tomb began with a twenty-five-foot-long descending passage cut into the floor of the valley. At the bottom and to the right, a level corridor led to an unfinished suite of six rooms. Ahead, the descent continued for another twenty-five feet to a second suite of rooms, also on the right. In one of these we will pick up the trail of Tutankhamen. The passage then ended in a cavernous room that contained the sarcophagus of Akhenaten. Reconstruction of the fragments found by excavators showed that Akhenaten abandoned tradition even in the design of his sarcophagus. He chose a simple granite rectangular box, whereas most of his ancestors had been buried in stone coffins shaped like cartouches, the sign of royalty. At each corner, traditionally, the figures of goddesses were carved whose outstretched arms protected the king. The goddesses were banished from Akhenaten's sarcophagus in favor of four images of his beloved Nefertiti.[2]

While the pharaoh's body was being prepared for burial (we have no records for this, so it is not known how, or even if, the bodies were mummified under the new religion), a matter even more pressing had to be settled. The country could not wait seventy days for a leader; a new pharaoh had to be crowned. There were few choices. As far as we can determine from inscriptions on the broken blocks at Amarna, Akhenaten's family was severely depleted. Nefertiti had died several years before him. Another shadowy member of the royal house who reached adulthood was a boy named Smenkare. He may have been Tutankhamen's brother, but is not mentioned as a child or shown with the other royal children, though he appears briefly as coregent with Akhenaten at the tail end of his reign. Smenkare, however, died after less than two years of sharing the throne, leaving Akhenaten alone until his death.

Of the six daughters born to Akhenaten and Nefertiti, Ankhesen-paaten is the only one we hear of after her father's death. One other may have lived, but there is no solid evidence. Not only did infant mortality approach fifty percent of the birthrate in ancient times, but child mortality was also high. At the very least, four daughters had died; Ankhe-senpaaten may well have been the only surviving member of the family with pure royal blood. The only other child with any royal blood at all was a young boy named Tutankh*aten*, who would later change the last part of his name to *-amen*. I believe he was the son of Akhenaten. Although many Egyptologists agree on this point, many do not. It is time to figure out who he was.

When Petrie began excavating the palace at Amarna, one of the first things he looked for were its rubbish mounds, a source for copious information about palace life. Royal objects—jars, dishes, lamps, cosmetic jars—were often inscribed with the owner's names, and, when broken, were discarded in the royal garbage heap. Petrie knew the value of carefully sifting through such debris, and put some of his diggers on the job. Hundreds of objects inscribed with the names of the royal family were found, including some with Tutankh*aten*'s name. It was clear to Petrie that this mysterious Tutankhaten, who at this time was a shadowy figure to Egyptologists, was in some way connected with the religious revolution at Amarna.

Fortunately, in Tutankhamen's day it was the fashion of the royal court to wear ceramic finger rings with the names of one member or another of the royal household. These bright blue ceramic rings, probably party favors, were fragile and broken easily. Among the royal trash Petrie found dozens of them with the names of Akhenaten, his queen Nefer-titi, the six princesses, and Tutankhaten. It was clear that he was a member of the royal household, but who were his parents and why was he never shown with the princesses? One question may answer the other, so let's start with Tutankhamen's father.

If the temples and palaces at Amarna still stood, scenes from their walls might have supplied the missing details of Tutankhamen's parentage. There would have been thousands of blocks that once composed the great temples, all carved with inscriptions; surely they were not all smashed to dust. Where were they? Petrie seems not to have wondered about this. Years after he left Amarna, a German expedition working across the river from the ghost city of Amarna discovered that the blocks had been floated across the Nile for reuse in other temples at a later city called Hermopolis. These provided the first real clue about Tutankhamen's parents.

When the German expedition translated the Hermopolis blocks, as they later became known, they found the inscription *"King's son, of his body, his beloved, Tutankhaten."* Other objects presented Tutankh*aten's* name in a cartouche which indicated that this Tutankh*aten*-amen was a king. The Hermopolis block established with certainty that this king was also the son of a king, but of which king?

Who Tutankhamen's parents were has been debated by Egyptologists ever since the Hermopolis block was found. Some believe he was the son of Amenhotep III and his Queen Tiye. I have never found this theory credible because of simple arithmetic. From other sources that I will talk about later, we know the year Tutankhamen died, and from a careful examination of his mummy we know he was about nineteen at the time of death. Working backwards from the time of death shows that he was born in the middle of Akhenaten's seventeen-year reign. Queen Tiye married Amenhotep, Akhenaten's father, early in his thirty-eight-year reign. Even if she were fifteen at the time, she would have been in her fifties when Tutankhamen was born, almost certainly beyond childbearing age. Also, Amenhotep and Tiye never mention a son Tutankhaten when their other sons are discussed. The records show they had six children, four girls and two boys. We know all their names. Finally, the name *Tutankhaten* is an Amarna name, associating him with the Aten, rather than with the god Amun or other traditional gods Amenhotep III named his children after.

The best candidate for Tutankhamen's father is Akhenaten himself. The problem, however, is that Tutankhamen is never shown with the rest of his family. The Amarna tomb walls show Akhenaten, Nefertiti, and six daughters, time after time—never a son. If Tutankhamen really was Akhenaten's son, why isn't he shown with the rest of the family? There are two good answers. The first is that royal princes in the Eighteenth Dynasty are rarely shown on monuments, only princesses. No one knows why. Perhaps pharaohs feared that pictures of sons would establish royal credentials for a competitor before the father was ready to give up his throne. Whatever the rationale, the omission of sons in royal family scenes, in this dynasty, in no way indicated that sons did not exist.

A second, more compelling reason, came to light in the 1960s when cosmetic vessels in both the British Museum and New York's Metropolitan Museum of Art were found to have the names and titles of a previously unknown Amarna queen named Kiya.[3] The Metropolitan's vessel had been purchased in 1920 from Howard Carter, before his discovery of Tutankhamen's tomb, during a time when he sold antiquities to make ends meet. The inscription, carved in the white stone and filled with blue pigment, gives Kiya's title: "Wife and great beloved of the King of Upper and Lower Egypt, who lives in truth, (Akhenaten) the beautiful child of the living Aten, who shall live forever, eternally, Kiya." The vase in the British Museum bears an almost identical inscription.[4] Once Egyptologists became aware that Akhenaten had a second wife, they searched for other traces of her.

Soon, blocks from the dismantled temples at Amarna were found with Kiya's name (fig. 2). Although she was not called the "King's Great Wife"—that was Nefertiti—Kiya was the king's second wife, still an important person of the court. The blocks recovered from Akhenaten's dismantled temples contain scenes of Kiya in the presence of Akhenaten, making offerings to the solar disk. Others show her worshipping the Aten in a temple built especially for her. She is never present, however, in any scene with the Great Wife, Nefertiti. They may have shared a husband, but certainly not the same prominence.[5]

Many of the blocks with scenes of Kiya came from the area of the city known as the Maru-Aten where her temple, called a sunshade, once stood. This "temple" was actually a large park enclosed with stone kiosks, probably closer to a meditation garden than a formal place of worship.[6] Kiya's sunshade was a place of beauty with a large central pool, pavements decorated with scenes of nature—marshes, water birds, plants and trees—everything that the Aten provided. The kiosk, inlaid with colored ceramics and stones, showed Kiya making daily offerings to the god.

Kiya's name ceased to appear on monuments around the ninth year of Akhenaten's reign, just about the time Tutankhamen was born, suggesting the possibility that she may have died while giving birth to the future king of Egypt. Soon after her death, her name was erased from her sunshade temple, replaced by that of the eldest Amarna princess. If Kiya were indeed Tutankhamen's mother, that would explain why the young prince did not appear in the official scenes of the royal family. Children of the king by a secondary wife occupied a lower status than children of "the Great Wife." Tutankhamen would not have been displayed with his more exalted half sisters.

All of this was merely abstract theory until some confirmation that Akhenaten was Tutankhamen's father was discovered in his isolated tomb at Amarna. From the era of the pyramids on, the tombs of the kings were rarely completed by the time of their burial. I think the idea was that it was bad luck to complete a tomb before the king died, and there generally was not enough time to finish it during the interval between death and entombment. So Akhenaten's tomb is incomplete, but wall decorations had been finished in several rooms. The scenes were like nothing ever found before in a pharaoh's tomb. Because of his religious beliefs, these were not scenes of gods welcoming pharaoh into the next world. Tradition had been replaced with intimate glimpses and tender moments from Pharaoh's private life. It had been known to Egyptologists[7] for a long time that one wall presented a touching scene of Akhenaten and Nefertiti mourning the death of their second daughter, Meketaten. The puzzle was that there are actually two such scenes in the tomb, remarkably similar, one in room Alpha and another in room Gamma. Both show a dead woman on a bed, Akhenaten and Nefertiti in attitudes of mourning, and an infant held in a nurse's arms. Most experts supposed that both recorded the death in childbirth of Meketaten. But why would there be two scenes of the same event? In the 1970s, Professor Geoffrey Martin of University College, London, in the course of making an accurate record of everything that remained on the walls of the tomb, found the confirmation that Akhenaten was Tutankhamen's father.

Martin noticed that, although the two mourning scenes are similar, only one (in room Gamma) names the dying woman as Meketaten, the daughter of Akhenaten and Nefertiti. The other scene, in room Alpha, does not identify either the mother or her infant. It could certainly be that two different women, each of whom died in childbirth, are separately mourned. In the scene with the unnamed mother in room Alpha, Akhenaten and Nefertiti lean over the mother who has just died, while behind them a woman (nurse?) holds a newborn infant. Most significant, the nurse and infant are shaded by a fan bearer, indicating a royal baby. Martin plausibly suggests that the scene in room Alpha shows the birth of Tutankhamen, and that the mother is probably Kiya, the second wife of Akhenaten.[8]

Put together, the case runs like this: Someone gave birth to a royal child (hence the royal fan bearer). Kiya, a secondary wife, received special honors, such as her own little chapel, which suggests she had done something to raise her above the role of a harem wife. As it turned out, this elevated status did not last (she died in childbirth); her chapel was rededicated to someone else. Presenting a daughter to Pharaoh would not excite a father who already had six others. The possibility of a son would, and it would earn a picture in the king's tomb if it came to pass, especially if he had none by his primary wife. Hence, in all probability, Kiya, Akhenaten's second wife, bore the king a son. We know that Tutankhamen was the son of some king (from the Hermopolis blocks), probably not Amenhotep III and his elderly wife. The conclusion is tenuous, but I believe it is correct. Tutankhamen was the son of Kiya and Akhenaten. This would explain why Tutankhamen was never shown with the other princesses. He was born of a minor, though honored, wife of the pharaoh.

Merely because Tutankhamen was not shown in the official family portraits, we should not think he was neglected or ignored. Unless and until someone else came along, Tutankhamen stood just one step behind the heir apparent, Smenkare. We can assume that Tutankhamen enjoyed all the benefits and attention befitting a member of the royal household, one who might be pharaoh someday.

We are now in a position to reconstruct what young Tutankhamen's life must have been like at Amarna. Born in the middle of the greatest religious revolution Egypt had ever seen, Tutankhamen started his life in a bustling, energetic family at its peak, full of the optimism and excitement of a new movement, but distant from the rest of Egypt and its traditional gods. As a young child he wouldn't have understood the ideas his father preached, but he would have sensed that his father, the king, was an important leader.

Tutankhamen grew up in the royal nursery, along with six princesses, his half-sisters, all but one older than he. The heir apparent, Smenkare, was probably an older brother, or half-brother, more than ten years his senior, and may have been on his own already. Tutankhamen began learning to read and write around the age of four. Learning to read hieroglyphs is more difficult than one might think. It's not just picture writing. When you see an owl or a foot hieroglyph, the inscription isn't talking about birds and feet. The owl represents the sound of *M* and the foot the sound of *B;* many hieroglyphs are phonetic just like our alphabet. Tutankhamen learned twenty-five letters of the Egyptian alphabet, and then he started on the hundreds of other hieroglyphs that are ideographic—pictures of the words or idea they represent.

Hours upon hours would be devoted to writing hieroglyphs correctly with a reed brush the student chewed on until the end splayed and was soft, like a paintbrush. The scribal palette was a rectangular block of wood or stone with pits for blocks of red and black ink and a hollowed slit to hold the reed brushes. Tutankhamen's palette, later found in his tomb, was carved from ivory and inscribed with his name. When he was ready to write, he dipped his brush in a little bowl of water, touched it to the solid ink, and drew his hieroglyphs on broken bits of pottery for practice, later on papyrus. The hieroglyphs for writing show the implements Tutankhamen learned with: 𓏞 the palette, the little bowl, and the reed brush. Tutankhamen practiced by copying texts of the wisdom of earlier generations. Traditionally, maxims that would improve the mind as well as penmanship were favorites. *"Let your name go forth, while your mouth is silent." "Report a thing observed, not heard."* I suspect that as Tutankhamen grew older, he was given prayers to the Aten to copy.

Life was not all study for Tutankhamen. He must have gone swimming off the banks of the Nile with his sisters and children of the courtiers, along with an entourage of royal guards and nurses to watch for crocodiles. A favorite love poem from Tutankhamen's time laments, "My love is on one bank of the river, I on the other, and there's a crocodile on the sandbank." Tutankhamen learned to hunt ducks with a small bow, especially made for a boy's short arms, and probably delighted in hiding in the reeds waiting for his target, often assisted by one of his sisters. It was a sport that he enjoyed all his life. The young prince had few cares. His older brother was going to be king, so Tutankhamen did not bear the responsibility or need the training to officiate at state and religious functions.

When he was about eight years old, Tutankhamen probably learned to drive a chariot. An experienced charioteer must have accompanied him to control its two prancing steeds, until Tutankhamen was strong enough to handle the reins alone. His teacher would make the young prince practice for weeks to master the fine points of driving over rough and sandy terrain. Tutankhamen's chariot training was not to prepare him for battle someday—his father had no interest in military matters. It was so he could present a virile figure driving along the royal road in a family procession.

There were some things Tutankhamen missed out on. His father had pledged never to leave the city, so it is unlikely that Tutankhamen was permitted a trip to the delta, 250 miles north of Amarna, where the best duck and bird hunting was found in papyrus thickets so dense that two people ten feet apart couldn't see each other. There, fowlers caught twenty birds in their nets at one time. Tutankhamen would have heard conversations in the palace about such fabulous hunts, but he could not participate. He must also have heard stories about Thebes, the grand city with temples even larger than those at Amarna, where his grandfather had ruled and his father had grown up. But he couldn't visit there either. That was where the priests of Amun lived, and only recently his father had sent servants to carve out the name of Amun from all the temples, even from the top of Queen Hatshepsut's obelisk—although it was so high that the unenthusiastic workmen left it alone, figuring that no one would see it anyway.

By the time Tutankhamen was eight or nine he would have sensed troubles in his father's court. The foreign office was receiving letters from distant lands, far beyond the borders of Egypt, on little clay tablets hard as rocks. The tablets, ranging in size from two and a half to three and a half inches wide, and two and a half inches to nine inches long, were covered with small wedge-shaped writing, quite different from the hieroglyphs he was learning to write. They were written in Akkadian, the international language of the day. Many of the letters had been sent to Egypt from kings of other countries, Byblos (Lebanon), Ugarit (Syria), Assyria (Iraq), and Hatti (Turkey.) Others were sent by vassals requesting favors from the pharaoh. Many expressed puzzlement—why doesn't the king answer their requests?

For example, a succession of letters from a loyal prince of Byblos named Rib-Addi, Akhenaten's man in Lebanon, were filled with desperate pleas. He wrote no fewer than sixty-four letters. Rib-Addi is known from earlier letters to Akhenaten's father, during better times, that reveal a man of good business sense, able to conduct matters of state with dignity and pride. During Akhenaten's reign, Rib-Addi's position in Byblos had weakened; the faithful prince wrote repeatedly to Akhenaten telling of his plight, pleading with to Pharaoh to send troops.

> *What is Abdi-Assuta, the servant, the dog, that he should take the*
> *land of the king to himself?*
> *. . . So send me fifty pairs of horses and two hundred infantry, so that I*
> *may remain in Sigata . . .*[9]

When the troops were not sent, he wrote to the Egyptian General Amanappa:

> *To Amanappa, my father, thus (saith) Rib-Adda, thy son:*
> *At the feet of my father I fall down . . .*
> *Why hast thou held back and not spoken*
> *to the king, thy lord, in order that thou mayest march*
> *forth with archers . . .*
> *So speak this word to the king, thy lord . . .*
> *That he send help to me as quickly as possible.*[10]

When even this pitiful plea went unanswered, Rib-Addi wrote to Akhenaten again:

> *Rib-Addi spoke to (his)lord, the king of the lands,*
> *The great king, the king of battles . . .*
> *At the feet of my lord, my sun,*
> *seven times seven I fall down.*
> *Let the king, the lord know that all is well with Gubla,*
> *The faithful handmaiden of the king, from the time of his fathers.*
> *But behold, now Abdi-Asirti has taken Sigata to himself*

and said to the people of Amnia: "Kill your princes. Then you will be
as we are, and you will have rest."
And they did according to his words,
And have become as the Gaz-People.
And behold now,
Abdi-Asirti has written to the warriors:
"Assemble yourselves in the house of Nimit and we will fall upon
Gubla. . . ."
Thus have they formed a conspiracy with one another,
and thus I have great fear that there is no man to rescue me
out of their hand.
Like a bird that lies in a net, so am I.[11]

The plea remained unanswered. Rib-Addi was nearly killed.

A stranger stood with drawn dagger . . . against me;
but I killed him . . .
I cannot go [out of the gate] and I have written to the palace.
(But thou has not) sent an answer.
I have been wounded [nine] times
And have so feared [for] my life . . .[12]

One can only wonder what end befell poor Rib-Addi. Tutankhamen's
father, an idealist and religious visionary, lacked all interest in dealing
with the complex business of governing a major country.

And so Tutankhamen passed his childhood in privileged circumstances, with everything at his disposal a young boy could wish for. Except that he was confined to the boundaries of just one city. Since little
was expected of him as long as Smenkare, his older brother, sat with his
father on the throne, his life was otherwise carefree, perhaps dimly
clouded by a sense that all was not right with Egypt. Then, one day,
Smenkare died. On that day Tutankhamen's life took a very serious turn.
He would one day be king. Within two years, his father, the pharaoh,
died as well.

This death left the affairs of Egypt in disarray. Predeceased by his wives and by his only adult son, Akhenaten's death extinguished the last royal adult. There must have been great confusion about what should be done, where to begin picking up the pieces, who should take control. Ankhesenpaaten and her half-brother Tutankh*aten* were the only surviving royals, but they were children. Yet the question of who would succeed Akhenaten on the throne of Egypt was settled almost by default. The ten-year-old Tutankhamen was simply the only male of the royal line and Ankhesenpaaten was the only royal female. Tutankhamen alone could be pharaoh, although his half-royal blood would have to be supplemented by the full royal blood of his sister. Ankhesenpaaten and Tutankhamen married; Tutankhamen's skinny ten-year-old frame was placed upon the very large throne of the pharaoh of Egypt.

With a power vacuum created by Akhenaten's death and the fate of Egypt at stake, there must have been furious jockeying for position among the officials of the Amarna court. A pair of ten-year-olds could not take charge, whatever their titles. Each member of the inner circle must have had a strong and varied reaction to what should be done now that their eccentric leader was gone. Several men must each have thought he was the right man to successfully steer the nation through this precarious time.

The ones with the most to lose must have been distraught when they found their positions suddenly at risk. Meri-Re, the high priest of the Aten, owed his elevated position, great wealth, and high social status to the dreamer he followed to Amarna. Examination of his tomb, one of the grandest in the necropolis, fleshes out the picture. Meri-Re held the prestigious title "Fan bearer on the right hand of the king," but also listed "High Priest of the Aten," "Royal Chancellor," "Hereditary Prince," and "One Known to the King," as evidence of his crucial role in the management of the nation.[13] His tomb walls display Akhenaten installing Meri-Re as High Priest of the Aten, and lavishing collars and necklaces of gold upon him. Meri-Re was a key player in the new religion, and close to Akhenaten. He was almost certainly alive when Akhenaten died in the seventeenth year of his reign.[14] So he would be there to make decisions for the boy-king and push him to continue the support and practice of the new religion.

Another nobleman, Panhesy, would have seconded this counsel. He was "Second Priest of the Lord of the Two Lands," "Superintendent of the Granary of the Aten," "Superintendent of the Oxen of the Aten," "Northern Chancellor of the King," and "Intimate of the King."[15] Although second to Meri-Re in religious matters, Panhesy administrated and controlled the wealth associated with the Aten and the priesthood. He, too, is shown on his tomb walls laden with gold necklaces, while servants carry the collars, bracelets, and other ornaments given to him by the king.[16]

Also glued to the king's side was the grand courtier Aye, a contemporary of Tutankhamen's grandfather, Amenhotep III. Aye may have served the royal family through two generations already. He was perhaps the oldest member of the previous regime to follow the odd-looking Akhenaten on his quest for enlightenment and seems positioned above all other officials in the court. Aye's declarations and some of his actions show him protective of the pharaoh and his family; other actions, however, suggest scheming ambition, as we will see. At this stage in our investigation, the only thing we can say with certainty is that Aye was one of the few people surrounding the new pharaoh who had direct knowledge of a different regime than Akhenaten's.

Aye was the highest-placed official in the government. His tomb, the largest and most elaborate of all the nobles, displayed his titles: Fanbearer on the Right Hand of the King, Overseer of all the Horses of His Majesty, the Royal Scribe, and, most important of all, the God's Father. "The God's Father" was a title given only to those very close to the pharaoh (the living god), and could even indicate a royal tutor, who stands in for the father. "Overseer of all the Horses of His Majesty" suggests a military connection, though in Akhenaten's time it may have been honorary because the military was neglected.

Aye's wife, Tey, also held a high position in the Amarna court—Nurse to Nefertiti. Politically, they were the best connected couple at Amarna. Tey had easy access to the queen, so knew intimate details about palace life. Her husband, Aye, had the pharaoh's ear. Together they formed the eyes and ears of the palace. Their prestige at court is confirmed on the wall of Aye's tomb, where Akhenaten is shown award-ing gold collars to both Aye and Tey in recognition of their services, making Tey the only woman placed in the ranks of "People of Gold," suggesting that she was a power in her own right. An inscription on Aye's tomb wall boasts:

> I was one favored by his lord every day, great in favor from year to year, because of the exceeding greatness of my excellence in his opinion. He doubled for me my favors like the number of sand; I was the first of the officials at the head of the people . . . My name has penetrated into the palace, because of my useful-ness to the king, because of my hearing his teaching.[17]

These do not sound like the words of a selfless family retainer. They convey a self-aggrandizing view of someone who relishes all the trap-pings of power earned because of his outstanding abilities.

Twice on the walls of his tomb, Aye shows himself and his wife re-ceiving honors and gold from the pharaoh. In one scene a man seated on a stool asks a young boy leaving the ceremony, "For whom do they rejoice, boy?" The boy replies, "They rejoice for Aye, the God's Father, together with Tey. They have been made people of gold" (fig. 4).

But work seems to have ceased on Aye's tomb long before Akhen-aten died, which is peculiar, even ominous. A number of signs tell us so. There are several ways to tell when work stopped on a tomb. Sometimes an inscription gives the date of its carving—for example, "Year 12 of Akhenaten." Another clue is to note the way the Aten's name is written. Before year 9, his name was: "Re-Horakhty lives, rejoicing in the Hori-zon in his name Shu, which is Aten." After year 9 of Akhenaten's reign the Aten's name was changed to "Re, the father who has returned as Aten." Still another way of dating a tomb is by the number of Akhen-aten's daughters shown. The fourth princess appears around year 9, the fifth around year 11, etc. The walls of Aye's tomb are inscribed with only the early form of the Aten's name, and just three princesses are shown in scenes of the royal family. It seems that work stopped on Aye's tomb around year 8 of Akhenaten's seventeen-year rule. Why? The answer may be that by year 8 of the new order, Aye, from his privileged position as an insider, saw that things were not going well at Amarna. He may have realized that Camelot was doomed. This is only speculation; what seems clear is that Aye had no intention of staying long enough in Amarna to be buried. The question is, what plans did Aye have for his future?

Someone had to rule the country in Tutankhamen's place, at least until the child approached adulthood. Meri-Re, Panhesy, and Aye are the three officials most likely to have imposed their wills on the immature king. Probably all three advised him, but there were crucial issues that divided the triumvirate. Who had the final say? Who was the real power behind the throne? Meri-Re, the high priest of the Aten, had the most to lose if the young king abandoned the Aten. Panhesy's wealth and position were also tied to the Aten's estates; he, too, would have advised Tutankhamen to continue his father's religion. Both would have urged, for their own sake if not the country's, that Amarna remain the religious and civil capital. But of the three possible regents, Aye held the highest rank—the only one titled "God's Father." Aye was not committed to either the new religion or the capital.

Almost immediately the real ruler of Egypt revealed himself. The decision was made to return to Thebes and resurrect the old religion. Only Aye, of the three Amarna leaders, makes the transition to the new regime. Meri-Re and Panehesy disappear from history; we can only imagine what happened to them. Although no inscription explicitly states that Aye became the vizier of Egypt, the equivalent of prime minister, most Egyptologists agree that he assumed that role.[18]

Now that he had control, Aye faced powerful interest blocks, such as the army and priesthood, grumbling loudly about the state of the country. Aye's power consisted of two very young royal children. His first step was to announce the restoration of the old regime by holding the coronation of the new pharaoh in Thebes, the traditional religious capital of Egypt. As soon as he could, Aye would have Tutankh*aten* and Ankhesen*paaten* change their names to show their association with the old god Amun, becoming Tutankhamen and Ankhesenamen (the "amen" part of their names is an English transliteration of Amun). Both acts would earn the support of the priests. The army would watch to see what lay ahead for them, but could take heart in the fact that the new pharaoh had at least ended the isolation in Amarna.

Sailing to Thebes for the coronation would have been the first time Tutankhamen and Ankhesenamen ever traveled outside of Amarna, distracting them from the death of their father and the turmoil of Amarna. As the boat sailed up the Nile they saw villagers lining the banks of the river hoping to catch a glimpse of their new king and queen. When they landed at Thebes, these children, raised in an isolated city with only one god, must have been overwhelmed by the bustling city, its multitude of temples and panoply of different gods. They were orphans separated from the only home they had known, about to denounce their religion. It must all have been quite terrifying.

Aye and his wife Tey would have identified the sights, but it would have been a dozen years since they had seen Thebes. No longer did the city glow with self-importance, beckoning with prosperity. It had become a darker, more dangerous place. Here the children would have been confronted with suspicious, even hostile looks, a frightening change from the pure adoring faces of simple farmers along the way. Tutankhamen and his bride must have clung to each other, perhaps holding hands, wondering what lay ahead for them in this frightening, large world. We know from portraits and inscriptions that a genuine love developed between them, perhaps nurtured by such shared, difficult early experiences (fig. 6).

They were installed in the once-grand palace of their grandfather, Amenhotep III. A king had not been in residence for almost two decades, so workmen and painters must have frantically prepared for the royal arrival. Built of mud brick, covered with plaster, beautifully painted with elaborate motifs, this palace was a sprawling affair, with gardens and lakes and spacious quarters for Pharaoh's queen, wives, concubines, and children. Tutankhamen's father had grown up here as Amenhotep IV. Aye may have been a visitor. No doubt old retainers would tell Tutankhamen and Ankhesenamen stories about their grandmother, Queen Tiye, and her fabulous pleasure lake, and about their grandfather, Amenhotep III, who had built as no one before him. They would tell them about tribute from foreign lands, paraded before the palace, exotic things like ostriches and giraffes, which the children had never seen. Compared to this busy palace in the center of a larger world, Amarna was an isolated ivory tower. Tutankhamen and Ankhesenamen would have to absorb a great deal, and quickly, in order to survive.

Then came the coronation. Tutankhamen stood before the gateway to Karnak Temple, the largest building he had even seen, looking onto a courtyard filled with thousands of priests who served the god his father had banished. For the crowd of Thebans thronging outside, this was their first glimpse of the new king who they prayed would return Egypt to the good old days.

Tutankhamen was purified with ritual waters poured from four gold vases. Now he could enter the house of the gods. The procession moved slowly past the obelisks of Tutankhamen's ancestors, Tuthmosis I and Hatshepsut, past the shrine erected by Tuthmosis III, stopping at various places for rituals and prayers. He was presented with the crowns of kingship—the tall white crown representing upper Egypt, then the red crown of lower Egypt—successively placed on his head. He became the "Lord of the Two Lands, " King of Upper and Lower Egypt." Then the blue "kepresh" crown (sometimes called the "War Crown") was conferred and he became the commander of the army (fig. 5).

The crowns of Egypt were revered as possessors of magical properties bestowing invincibility on those who wore them. Probably only one of each type existed at any time, passed from pharaoh to pharaoh on the day of his coronation. No such crown has ever been found in an excavation—these were the only royal objects the kings of Egypt were not allowed to take to their graves.

As the procession moved along the passageways between the temples, Tutankhamen neared his child-sized throne covered in gold. There he was presented with the royal symbols of his authority, the crook and the flail—Pharaoh was both the shepherd of his flock and its dominating master. Two sets of crook and flail were found in Tutankhamen's tomb, one child-sized set, used at Tutankhamen's coronation, the other was that of a full-sized pharaoh. The small set bore the name of the Aten, a last reminder of the life he was about to leave behind.

As Tutankhamen sat for the first time upon the throne, the high priest of Amun recited his five royal names:

1. The Horus name, associating the king with Horus, the Falcon god:

   "Horus, Strong Bull, whose Images are Born."

2. The Two Ladies Name, associating the pharaoh with the cobra goddess and the vulture goddess:

   "Whose Laws are Good, who Pacifies All the Gods."

3. The Golden Horus Name, a second association with Horus:

   "Who Brings Together Divine Order, who Pleases the Gods."

4. The Prenomen, the first of the king's two names written in a cartouche, the oval signifying royalty, preceded by the hiero-glyphs of a bee and a sedge plant, symbols of Upper and Lower Egypt:

   "Re Manifests himself as Lord." "Lord of Re's Being"
   (Neb-Keperu-Re).

5. The nomen, the second name in a cartouche, preceded by hiero-glyphs for "Son of Re," asserting the king's descent from the sun god Re:

   "Tutankhaten, living image of the Aten." (At this stage his name had not yet been changed.)

After the five royal names had been bestowed on Tutankhamen, he was officially the Pharaoh of Egypt. The procession retraced its steps through the temple back to the entrance pylon; the ceremony was over. On his way to the palace for his own celebration with more lavish entertainment, the new king passed crowds feasting and rejoicing in the streets, thanks to liberally distributed gifts of bread and beer. There were dancers with weights in their long hair, so it swayed as they moved, musicians, hand clappers, and singers, all for the enjoyment of the new king. One can imagine the excitement that Tutankhamen and Ankhesenamen felt as they talked about the coronation and the fantastic gods and rituals. They must have been amazed to see the temple walls with images of strange gods who had human bodies and animal heads—lionesses, falcons, and rams. Why did the pharaohs shown on the walls offer incense and beer to them? Their father would never have done that. As grand as Thebes was, they must still have thought wistfully about the more familiar, quieter surroundings of Amarna. Thebes was too big and complicated.

After a short time, the young king and queen did, indeed, return to Amarna, but stayed only a year or so. With their father dead, the city had lost its soul. The decision had been made not to reconcile two estranged religious camps; one or the other must be abandoned if Egypt were to be unified. By now the children had grieved long enough, had learned that Amarna was not the world. The royal couple changed their names to reflect the return to Amun, the god of Thebes, becoming Tutankhamen and Ankhesenamen.

Within two years the royal court and government all moved to Thebes. The old religion and traditions of the past were fully reinstated. With no support or reason for existence, Akhenaten's holy city was virtually abandoned and his god declined into obscurity. But there were a few who could return to Thebes. Priests of the Aten may have had to remain in Amarna, unless they converted. Akhenaten's courtiers would face hostility in any other city for their participation in Akhenaten's hated policies. None of their names are found in any Theban records.

Of Akhenaten's high officials, only Aye seemed able to transcend the heresy and resume his career. He was guiding the policies of Tutankhamen in the right direction. Some would have viewed him with suspicion, but the priesthood enthusiastically greeted the restoration of Amun and the temples. Any criticism of Aye would have waned as skeptics observed a trend back to the old traditions. Under Aye's guidance,

Tutankhamen seemed to be doing everything right. It was a delicate balance, but Aye was a master of the high wire. He had earned the confidence of his young boss *and* the admiration of his priests. Aye must truly have been proud of his "excellent" work.

The Amarna dream had turned rancid. Ordinary citizens abandoned Amarna, moving en masse to Thebes, creating an overnight ghost town walked through only by priests of a religion that no one wanted, and courtiers without a court. One indication of how the Amarnans felt about their time in the city they abandoned is shown by what they left behind. In 1912 the German expedition to Amarna, led by Ludwig Borchardt, made a dramatic discovery while clearing debris from the house and studio of a master sculptor called Tuthmosis. When they entered a locked storeroom in the sculptor's house, the excavators found exquisite busts and heads of statues that Tuthmosis had not completed when the exodus from the city began. Among these pieces was the famous bust of Nefertiti. That such a work of art should be left behind can only mean that people did not want to remember the era they had helped create.

Akhenaten was branded a heretic. Less than fifteen years after his death, gangs of workmen were sent to Amarna to dismantle the temples and to reuse their blocks in building projects elsewhere. Amarna was razed to the ground. What had once been an oasis of beauty on a barren landscape became a lost city in a desert. Egypt's brief encounter with the Aten was over, monotheism would not return to the Nile Valley for 1,500 years. Egypt had shown it would not tolerate any change in its religion or the role of its pharaoh, not for another thousand years and not until it had lost its special place of dominance in the world.

The Amarna heresy was a unique departure from Egypt's tradition-bound history, what physicists today call a "singularity," an unparalleled event. The seeds of social revolution often take root in poverty and discontent; this movement sprang from prosperity. Most revolutions that shake political foundations are fraught with violence; Akhenaten's was peaceful. His dream was realized for a while because the person with vision carried the awesome power of a pharaoh, almost enough to pull it off. But he died too soon, ending what could have been a turning point in the history of the world. Today, we are so comfortable with mono-theism that it is difficult to imagine just how revolutionary an idea this was for the inhabitants of the Nile Valley. For two thousand years Egyptians had worshipped numerous gods, their deities rising and falling in importance and evolving into aspects of each other, but they were never discarded. Often foreign gods, seen as aspects of Egyptian gods, were welcomed into the pantheon. When you already have a number of gods, a few more are no problem. Rather, why take any chance by excluding one who may be powerful? There was no reason to choose only one deity when many gods suited them so well. Monotheism forced people into a mode of thinking that seemed, if not unnatural, at least unreasonable. Even Akhenaten didn't comprehend the great danger of monotheism—that it is divisive. If there is only one god, then those who don't accept that god are wrong. Monotheism draws a line between "us" and "them," divides people and nations into believers and non-believers. No war was ever fought between polytheistic countries over whose gods were the true one. Compare this with the number of wars fought on behalf of the Jewish, Christian, and Islamic religions. Akhenaten had not realized that.

If a modern parallel would help us understand the Amarna revolution, consider the changes now taking place in Germany. Two halves of that nation had long been ideologically divided. One was led by a leader whose vision was out of touch with reality, who could support his ideal only through intolerance. In the end, he lost. The interesting part of the parallel is to observe what happened to his former followers and to all he had created after the movement failed. Today, almost no one in East Germany acknowledges support for the former regime. They rush to help pull down the old statues and buildings they themselves had erected. In ancient Egypt, too, there was a general denial of ever having been a part of Akhenaten's movement. Even names were changed to make assimilation possible—I can't imagine a citizen of Amarna named Aten-Em-Heb—"The Aten is in Festival"—returning to Thebes with his name intact. This is why there are so many unanswered questions about what happened at Amarna, as there are about the inner workings of communist Germany. Just as most communists did not keep souvenirs of their membership, the inhabitants of Amarna did not preserve artifacts of the revolution. The bust of Nefertiti was left behind because no one wanted it.

The man who caused it all assuredly did not rest peacefully deep in the confines of his Amarna tomb. Soon after the city was abandoned, all its tombs were robbed for the treasures they contained. The bodies of Nefertiti, Kiya, and the five princesses who died at Amarna have never been found. Like Akhenaten's, they were probably torn to shreds.

6

The Return to Thebes

Take a wife while you're young
That she make a wife for you
She should bear for you while you are young,
It is right to make people.

—The scribe Ani
circa 1400 B.C.

Tutankhamen had mounted a throne that wobbled uneasily from the neglect and divisions of the previous reign. Aware of the internal problems that beset Egypt, her foreign neighbors had grown defiant. The confederated tribes of Nubia, for example, brazenly joined forces in an effort to rid themselves of Egypt's domination. They halted shipments of gold and attacked the southern military outposts, sacking and burning. To the west of Egypt the countries of "Asia," as the Egyptians called them, claimed one excuse after another for reneging on their agreed tribute, cutting off necessary goods for Egypt. The revitalization of Egypt's economy depended on regaining control of "Asia" and Nubia for their irreplaceable resources. This would be the new administration's first priority—securing the wherewithal, that could then be used to resurrect the temples that had suffered so greatly from both neglect and religious fanaticism. The motto for Tutankhamen's reign would be: Restoration.

First, something had to be done about the army which had languished for years without direction, serving primarily as Akhenaten's personal bodyguard at Amarna. The troops had not marched north to Syria, west to Libya, or south to Nubia to gain territory and tribute, nor had they fought a war in years. The army had to be retrained and enlarged. Infantry had to be provisioned with the best weapons—spears, bows and arrows, and leather shields. The charioteers, the elite of the Egyptian army, had to be provided with horses, chariots, harnesses, and ornaments. A side effect of this renewal would be hundreds of jobs for the craftsmen who would provision the new army. Prosperity would begin.

To rebuild, Egypt would need timber from Lebanon, but the flourishing trade had practically ended. Choice cedar logs were going to other, more persuasive neighbors. Shrewd negotiators would have to be found so that this lucrative trade could be restored. Fear of a revitalized Egyptian army would aid immeasurably in the negotiators' ability to make favorable terms. The army was the key to all the problems, but rearmament cost money.

Administrative offices at Memphis were reopened, the languishing bureaucracy dusted off, revamped, and set into motion. While Akhenaten was lost in his own world at Amarna, the great bureaucracy of Egypt had deteriorated. Taxes were still collected, but inscriptions suggest that corruption was rampant throughout the system, as officials extorted grain from the farmers. An entirely new group of ministers and officials would be appointed to assure the smooth running of an improved bureaucracy.

Throughout Egypt's history, two constants remained—the river and the land. These elemental sources of Egypt's wealth had never failed before and would not fail this time. Crops would grow and be harvested just as they always had been, and the new tax collectors would be, it was hoped, honest. With careful supervision local governors could again be held accountable for their actions and the tax structures fairly revised.

Once trade goods and tribute again flowed into the country, the temples and shrines Akhenaten had closed would be reopened, sanctuaries of the gods would be rebuilt, and their gold cult statues restored. Craftsmen would again cast and carve statues by the thousands. Thebes would be reinstated as the religious capital of the great god Amun. Everything would return to normal. All this would require years of effort and a great deal of wealth.

The complex interdependence of funds and a stronger army leading to capital for rebuilding, all of which depended on more efficient collection of taxes, was more than an eleven-year-old pharaoh could comprehend. He would need the help of some very capable people. Nature would provide the natural resources, his new cabinet the guidance that would determine the direction of the country during the next decade, as Tutankhamen and Ankhesenamen literally grew up. To be sure, the young king and queen were visible—dedicating temples, officiating at festivals, commissioning works and restorations in the temples, no doubt greeting foreign dignitaries and appearing at banquets—but they were children who needed to learn.

While Tutankhamen grew and matured, so did his understanding of what it meant to be the king of Egypt. There is no reason to believe that he did not welcome this task and willingly assume more responsibility as time passed. He would have requested meetings with his officials, the viziers of Upper and Lower Egypt, the Overseer of the Treasury, Overseer of the Royal Works, and the Overseer of the Army, asking questions about every area of his vast domain. The country was vast, and the young pharaoh could not keep his eyes on everything, so his officials retained tremendous power. It was crucial that they be trustworthy and fair. The ancient proverb was: "Gracious king, lawful vizier."

Public-relations efforts showed the people that their new pharaoh understood what they had endured. An eight-foot-high stela was carved and prominently dedicated in front of Karnak Temple. Given that this is the earliest campaign speech in history, Tutankhamen's writer was truly inspired. At the very top of the stela, carved in relief, is a scene of Tutankhamen making offerings to Amun. Even if you couldn't read the hieroglyphs, the message was clear. Here was the pharaoh presenting incense to Amun. How things had changed from the past regime! In the text below, Tutankhamen laments the deplorable state in which he found the temples of Egypt, and describes all his efforts to restore them to their former glory.

> Now when this majesty arose as king, the temple of the gods and goddesses beginning from Elephantine to the marshes of the Delta . . . had fallen into neglect.
>
> Their shrines had fallen into desolation and became land overrun with the *Rata*-plants.
>
> Their sanctuaries were as if they had never been, their halls were a trodden path.
>
> The land was in confusion, the gods forsook this land . . .
>
> His majesty was administering this land, and making daily governance of the two river-banks.
>
> Then his majesty took counsel with his heart, searching out every excellent occasion, seeking what was beneficial to his father Amun, for fashioning his august image of real fine-gold . . .
>
> All the (offerings) of the temple are doubled, trebled, and quadrupled with silver, gold, lapis-lazuli, turquoise, all rare costly stones, royal linen, white cloth, fine linen, olive oil, gum . . . incense and myrrh, without limit of all good things . . .
>
> The gods and goddesses who are in this land, their hearts are joyful.
>
> The possessors of shrines are glad,
>
> Lands are in a state of jubilation and merry making,
>
> Celebration is throughout [the whole land] and good [conditions] have come to pass.[1]

There is a clear acknowledgment that, under his father's rule, the "Land was in confusion," the temples from north to south had "fallen into neglect." The text goes beyond citing religious problems and strikes at the

FIG.1: Colossal statue of Akhenaten, Tutankhamen's father. *Egyptian Museum, Cairo.*

FIG.2: Akhenaten's second wife, Kiya, Tutankhamen's mother, carved relief from Hermopolis. *Ny Carlsberg Glyptotek, Copenhagen. Photograph by Pat Remler.*

FIG.3: Lid from a canopic jar found in Tomb 55. Possibly Kiya, Tutankhamen's mother. *Metropolitan Museum of Art, New York. Photograph by Pat Remler.*

FIG.4: Aye and his wife Tey worshipping the Aten.
Tomb of Aye at Amarna. Photograph by Pat Remler.

FIG.5: Head of young
Tutankhamen, from a
statue possibly made
for his coronation.
*Metropolitan Museum
of Art, New York.
Photograph by Pat Remler.*

FIG.6: Ankhesenamen offering lotus blossoms to Tutankhamen, detail of an ivory
and wood chest found in Tutankhamen's tomb.   *The Metropolitan Museum of Art,
previously on loan from the Cairo Museum. Photograph by Lee Boltin.*

FIG.7: Small golden shrine decorated with scenes of Tutankhamen and Ankhesenamen. *The Metropolitan Museum of Art, previously on loan from the Cairo Museum. Photograph by Lee Boltin.*

FIG.8: Tutankhamen pouring perfume into Ankhesenamen's hands. Detail from small golden shrine. *The Egyptian Museum, Cairo.*

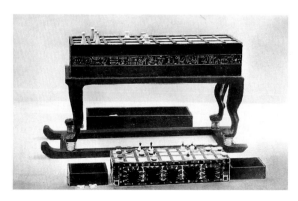

FIG.9: Ivory and wood game boards used by Tutankhamen and Ankhesenamen. *The Egyptian Museum, Cairo.*

FIG. 10: The head of Aye, Tutankhamen's vizier. *Agyptisches Museum, Berlin. Photograph by Pat Remler.*

FIG. 11: Statue of General Horemheb as a scribe. The inscription on the base boasts that he suppressed crime and lawlessness during Tutankhamen's reign. *The Metropolitan Museum of Art, New York. Photograph by Pat Remler.*

FIG. 12: Huy, Tutankhamen's viceroy to Nubia. *Bode Museum, Berlin. Photograph by Pat Remler.*

FIG.13A: Interior of gilded coffin for the larger fetus found in Tutankhamen's tomb with the wrapped mummy inside. *Photograph by the Egyptian Expedition, The Metropolitan Museum of Art, New York.*

FIG.13B: Larger fetus partially unwrapped. *Photograph by the Egyptian Expedition, The Metropolitan Museum of Art, New York.*

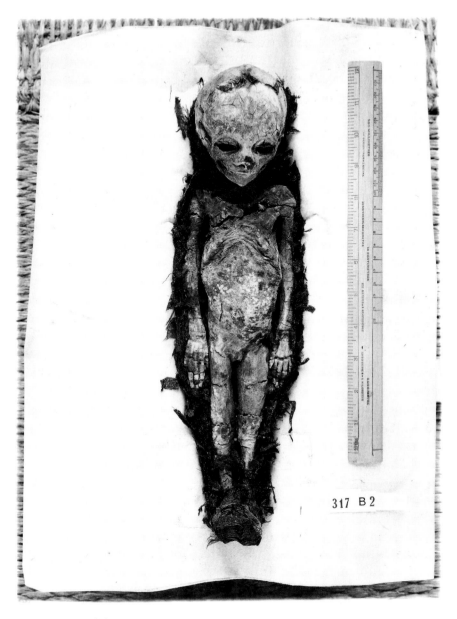

317 B 2

FIG. 13C: The larger fetus. Note the damage at the top of the skull where Derry opened it to remove the linen inserted by the embalmers. Had the little girl lived, she would probably have been deformed. *Photograph by the Egyptian Expedition, The Metropolitan Museum of Art, New York.*

FIG.14A: External coffin (with lid removed) for the smaller of the two fetuses found in Tutankhamen's tomb. *Photograph by the Egyptian Expedition, The Metropolitan Museum of Art, New York.*

FIG.16: Floral collar worn by one of the mourners at the ritual meal during the burial of Tutankhamen. *The Metropolitan Museum of Art, gift of Theodore Davis, 1909.*

FIG.14B: The smaller fetus. *Photograph by the Egyptian Expedition,*
The Metropolitan Museum of Art, New York.

FIG.15: The author with
Dr. Fawzi Gaballah examining
one of the fetuses from
Tutankhamen's tomb.
Kasr El Einy Hospital, Cairo.
Photograph by Pat Remler.

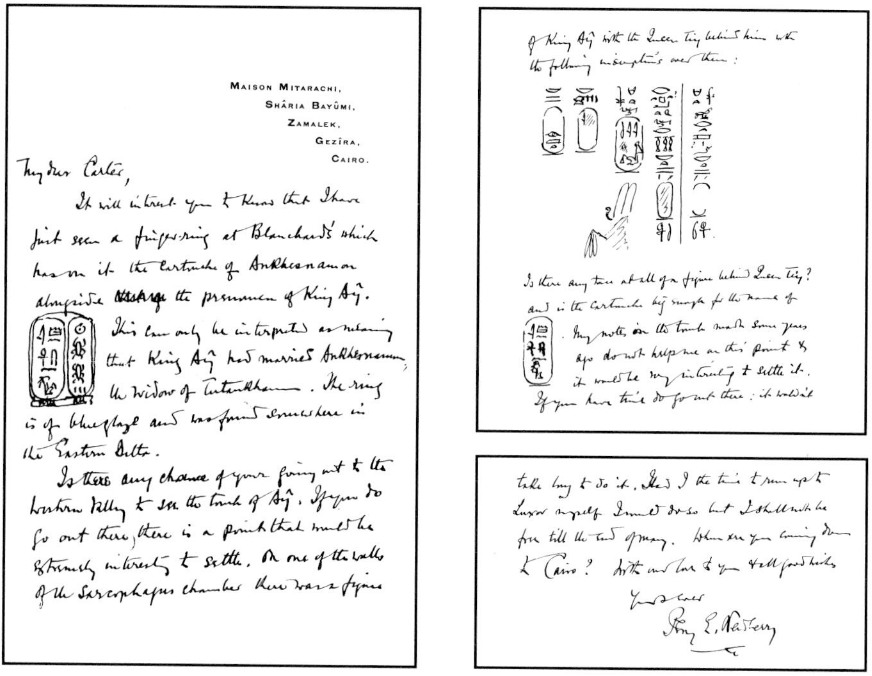

Maison Mitarachi,
Shâria Bayûmi,
Zamalek,
Gezîra,
Cairo.

My dear Carter,

It will interest you to know that I have just seen a finger-ring at Blanchard's which has on it the cartouche of Ankhesenamon alongside the prenomen of King Ay. This can only be interpreted as meaning that King Ay had married Ankhesenamun the widow of Tutankhamon. The ring is of blue glaze and was found somewhere in the Eastern Delta.

Is there any chance of your going out to the Western Valley to see the tomb of Ay. If you do go out there, there is a point that would be extremely interesting to settle. On one of the walls of the Sarcophagus chamber there was a figure of King Ay with the Queen Tiy behind him with the following inscriptions over them:

Is there any trace at all of a figure behind Queen Tiy? and is the cartouche big enough for the name of . My notes on the tomb made some years ago do not help me on this point & it would be very interesting to settle it. If you have time do go out there: it would not take long to do it. Had I the time to run up to Luxor myself I would do so but I shall not be free till the end of May. When are you coming down to Cairo? With our love to you & all good wishes

Yours ever
Percy E. Newberry

FIG.18: Letter written by Percy Newberry, telling Howard Carter of the ring indicating that Aye married Ankhesenamen. *Courtesy Griffith Institute, Oxford.*

FIG.17: Aye performing the opening of the mouth ceremony on Tutankhamen's mummy. Wall painting in Tutankhamen's tomb in the Valley of the Kings. *Photograph by Pat Remler.*

FIG.19: One of the hundreds of servant statues (*ushabtis*) placed in the tomb to accompany Tutankhamen to the next world. *The Metropolitan Museum of Art, on loan from the Cairo Museum. Photograph by Lee Boltin.*

FIG.20: Colossal statue of Tutankhamen from his mortuary temple. His name has been erased and the statue now bears the cartouche of Horemheb. *The Egyptian Museum, Cairo. Photograph by Pat Remler.*

FIG.21: The only place in Luxor Temple where Tutankhamen's name has not been erased is high on the east wall of the Colonnade Hall. *Luxor Temple. Photograph by Pat Remler.*

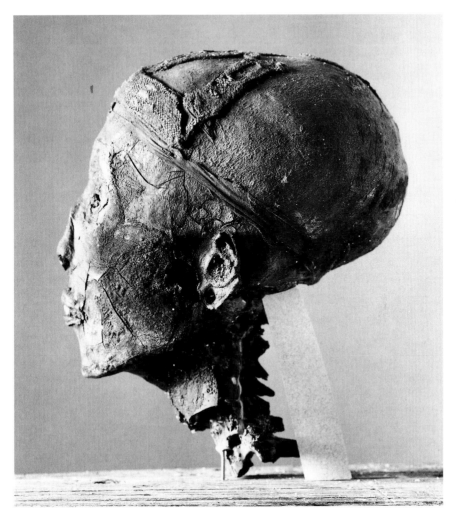

FIG.22: Skull of Tutankhamen, showing the elongated head typical of the royal family in the Amarna Period. *Photograph by the Egyptian Expedition, The Metropolitan Museum of Art, New York.*

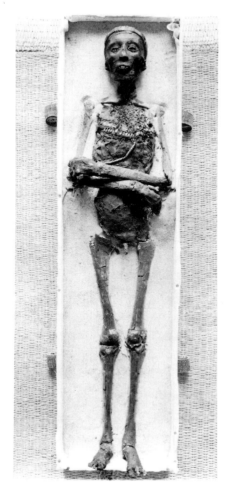

FIG.23: The mummy of Tutankhamen reassembled on a sand tray after the autopsy by Dr. Derry. His mummy still rests in his tomb in the Valley of the Kings. *Photograph by the Egyptian Expedition, The Metropolitan Museum of Art, New York.*

FIG.24A: One of four miniature canopic coffins that contained Tutankhamen's internal organs. *Photograph by the Egyptian Expedition, The Metropolitan Museum of Art, New York.*

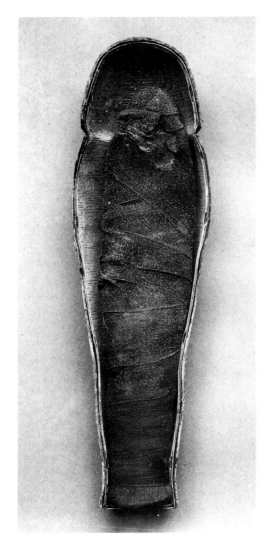

FIG.24C: The unwrapped contents of the canopic coffin: Tutankhamen's liver. *Photograph by the Egyptian Expedition, The Metropolitan Museum of Art, New York.*

FIG.24B: One of Tutankhamen's miniature canopic coffins with its lid removed and the wrapped organ still inside. *Photograph by the Egyptian Expedition, The Metropolitan Museum of Art, New York.*

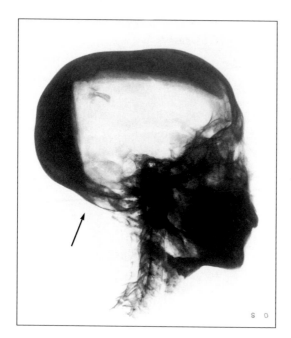

FIG.25: X ray of Tutankhamen's skull. The bone fragment visible in the upper left corner is the result of postmortem damage to the skull. Arrow points to the location of the possible blow to the back of the head. *Courtesy Department of Human Anatomy and Cell Biology, University of Liverpool.*

FIG.26: Author with Dr. Gerald Irwin, medical director of the Radiologic Technology Program at the C.W. Post Campus of Long Island University. Irwin was the first to suggest Tutankhamen may have lingered before dying from a blow to the back of the head. *Photograph by Gina Mosti.*

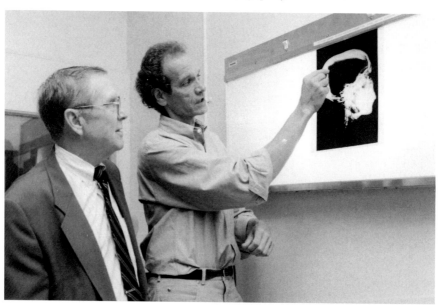

heart of Egypt's malaise. The army had been unsupported for years. The text carved on the stela states that during this time if Egypt's army were sent to Syria, "It met with no success at all." This isn't just a politician's campaign speech, it's a plan of action: build up the military, restore Egypt's wealth, and reopen the temples.

There is even a subtle, but unmistakable, declaration that the isolationism of Akhenaten's Amarna days was over. The stela refers to Tutankhamen on his throne in the palace in Memphis, where the stela was probably written, but the stela was erected in Thebes. This shows how far the country had already come. Egypt had a true king of both Upper and Lower Egypt, a pharaoh for all of the country.

Tutankhamen was about eleven years old when the Restoration Stela, as it is known, was carved. Someone was putting words into his very young mouth, but they were words the Egyptian public and the Amun priesthood wanted to hear. Their temples would be restored and the gods' offerings reinstated. But promises were not deeds—every proclamation issued by Tutankhamen must have been viewed with some doubt. Deeds required effective, intelligent administration. Who was going to implement all these wonderful plans?

The officials in charge were new players, men untainted by the Amarna days. Aye must have been instrumental in their recruitment, and he chose well. Maya, Tutankhamen's new treasurer, was central to the restoration plan. We know a great deal about the internal workings of the government during Tutankhamen's reign because Maya inscribed his autobiography on his tomb wall. He was in charge of collecting the taxes, overseeing their registry in the royal treasury, then allocating their distribution. He even supervised the casting of gold statues for the temples. From his office in Memphis, Maya dispatched an army of scribes to all the nomes (provinces) of Egypt to record how much grain was collected from each farmer.

Peasants were taxed not on how much they harvested, but on how much they *should have* harvested, as estimated by reading the Nilometer. Boulders along the banks of the Nile, "Nilometers," were inscribed with high water marks from centuries of Nile floods. During inundation each year, the Nilometers recorded how high the river rose in every part of Egypt. Once it was known how bountiful the Nile had been that year, officials calculated how much grain could be grown per acre. The farmers were taxed one portion of their predicted harvest. This system prevented tax collectors from having to search for hidden caches of grain. If a farmer's fields didn't produce what was expected, he still had to pay his full share. If, however, he was diligent and his land yielded more than the Nilometer estimate, the excess was his alone.

Maya's job was all the more difficult because money had not yet been invented. Grain was collected, transported to the royal warehouses, tallied, and stored. Once an order for disbursement came to Maya's office, the grain was weighed, counted, delivered and recounted again. Armies of scribes worked under Maya's direction up and down the Nile. Maya's brother, Nahuher, was a "Royal Scribe," indicating not that he took dictation from the pharaoh, but that he worked in the royal treasury, much as the "royal mail" in England consists of more than letters to the Queen. Eventually, there were so many "Royal Scribes" that a scribe who actually worked in the palace was given the designation "*True* Royal Scribe."

Maya's tomb lies just a few miles from Memphis at the ancient cemetery at Saqqara, the site of the first pyramid built more than a thousand years earlier. In Maya's day the necropolis had become a tourist attraction. Egyptians visited the ancient tombs in much the same way people visit famous cemeteries today. In times of difficulty, Egyptians could stroll through Saqqara to be reminded of Egypt's better days. So when Maya carved his autobiography on his tomb wall, he addressed it to "the people who come and want to divert themselves in the west and to have a walk in the district of eternity."[2] Maya was proud of the role he played in putting Egypt back together. He summarized his career: "In the beginning I was good, in the end I was brilliant."

But all these good deeds, reopening temples, recasting gold statues of the gods, and supporting the military, had to be paid for. In the eighth year of Tutankhamen's reign Maya was instructed "to tax the entire land and to institute divine offerings [for] all [the gods] of the land of Egypt."[3] When the new tax was levied Tutankhamen was nearly eighteen. He may well have engaged in long discussions with Maya revolving around the mark on the Nilometer that year and how much revenue could consequently be expected. Aye would have been party to their meeting, no doubt subtly guiding its direction. Although no one likes a tax increase, at least the farmers knew their payments were going toward reopening their temples and fashioning new statues of their gods. No longer did their grain flow to a city they had never seen, to support a god they did not worship and a pharaoh they did not understand.

Just a short walk from Maya's tomb is the tomb of a contemporary who was as important as Maya in the revitalization of Egypt, though in a very different way. Like most accountants, Maya would spend most of his life counting other people's "money." General Horemheb made sure there was something to count.

Horemheb, who had been elevated to the position of overseer of Tutankhamen's army, was a self-made man from the northern town of Hierakonpolis, home of the ram-headed god Herishef. He would have begun his military career as a young infantryman, either at the end of Amenhotep III's reign or at the beginning of Akhenaten's. As a young soldier working his way through the ranks, he must have found it disheartening to serve at a time when there were no wars providing the opportunity to distinguish himself, but Horemheb persevered. He must have been a man of determination, with the confidence and strength to command. Now a man in his prime, he held a crucial appointment in Tutankhamen's administration. As Overseer of the Army, Horemheb was the one who would reassert Egypt's control over western Asia and Nubia. With funds supplied by Maya, Horemheb recruited, equipped, and trained an Egyptian army that finally "marched out," to subdue Nubia. Once again, the supply of gold necessary for trade flowed into Egypt's treasury. There remained Syria–Palestine to conquer, which was also crucial to Egypt's well-being. Egypt had no forests, so it desperately needed cedar logs from Lebanon to build ships and the great doors and flagpoles of its temples. The hieroglyph for the word "god" is a banner on a staff ⸜, a staff of cedar.

Of course, we cannot know when meetings took place, or whether they occurred in Thebes or Memphis, but we can imagine the young pharaoh growing into manhood, eager to take the responsibility to lead his country, consulting with his treasurer, Maya, his general, Horemheb, and his faithful adviser, Aye. Should Horemheb's forces strike Libya first because they were the weakest, thereby seasoning the young troops for the big campaign into Syria? Or was it advisable to strike first at Nubia for more gold? At meetings like this the details for Egypt's recovery were hammered out. I imagine "the big three"—Maya, Aye, and Horemheb—each working in different ways. Maya ensconced in his office, surrounded by papyrus scrolls with scribes rushing to and fro reporting on revenues and losses. He was the accountant, conservative, orderly but always in the middle of things, the one who understood the finances of Egypt.

Aye worked in a very different way. He was the politician, working quietly from behind the scenes, orchestrating the moves of the other players. Perhaps, as at Amarna, he continued to be the eyes and the ears of the palace, remaining close to Tutankhamen, diverting contact with anyone else who sought the king's ear. An old Egyptian maxim says: "Do not reveal your heart to a stranger, he may use your words against you." That was Aye. We can begin to understand what a remarkably ambitious man he was. A small piece of inscribed gold foil discovered in the Valley of the Kings[4] adds a particularly interesting insight into his personality. Embossed on this foil is a scene in which Tutankhamen assumes the traditional conquering-hero posture, grasping a Libyan captive by the hair, ready to smite him with a curved sword. Behind Tutankhamen stands Ankhesenamen, his support. Traditionally, in front of the king would be the god to whom the enemy is being offered as a kind of sacrifice. But on this bit of gold, probably from a piece of furniture in Aye's tomb, Aye stands before the king in the position reserved for the god. Aye has not so subtly elevated himself to a divine position. Here was a man with truly grandiose dreams.

Horemheb was different. Although he, too, was an essential player in Tutankhamen's plan for recovery, he stood neither in the middle of things, nor behind the scenes pulling strings. Horemheb, like Aye, was an ambitious man, but he was more straightforward in his dealings. Approve a campaign and he would begin the march. As soon as his quartermaster submitted a list of the supplies needed—bronze battle axes, bows, arrows, shields, sandals, water skins, etc.—and they were received, he would be gone. Before long he would return with captives and tribute. Horemheb, campaigning for months at time, was not privy to the inner workings and politics of the palace He was the outsider, but an outsider holding a great deal of power.

In just a few years Horemheb's military expeditions regained all the territories that had slipped away from Akhenaten. Upon returning from a northern campaign, Horemheb paraded Asiatic prisoners before Tutankhamen; when he went south he returned with Nubian captives for his king. No one was safe from Horemheb's military raids, even Libyans—with their characteristic goatees and side locks—were captured and brought to work on the temples of Egypt.

Horemheb's successes were rewarded by a grateful Tutankhamen. As Egypt grew in strength, Horemheb grew in power. No longer was he only the commander in chief of the army; he was promoted to "Overseer of all Works of the King" and "Deputy of the King in the Entire Land." One of the titles that pleased him most had nothing to do with his military career, it was more like an honorary academic degree—"Royal Scribe." The general was so delighted that he commissioned a life-sized granite statue of himself seated in the scribal position with a papyrus scroll across his lap (fig. 11). The inscription on the base of the statue confirms his attention to regulations and their enforcement:

> *I am the recorder of the law,*
> *Who gives direction to courtiers*
> *Wise in speech, there's nothing I ignore.*[5]

Horemheb constructed a tomb at Memphis, the most beautiful and elaborate in the entire cemetery. As Overseer of the Royal Works he commanded the best craftsmen in the land. The sculptures and wall carvings are among the finest ever produced in ancient Egypt, master-pieces by any standard. Although they are traditional in their style, a fluidity of line and an attention to detail shows the hands of craftsmen trained in Amarna who survived that era. Horemheb's tomb was topped by a small temple above the ground, complete with a courtyard and columned hall. His descendants could come, sit in the shade of the columns, and have a meal in honor of their ancestor. As they ate, they would be surrounded by carvings of Horemheb's great battles against the "wretched Asiatics," the inhabitants of "Vile Nubia," the "barbarians of Libya." They would see Horemheb receiving collars of gold from the pharaoh he served, Tutankhamen. It was a military man's version of paradise regained.

While Horemheb, Aye, and Maya worked to resuscitate Egypt's economy and dominions, Tutankhamen's task was to reassure the priests that he embraced the old gods of Egypt. His first major building project in Thebes—the completion of the Colonnade Hall in Luxor Temple—was a stroke of genius. His grandfather, the great King Amenhotep III, had built the 150-foot-long hall, but died before it was decorated. When Akhenaten banished the gods of Thebes and moved to Amarna, the columns stood bare, and remained so for more than a decade. Tutankhamen was advised by Aye, no doubt, to decorate the hall with scenes from Egypt's most important religious festival.

This was a project that Tutankhamen and Ankhesenamen could become fully involved in. They no doubt visited the temple often and asked questions while the priests, scribes, and artists discussed how to best illustrate the story of the Festival of Opet. These meetings also provided classes for Tutankhamen on the nature of a religion that was completely new to him. It must have been something like Bible school or catechism through pictures.

This shrewd decision to complete the colonnade identified Tutankhamen with his grandfather whom the priests of Amun respected for his works. In this way he emphasized his continuity with the royal line, and could be recognized by the priests as the legitimate heir to the throne, yet distanced him from his father's aberrations. This worked elegantly to extinguish priestly fears that he might be too much his father's son.

We can only wonder what Tutankhamen's private reactions were to the new religion. Was he willing and receptive, or did he secretly still pray to the Aten? What was he thinking as he played his prominent part in religious festivals?

The Colonnade Hall was decorated with scenes of the most glorious of all the festivals in Thebes—the Opet Festival. It celebrated the annual visit of Amun and his family to Luxor Temple. Opet was the ancient name of Karnak, the temple where the festival originated, and home to the Theban trinity: Amun (the father), Mut (his wife) and Khonsu (their son). At the opening of the Opet festival the statues of Amun, Mut and Khonsu were taken from their shrines in Karnak temple, placed in divine barques, and sailed one and a half miles along the Nile to Luxor Temple (southern Opet). Tutankhamen's decorations show precious details of the joyous procession as it traveled south to Luxor Temple, and the return of the procession to Karnak at the end of the festival. Tutankhamen himself is prominently featured in the reliefs on the west wall of the colonnade. He makes offerings to the gods Amun, Mut and Khonsu, accompanies the barques to the edge of the Nile, sails with the gods on their journey up the Nile, follows the barques from the banks of the Nile to the facade of Luxor Temple, and makes an offering to the gods in their sanctuaries in Luxor Temple.[6] Could anyone demonstrate greater devotion?

When the festival of Opet was reinstated, the people of Thebes must have been overjoyed, lining the east bank of the Nile to see the boats of the gods and to catch a glimpse of this Tutankhamen who had restored the old religion. When the procession moved inside Luxor Temple, thousands crowded into the open courtyard to view the shrines as they were carried to their temporary homes deep inside the temple, where the common people could not go. Knowing, at least from the scenes on the temple walls, that Tutankhamen presented offerings of incense, meat, vegetables, beer, and wine to the gods, the common people must have been filled with joy. It was the first time in years that their pharaoh had honored their gods. I am sure that many wept.

Despite the excitement of the people and their own busy days, Tutankhamen and Ankhesenamen must have missed their father, and their former life at Amarna, where their days were more free. Gradually, however, the pleasures of living in Thebes and Memphis, with all the variety that Egypt offered, must have seemed the better course.

From their palace in Memphis it was a short trip to the Delta for the finest bird hunting in the land. Skimming the marshes in flat-bottomed skiffs made of papyrus stalks, fowlers set nets and waited to snare passing flocks. Tutankhamen especially loved hunting with a bow and arrow. Lightweight wood shafts with tiny sharpened wood arrow-heads—bird points—were best, which traveled faster than a bird could fly. (Tutankhamen's bows and arrows were found in his tomb.) Along with Ankhesenamen, the two spent some of their happiest hours together in the marshes, he shooting at passing ducks and she readying the next arrow for him. When they tired of the bow and arrow, there was the throw stick, far more difficult to master—shaped something like a boomerang. It took a strong arm to throw it hard enough to down a bird in flight.

From their southern palace in Thebes they went ostrich hunting in the desert, which was always an adventure. While his charioteer chased the birds, Tutankhamen, beside him, shot his arrows from the bouncing chariot. The diversions of the young king and his queen were many, and it seems likely that his advisers were happy to have them occupied with hunting and sports.

Another endeavor that occupied Tutankhamen's time was building his tomb. The young king chose a site next to his grandfather's tomb in the West Valley. Amenhotep III had dug the first tomb in the area, and not far from it stood an unfinished tomb (WV25) that most Egyptologists agree was begun by Amenhotep IV, before he changed his name to Akhenaten and moved to Amarna.[7] If the identification of this tomb is correct, Tutankhamen's tomb was sited next to his grandfather's and near a tomb once intended for his father. Work began on Tutankhamen's tomb when he was just entering his teens. Construction would have proceeded at a leisurely pace, for the overseer of the works surely believed he had years and years before the finished tomb would be needed.

A royal architect drew the floor plan, then presented it to the Overseer of the Royal Necropolis. A draftsman marked the cliff wall with the outline of the doorway; then, starting at the top, carvers began to chip away the rock with bronze chisels hammered by wooden mallets. Tombs always began at the top so that the carvers swinging their mallets were assisted by gravity, rather than having to constantly raise their mallets higher and higher. As the chips mounted, young boys scooped them into straw baskets and carried the rubble away from the tomb. In a few weeks a descending passageway became evident that daily went deeper and deeper into the bedrock until assistants with bronze mirrors were called to reflect sunlight down the shaft so the workmen could see. After the passage reached the depth prescribed by the architect, a large room was carved from the living rock, but leaving square pillars to support the ceiling. As soon as the rough work was completed, more experienced carvers smoothed the walls to prepare them for decoration. The tomb was now large enough for a left-hand gang and a right-hand gang to work simultaneously. As chisels dulled, boys would carry them to the surface for sharpening. It was a team effort. All the workmen and their families lived together in a small village near the Valley of the Kings, a village that was walled so that it could be sealed shut at night. These people included draftsmen, carvers, painters, sculptors, artisans who carved hieroglyphs, and overseers—all necessary to prepare a tomb for eternity.

As Tutankhamen grew up, he could more actively participate in the discussions with Aye and Maya about finances, meet with foreign envoys when trade agreements were discussed, select his own servants and tutors, and decide whom to reward for faithful service. He was, after all, the grandson of Amenhotep III, the great diplomat and shrewd administrator. Governing was in his blood. Fortunately, the tomb of Huy, one of Tutankhamen's most trusted ambassadors, has been preserved. It provides a clear sense of the role Tutankhamen played. At this point, he was a teenager. Horemheb had just subdued Nubia; so a viceroy was needed to administer the territory. Nubia was counted on for tons of gold annually, along with luxury items such as ebony for furniture, ivory for jewelry, giraffe and leopard skins—all symbols of Egypt's opulence. The viceroyage was a critical position (fig. 12).

Huy records on his tomb walls that he was summoned to the palace to receive the seal of the viceroy for stamping the gold that would be shipped back to Thebes. Since the bygone days of the Old Kingdom, small cylinder seals had been signs of authority. In fact, the hieroglyphic word for treasurer included a seal on a cord, worn as a badge of office around the neck. So when Huy was called to the palace at Thebes, it was a great day in his life. Huy's entire family was permitted to watch the great event. He was led before his pharaoh, where he bowed and was greeted by a member of Tutankhamen's cabinet who said: "The Land from Nekhen to Nesut-Towey has been given to thee." Huy answered: "May Amun of Nesut-Towey grant all that you have commanded, oh sovereign, my lord." Tutankhamen then commanded that he depart and return with gold, ivory, ebony, giraffes, all good things found in Nubia. Note that it was not Tutankhamen but a member of the cabinet who gave the commission to his agent. Tutankhamen merely seconded that order.

With his seal of office firmly in hand, Huy left the palace to prepare for his expedition to Nubia. One of his sons bore the title "Master of the Horse." On the walls of Huy's tomb we see horses peeking out of their stalls as his ship heads for Nubia. There are no records of the voyage to Nubia or his stay there, but we can imagine that Horemheb's recent campaign had removed any obstacles that could have prevented Huy from performing his duties. Not surprisingly, the expedition was a complete success. Huy returned north to Egypt with a fleet loaded with treasure so extensive that its presentation to Tutankhamen had to take place outside in the courtyard of the palace. There were endless piles of gold, cast into rings the size of bracelets, heaps of ivory and ebony, a live giraffe, and more. Slaves in manacles were paraded before the young king so he could select those that pleased him. There was a herd of especially fat Nubian cattle, highly prized as offerings to the god Amun. During the feast of Opet, a cow's horns were topped with carved hands; between them was a tiny Nubian head. When the animal lowered its head, Nubia symbolically paid homage to Egypt.

Pleased with the procession—he must have loved the giraffe—Tutankhamen rewarded Huy with gold necklaces. I wonder if he thought of the times at Amarna when his father had distributed gold necklaces from the Window of Appearances. But, in the case of Huy, these were not bribes for following the faith, but rewards for a job well done. Many of the gold objects placed in Tutankhamen's tomb were due to Huy's labors. The famous solid gold coffin may have been fashioned from massive gold shipments from Nubia, thanks to Huy.

As the years passed, Tutankhamen and Ankhesenamen grew into young adults and fell in love. She had been at his side since they were both ten years old and was now portrayed, either standing or kneeling, beside her pharaoh in almost every depiction. The royal workshops produced statues of the handsome couple, seated side by side, wearing the crowns, respectively, of the god Amun and his wife Mut. One pair of these statues of the young king and queen, in Luxor Temple, still smiles down on passing tourists.

Unlike all his predecessors with harems, Tutankhamen never married additional wives, another indication that he and Ankhesenamen were very close. But, since they were the last survivors of the Eighteenth Dynasty, they would have to produce children if the royal line was to continue. Otherwise, when the time came to choose the next pharaoh, Divine Order could be disrupted and Egypt could be thrown into turmoil.

The couple did their best to fulfill this obligation. Ankhesenamen became pregnant. While the court prepared for the birth of the next king or queen of Egypt, she was tended by the Royal Physician, a man renowned for his skills and healing abilities.

Ancient Egyptians called medicine "the necessary art" and regulated the profession carefully, with specialists in various areas. The highest ranking physicians were priests. Since Sekhmet was the most important god associated with the medical arts, it was the priests of Sekhmet who produced the best doctors. This is somewhat surprising since their lioness-headed goddess was feared throughout Egyptian history for her temper, and at one time she almost destroyed mankind. Priests of Sekhmet often had several titles, one medical, another magical. Nedjemou, for example, was "Chief of the Priests of Sekhmet" and "Chief of the Physicians," while Heryshefnakht was "Chief of Magicians," "High Priest of Sekhmet," and physician to the pharaoh. In addition to priest-physicians, the *wabu*, there were the *sunu*, who were the lay physicians. Since the medical profession was carefully regulated with severe penalties for improper practice, the *sunu* were almost certainly trained in medicine, although they were not associated with any particular temple nor devoted to a particular god. Thus their practice was probably more eclectic than the priest-physicians, as they could draw from all available sources.

While both the priest-physicians and the lay physicians used a combination of sound clinical medicine and magic, there was a third kind of physician who was not trained in medicine, but used only incantations, amulets, and magic to cure his patients. Most of the medical papyri that have survived come from this third class of medical men, for they list spells and potions with little evidence of scientific knowledge or careful observation.

Ankhesenamen's personal physician would have specialized in gynecology, "diseases of women." This was her first child, "the opener of the womb," and as she neared the end of her term a birthing stool was prepared. Egyptian mothers sat on a mud-brick stool so that gravity would assist the birth process. (The slang for giving birth was "sitting on bricks.") This was such a basic part of Egyptian life that the hieroglyph for "born" shows a seated woman with the baby's head emerging.

But before Ankhesenamen used the birthing stool, misfortune struck. As she entered her eighth month, she miscarried and lost her child, a little girl. Had the child lived, she would have been deformed, with a curved spine and one shoulder higher than the other. There were probably whisperings in the palace of a curse on the child or the mother.

The Royal Magician would have been summoned. Because medicine in ancient Egypt was practiced by both clinical physicians and magical healers, the specific kind of illness determined the method of treatment. If the cause was known, as with broken bones or crocodile bites, then the treatment would be nonmagical. For a crocodile bite, the wound was sewn closed and raw meat placed on it. If, however, the illness was something such as a fever, where the cause would be unknown to Egyptians, it might be attributed to demons or malicious magic, consequently the treatment would be magical. There was even a specialist trained in "unknown diseases," who probably dealt with illnesses of no known cause. Reproduction was not fully understood in ancient Egypt, so the cause of the miscarriage may well have been attributed to a curse. Ankhesenamen's miscarriage, combined with the fetus's deformity, would require a magician healer to assure it would not happen again. In such cases a wax image of Toth, the god of writing and magic, was fashioned and placed on burning coals under the birthing stool. Ankhesenamen may have sat on the birthing stool so that the smoke could enter her womb and purge it of whatever malicious forces were at work. The miscarriage was more than just a tragedy of state. Egyptians loved children, had large families typical of agrarian societies—lots of children to help in the fields. Tutankhamen and Ankesenamen suffered personally. A popular maxim was: "Marry young and have many children." At the age when they should be starting their family, Tutankhamen and Ankhesenamen were off to a shaky beginning.

Because the fetus was stillborn and had never breathed life, it was unnamed. Had the baby lived to take its first breath she would have had a soul—a Ba and a Ka, the two most important aspects of the soul. The Ba of the deceased was always shown on tomb walls as a bird with a human head that could fly in and out of the tomb while waiting for the resurrection of the body in the west. The Ba was the personality, essential for resurrection. In one ancient Egyptian literary work,[8] a man contemplating suicide is scolded by his Ba who tells him that if he kills himself, the Ba will desert him and ruin any chance for immortality. Another part of the soul was the Ka, a kind of spiritual double that resided within the mummy. Without a Ba and a Ka the fetus had no chance for resurrection. This was the Egyptian religion but it meant little to a pair of young parents who had experienced all the hopes and dreams of parents in every age and seen them crushed. Going against all tradition, they had the little girl mummified.

The fetus was only twelve inches long, so small that special tools had to be crafted for the mummification. A tiny wire was inserted through the nasal passage into the cranial vault to remove the brain. Small strips of linen soaked in resin were next inserted into the skull to dry and preserve the tissue to prevent putrefaction. Then an incision, less than an inch long, was made in the left side of the abdomen to remove the internal organs. But here, even the considerable skills of the royal embalmers failed them. The fetus was too small. No tool could be devised to enter the cavity and remove the stomach, liver, kidney, and intestines without terribly damaging the body. The embalmers left the organs where they were, injecting resin into the abdominal cavity, sealing it for eternity. Bandagers carefully wrapped the baby in pure linen strips while priests recited the ancient prayers. A miniature coffin was carved for the fetus and coated with black resin. Thin gold leaf bands, imitating mummy bandages, placed on the outside of the coffin, were inscribed with the phrases "The venerated one" and "The Osiris"—for the child had no name. A second, smaller coffin rested inside the first with a prayer to Osiris inscribed on the front, in the hope that the god of the dead would intervene and assist the child in the next world. The priest laid the fetus inside the smaller coffin and recited spells from the Book of the Dead, continuing the recitation as the coffin was placed inside the larger one and the whole package wrapped with pure linen bandages. When the bandages were in place, the clay seal of the royal necropolis—a jackal above nine bound captives (symbols of Egypt's traditional enemies)—was attached. The little mummy was ready for burial with her parents one day. The tragedy of the miscarriage, yet another sad misfortune in their young lives, must have drawn Ankhesenamen and Tutankhamen even closer.

As Tutankhamen entered his eighteenth year, the three threads of Egyptian society—the priesthood, the military, and kingship—finally had become woven into a whole fabric. The temples of Amun thrived. Thebes was again dominated by the activities of Luxor and Karnak Temples, the centers around which much of Tutankhamen's restoration revolved.

Constant activity hummed in the temples. The decoration on the colonnade was nearing completion; its dazzling bright colors made the temple live. Other walls were repaired, new plaster added where the old had fallen away, so skillfully repainted that the repairs couldn't be seen. Shining bronze decorations were affixed to the great temple doors and shrines. All was attended to by the growing ranks of priests. Now, each morning the priests opened the doors to the inner sanctuaries to let the first rays of the sun enter the chamber, as they anointed the gold statues of the gods with perfume and sacred oils, painted their eyelids with eye shadow, and placed bread, onions, beer and fruits before each god for its morning meal. Then the priests chanted the prayer to Amun:

Pilot who knows the water,
Helmsman of [the weak],
Who gives bread to him who has none,
Who nourishes the servant of his house.
I take not a noble as protector,
I associate not with a man of wealth,
I place not my share in another's care,
My wealth is in the house of my [lord].
My lord is my protector,
I know his might, to wit:
A helper strong of arm,
None but he is strong, ·
Amun who knows compassion,
Who hearkens to him who calls him,
Amun-Re, the King of Gods,
The Bull great of strength, who loves strength.

Workshops had reopened next to each temple, producing the sacred oils and white linen required by the priesthood. Bakeries and breweries flourished. Storehouses began to fill with goods, animals were gathered for sacrifice, petitioners left offerings. Dreams were interpreted from the dream book in the temple library. For example, "if a man sees himself in a dream with a dwarf—bad. Half his life is gone." The old religion was running at full steam again.

The military was also strong—Horemheb had forged Egypt's army into a force to be feared. The tradition of Egypt's kingship had been restored, Tutankhamen made offerings at the altars of Amun and participated in the Opet festival. Under Maya's watchful eye, the storehouses of Egypt had filled. As all could see for themselves: the promises of the Restoration Stela were being kept.

Tutankhamen began construction of his mortuary temple on the west bank of the Nile. He chose a site a few miles from his tomb. It was a handsome rectangular building, with several colossal statues of the king standing at the entrance, intended as a memorial where Tutankhamen could be worshipped for centuries after his death. When Maya allotted funds for the temple, he also donated land, as a kind of annuity, to the Ka priests who would be the caretakers of the temple, making offerings for the soul of Tutankhamen. The produce of the land would pay for generations of caretaker priests and the eternal upkeep of the temple. Tutankhamen decorated the temple with scenes of himself in his chariot, leading the army into battle. Probably he had not yet ridden out with Horemheb on a campaign, but he expected to someday; he was young. The scenes on the temple walls reassured the people that their king was strong enough to lead the army, just as the great Tuthmosis III had.

So far Tutankhamen's reign had returned Egypt to the good old days, an era of prosperity, expansion, and tolerance. But, just as Divine Order seemed to have been restored in Egypt, two more tragedies struck the ill-fated teenagers. Ankhesenamen, five months into her second pregnancy, miscarried—another little girl. It must have been devastating. Surely they were cursed. Well aware that they were the last survivors of the great Eighteenth Dynasty, Tutankhamen and Ankhesenamen had to produce an heir; Ankhesenamen must bear a son. The second tiny fetus was wrapped and placed in a small coffin similar to her sister's, in the hope that Osiris, god of the dead, would at least grant her life in the next world.

Despite the revitalized economy and religion, if Tutankhamen were to die without an heir, Egypt would again be thrown into turmoil. Those wielding power would be pitted against each other in a wrestling match to win the throne. Egypt could be torn apart again. No one worried much about such a slight possibility; Tutankhamen was young, there was abundant time to produce an heir. Then the unthinkable happened.

In January of 1323 B.C., Tutankhamen, the eleventh ruler of the Eighteenth Dynasty, died under mysterious circumstances. He was nineteen years old. Shortly thereafter, his name was erased from history, lost for 3,000 years. To understand why, we must turn now to the Valley of the Kings.

7

The Most Famous
Tomb in History

Furnish your station in the Valley,
The grave that shall conceal your corpse;
Set it before you as your concern . . .
Emulate the great departed,
Who are at rest within their tombs.

—The scribe Ani
circa 1400 B.C.

Normally, Egyptologists excavate tombs that have been plundered practically bare, with only the walls to study. As we have seen, tomb wall scenes do supply a great deal of information, but imagine what could be learned if a tomb still contained everything that was buried with the deceased, including his most intimate objects, and imagine if the occupant were the pharaoh. Only one tomb in the history of Egyptology has been able to deliver that information. It was found across the Nile from Luxor in an area archeologists call "The Valley of the Kings."

The Valley of the Kings has a mystique all its own. It's the Board-walk and Park Place of archaeology—the site where every excavator would like to land. It's not just what might be discovered that draws Egyptologists to the site; it's the overpowering sense of the history of the place, big history. This is where Ramses the Great, the pharaoh of the Exodus, was laid to rest, and where Hatshepsut, the Queen who would be King, was buried. All these tombs are in an area even a tired tourist can walk in fifteen minutes. A visitor with no knowledge of the area's history still feels something special here. Gazing across the barren landscape at the white limestone cliffs shimmering in the heat somehow evokes a sense of eternity, the sense that thousands of years have changed nothing. Three-thousand-year-old graffiti on cliff walls, where pious priests paused to inscribe their names, are still as bright as the day they were drawn.

Today, a visitor to the Valley first flies to Luxor and then takes the tourist ferry across the Nile to the west bank, before boarding a bus for the ten-minute ride to the site. Quickly, the occasional village disappears and fields of sugar cane give way to desert. Passing through a cleft in the hills—the entrance to the Valley of the Kings—nothing appears for a long minute except limestone cliffs on either side of the road. The tourist rest house suddenly appears, and then a quarter of a mile later, the bus stops in the middle of an arcade of peddlers' stalls heaped with souvenirs. Once past the entrance gate a visitor can leave the gauntlet of vendors behind and follow neatly painted signs to the tombs of Tuthmosis III, Ramses VI, and, straight ahead, Tutankhamen. Of the more than sixty known tombs in the Valley of the Kings, only a dozen or so are open to tourists.

When the Greek traveler Diodorus Siculus visited the Valley in the middle of the first century B.C., the priests of Thebes told him their lists recorded forty-seven tombs, but only fifteen remained, the others having been destroyed by treasure hunters.[1] Fifteen centuries later the English clergyman Richard Pococke sailed up the Nile to visit the Valley in 1739, but could find only nine tombs that could be entered.[2] When Bonaparte[3] invaded Egypt in 1798 he brought along a group of scientists who explored the Valley, and charted sixteen tombs, eleven of which were open. Their "quick and dirty" survey was a remarkable achievement, considering that Napoleon's soldiers were fighting the Mameluke warlords who controlled Egypt at the time, and bullets were flying as the savants risked their lives to measure and record the tombs.

The first systematic excavations in the valley were conducted in the nineteenth century by Giovanni Battista Belzoni, the Italian giant turned adventurer. Trained as a hydraulic engineer, the six-foot-seven-inch Belzoni made his living as a circus strongman before traveling to Egypt in search of treasure. From 1815 to 1819, Belzoni excavated sites up and down the Nile. He was the first person in modern times to enter the pyramid of Khephren, the second largest at Giza, and also the first to enter the great temple of Abu Simbel, built by Ramses the Great, in Nubia. But Belzoni concentrated much of his efforts in the Valley of the Kings, where he believed the greatest treasure would be found. He wasn't so much interested in increasing knowledge as in finding ancient artifacts he could remove from Egypt to sell.

When tombs were cut into the valley walls, vast quantities of stone chips had to be removed and dumped outside, where they remained untouched for thousands of years. Belzoni used the mounds of chips to guide him to a tomb's location. Entrances to many of the tombs had been covered and lost. Sometimes an overhanging cliff collapsed and fell over the entrance, but more often an occasional torrential rainstorm passing through the valley washed mud, sand, and even boulders into the entrances. As centuries passed, the tombs gradually filled with rubble, hiding their entrances for centuries, sometimes forever.

Employing about twenty local workmen at a time, Belzoni excavated the most likely spots, and, although he uncovered several tombs, all had been plundered in antiquity. The most beautiful of these was the tomb of Seti I. Magical spells carved on the walls of Seti's tomb ensured his safe journey to the next world. "The Book of Gates," "The Book of Praising Re in the West," and "The Book of What Is in the Netherworld" were illustrated with paintings of the gods who would assist Seti in defeating his enemies. Above his burial chamber, an astronomical ceiling showed the Egyptian constellations against a dark blue sky. Belzoni, bedazzled by the tomb's brilliant colors, as bright as the day Seti was laid to rest, spent a full year making wax impressions so he could build replicas for an exhibition in London. The show was a sensation, creating one of the first waves of Egyptomania in Europe. Belzoni never knew that just a hundred yards away from Seti's tomb lay the greatest archaeological treasure ever, the tomb of Tutankhamen.

Following in Belzoni's footsteps, Jean-François Champollion, the decipherer of hieroglyphs, made his pilgrimage to the Valley of the Kings soon after Belzoni, but he wasn't interested in excavating. Thrilled with his newly acquired ability to translate hieroglyphs, Champollion was content to copy inscriptions on tomb walls.

Although known as the Valley of the Kings for centuries, no pharaoh's mummy had ever been found until a dramatic discovery in 1881. During the 1870s, antiquities of great beauty, bearing names of the kings and queens of Egypt, began to appear in the antique shops of Luxor. These rare pieces began arriving on the market at a time when bankrupt Egypt was being administered by a triumvirate of England, France, and Italy, to all of whom she was in debt. Each European country controlled a different segment of the Egyptian government; France was in charge of antiquities.

The Egyptian Antiquities Service had been founded by Auguste Mariette, who came to Egyptology in a rather circuitous way. When the papers of a relative who had made extensive drawings of the monuments of Egypt were sent to his family, Mariette studied them intensely, became so enthused about Egypt that he taught himself the hieroglyphic alphabet, and eventually landed a position at the Louvre Museum in Paris. Dispatched to Egypt to purchase manuscripts in 1850, he used the money instead to excavate the Serapeum, the burial place of the sacred Apis bulls. He returned to France with huge crates packed with antiquities—antiquities that are still on display at the Louvre. His greatest achievement was the founding of the Egyptian Antiquities Service, an attempt to stop the kind of looting that had initiated his own career.

The high quality of the royal objects being sold by Luxor dealers attracted collectors and museum curators from all over the world. Mariette himself purchased a *Book of the Dead* (a collection of magic spells buried with a mummy to assure resurrection in the next world) that had been prepared for Queen Henettowey, who lived some 300 years after Tutankhamen. Often incorporated in these papyrus scrolls were beautifully painted pictures of the gods and scenes of the next world. Egypt's dry climate allowed these papyrus rolls to retain much of their original color and vibrancy even after thousands of years. Henettowey's was nearly one hundred feet long and a remarkable work of art.

The next few years saw additional versions of the *Book of the Dead* appear on the market, all belonging to kings, queens, princes, and princesses of the family of Queen Henettowey. When, in addition to these papyri, beautiful jewelry also surfaced, it grew clear to Mariette that an intact royal tomb had been discovered and its contents were being sold piecemeal. He was determined to find the tomb before everything was dispersed or destroyed, but died in 1881 before he could complete his search. His successor, Gaston Maspero, made the search his top priority.

Evidence eventually pointed to the Abd er Rassouls, a family living close to the Valley. After intense questioning, one of the Rassouls revealed the location of the tomb. Two days later, the Rassoul brothers led Emile Brugsch, Maspero's assistant, to an elevated, winding path overlooking the Valley of the Kings that wound through the area known as Deir el Bahri—"the place of the northern monastery," the former site of an old Coptic monastery. Chimneylike outcroppings of rock lined the way through an uninhabited area, about a mile from the ruined temple of Queen Hatshepsut. Near the base of one rocky outcrop, a rectangular eight-by-ten-foot shaft descended forty feet straight down. After placing a palm log across the top of the pit to anchor a rope, first one of the Rassouls, then Brugsch descended. When the young assistant squeezed through the entrance at the bottom, the first thing he saw was a huge coffin, behind which were three more coffins, and past those, on the right, a corridor that ran more than seventy feet into the cliff. Littering the length of it were hundreds of small bright blue mummy-shaped statues, or *ushabtis*, buried with the deceased to serve him in the next world.

The corridor opened onto a room seventeen feet square, the floor of which was almost entirely covered with splendid coffins containing kings of the New Kingdom. Here lay Amenhotep I, Tuthmosis I, Tuthmosis II, and Tuthmosis III of the Eighteenth Dynasty—Tutankhamen's ancestors. Along with them were the Nineteenth Dynasty pharaohs Ramses I, his son, Seti I and *his* son, Ramses the Great. Further back in the tomb, the last room, higher than the others and twenty feet long, was strewn with the coffins and mummies of the Twenty-first Dynasty royal family whose *Books of the Dead* had initiated the quest. Here were the mummies of Pinedjem II, Queen Henettowey, and other members of that august family. The Rassouls had discovered the remains of kings and queens whose reigns spanned four centuries, from the Eighteenth Dynasty through the Twenty-first.

Brugsch, merely an assistant at the museum, was not a great scholar but had attended Egyptology classes in Cairo conducted by his more learned elder brother, Heinrich, so he was able to read the cartouches on many of the coffins. He realized that he was in the presence of the greatest pharaohs in history and that this was the most important find ever made in Egypt. But how had kings of so many different dynasties come to be together in one tomb?

By the Twentieth Dynasty, two centuries after Tutankhamen's death, most of the tombs in the Valley of the Kings had been robbed. An inspection of the Valley of the Kings during the Twenty-first Dynasty revealed this wholesale violation. Rather than continue futile attempts to protect isolated tombs, the violated bodies of the pharaohs were repaired, rewrapped, labeled with wooden tags, placed in new coffins when necessary, and removed to the communal tomb the Rassouls were later to discover. Hastily written accounts on the walls of the original tombs and inscriptions on the pharaohs' coffins and bandages detailed the dates and places of transit. Combining these records made it possible to reconstruct the steps priests of the Twenty-first Dynasty took to preserve the mummies of their ancestors.

The Deir el Bahri cache was considered secure enough that the priest-king Pinedjem II chose it for his own resting place. The inscriptions recording the last movements are written in black ink on the wall at the bottom of the shaft of the Deir el Bahri tomb. On Pinedjem's burial day, the bodies of Seti I and Ramses II were interred with him, and there they remained, undisturbed, for 3,000 years.

As important and unique as the Deir el Bahri discovery was, the findings were poorly documented. After two hours in the tomb, Brugsch realized that the crew's candles might set fire to the dry wooden coffins, so he quickly left the tomb. He then decided that the mummies and the funerary equipment had to be moved to Cairo as soon as possible. The inhabitants of nearby Gourna had for years made their living by robbing tombs. When they learned how much they were soon to lose, there was no telling what they would do. No time was taken to record where each coffin was found in the tomb, and not a single photograph was snapped nor a drawing made of the items *in situ*. Within two days all the coffins, canopic chests, and funerary equipment were hoisted to the surface. Three hundred men carried these treasures to the west bank of the Nile where the coffins, mummies, and statues were ferried to the east bank and loaded onto the museum's steamer for their journey to Cairo. When word of the boat's royal cargo became public, fellaheen women lined the banks of the Nile and wailed mourning cries, just as their ancient ancestors must have done in marking the passing of their kings.[4]

The Deir el Bahri cache had an important effect on excavations in the Valley of the Kings. The find showed how extensive tomb robbery had been in ancient Egypt and how unprotected the tombs were. As a result of the Deir el Bahri discovery, the mummies of Tuthmosis I and II were now in the Cairo Museum, and, although their tombs had not yet been discovered, it was certain they had been plundered, emptied of anything of value. There was good news as well: even with all the royal mummies contained in the cache, there were still plenty of important pharaohs unaccounted for—Tuthmosis IV, Amenhotep III, Merneptah, as well as other lesser known kings. Perhaps their tombs had escaped destruction and plunder.

In 1898, when Victor Loret discovered a second royal cache containing the mummies of Amenhotep III and other kings, attention began to focus on Tutankhamen, until then a practically unknown pharaoh. If Cleopatra, who ruled Egypt a thousand years after Tutankhamen, had been asked about him, she would have responded with a blank look.

Petrie's excavations at Amarna had shown that Tutankhamen was part of a religious revolution, making Amarna a hot subject among Egyptologists. At the same time, various royal tombs—all robbed—had been found in the Valley of the Kings, but not Tutankhamen's. Nor was his mummy among those saved by pious priests from the plundered tombs. It was not unreasonable to think that somewhere in the Valley of the Kings the mummy of Tutankhamen might still rest undisturbed in his tomb. The search for Tutankhamen began in earnest.

To excavate in Egypt, an archaeologist needed the permission of the Antiquities Service, which was not difficult to obtain at the beginning of the century. The "concession," as it was called, usually stipulated the area in which the excavator could dig and the length of time, during which everyone else was excluded from that area. Objects found would be divided between the Antiquities Service and the excavator. It was a good deal for both parties. The Antiquities Service with its limited funds got free labor and new objects for its museum; the excavator got what he wanted—knowledge, objects, or both. Some, like Petrie, came for knowledge. When Petrie received his share of the division of funds at the end of a season, he kept the most interesting pieces to form a study collection that evolved into the Petrie Museum at University College in London. The rest he divided among the patrons who had funded his excavations.

Other excavators came primarily for objects to enhance their own collections, or simply for the thrill of the hunt. Theodore Davis, a wealthy American lawyer and businessman, came for the hunt. Davis wintered in Egypt on his houseboat, *The Bedouin,* a rather elaborate affair complete with piano and crystal chandelier. Looking for a diversion, he decided to excavate but needed an experienced hand working with him to garner the permission. Enter Howard Carter, who began his career under Flinders Petrie.

Carter's introduction to Egyptology came via his natural talent as an artist. His father made a living painting animal portraits for wealthy patrons. His children—Howard was the youngest of eleven—inherited their father's talent. Howard's father had for years been the family portrait painter for Lord Amherst's family, so as a young boy Howard had accompanied his father to Didlington Hall, the family seat that housed Lord Amherst's collection of Egyptian antiquities. Amherst was involved with the Egypt Exploration Fund, a British society recently formed to excavate and record the monuments of Egypt. One of its excavators, in need of an artist to help draw the tomb walls at Beni Hassan, not far from Amarna, suggested that the artist be a "non-gentleman," as such a person would require less than a person of high breeding and thus some expenses could be saved. Young Howard Carter, since he had almost no formal schooling, fit the bill perfectly. Lady Amherst recommended the boy and he boarded a steamer bound for Alexandria. Carter quickly proved to be both competent and hardworking, able to live happily in the simple surroundings of an expedition camp. Soon he was sent to learn the rudiments of excavation techniques from Petrie at Amarna, skills that would later serve him well.

Petrie, who didn't know the young excavator well enough to trust his work, commented:

> . . . Howard Carter came as a lad of seventeen to join me in order to do some excavating for Mr. Tyson Amherst. His interest then was entirely in painting and natural history, and I little thought how much he would be enabled to do. To keep his work distant, I left him to the clearing of a temple site. There he found the broken statues of the queen, torsos and masses of chips from them.[5]

This was one of those curious quirks of history where the paths of two great men cross and neither realizes the significance. Petrie, though still a young man, was by now the most skilled excavator in Egypt, and had begun uncovering early clues to the life of Tutankhamen. Neither

Petrie nor Carter could have had any idea that a quarter of a century later, Carter would discover the tomb of Tutankhamen and become the most famous Egyptologist of all time. Indeed, as Carter worked on the site, he probably handled objects inscribed with Tutankhamen's name but had no idea who Tutankhamen was.

Carter went on to work on other excavations, learning the techniques of archaeology so well that in 1899, at the age of twenty-six, Carter was appointed by Maspero as Chief Inspector of southern Egypt for the Antiquities Service. Carter was energetic, hard working, and concerned about preserving Egypt's monuments. His duties included constructing iron doors on tomb entrances to prevent vandalism and theft, installing electric lights so tourists could see the wall paintings, restoring temples, and preventing thefts. Carter seems to have taken a special interest in the latter duty. He recorded one incident that verges on a Sherlock Holmes story.

Carter had prepared the tomb of Amenhotep II for tourism. He placed the king's mummy in its sarcophagus, displayed many of the objects that Loret had found, and installed an iron gate so the tomb could be locked at night. In spite of these precautions, on November 20, 1901, the tomb was broken into, the mummy of Amenhotep II damaged, and some objects stolen. Carter's report shows just how determined he was in tracking the criminals.

Nov. 28th 1901.—The following day I again went to the tomb of Amenophis II . . . It had been reported to me formerly by the parquet that the padlock of the tomb had been stuck together and made to look all right by means of little pieces of lead paper. . . . I found more small pieces of lead paper beneath the door and a little round piece of resin, probably from a sont-tree. This piece was the exact size of the socket for the tongue in the padlock and gave me a small clue; for on 11th Nov., it had been broken into, the lock being forced by a lever and made to look all right by the means of resin that stuck it together, the material and method in both cases being exactly the same.

I must add before going on further that I had grave suspicions against Mohamed Abd el Rasoul in the case of the Yi-ma-dua tomb, and I watched this man whenever possible, he being a well-known tomb plunderer and his house being quite near the tomb.

. . . I carefully compared the footprints in both tombs and found them to have a strong resemblance. In both cases, *the footprints, being prints of bare feet, are of one person only . . .* I then took photographs, to scale as near as possible, of the foot marks of bare feet, and measured them up very carefully.

During the meantime the spoor-man tracked footprints from Biban El Moluk to the village of Goorneh and to the house of Soleman and Ahmed Abd El Rasoul. These men were arrested . . .

30th Nov. 1901—I went to the parquet and . . . requested to leave to inspect the footprints of Mohamed Abd El Rasoul. This I did at Markaz, and found them to agree totally with my photographs and with the measurements which I had taken in the tomb of Amenophis II and Yi-ma-dua. The measurements agree to a millimeter.[6]

When Carter heard that Davis was interested in excavating, he suggested that he could arrange a concession in the Valley of the Kings for him, and, when Carter's duties as chief inspector permitted, he would supervise the work. In their first year of excavation they found the plundered tomb of Tuthmosis IV. Many of the funerary objects had been left by the ancient robbers including beautiful blue ushabti figures, and part of the pharaoh's chariot that was decorated with battle scenes. Davis was elated, and although the partnership was favorable to both men, it was not to last. In 1904, Carter was transferred north to oversee the monuments of Saqqara, fourteen miles south of Cairo. There he was involved in an altercation that ended his career with the Antiquities Service.

An unruly group of French tourists had tried to enter a tomb without tickets, forced their way past the guard, and refused to leave the tomb. Carter was called. When the French attacked the local guardians, Carter told them to defend themselves and a melee ensued. The French were outraged that an Egyptian workman had hit them, but Carter defended the guards' actions and wanted to prosecute the French. In colonial Egypt, it was unheard-of for an Egyptian to strike a European. The matter reached the highest European diplomatic levels in Egypt and Carter was asked to apologize. He refused. Maspero sympathized with Carter, but was forced to reprimand him and the outraged Carter resigned, never to return to the Antiquities Service. He was a free agent.

In the meantime, Davis, now without the services of Carter, employed twenty-two-year-old Edward Ayrton to continue the excavations in the Valley. The son of a diplomat, Ayrton was born in China, and at nineteen traveled to Egypt to excavate with Petrie. Like most of Petrie's disciples, he was well trained and served Davis well, discovering the plundered tomb of the pharaoh Horemheb, one of Tutankhamen's generals who later became king. He also found the first clue to Tutankhamen's tomb—lodged under a rock—a faience cup bearing the pharaoh's name. This provided the first solid link between Tutankhamen and the Valley of the Kings. Excited by this find, Ayrton and Davis continued the search, and, in 1907, came upon a small pit containing the remains of an ancient meal. Mixed with the food, cups, wine jars, and floral garlands were mummy wrappings that bore the name of Tutankhamen. Clearly, Tutankhamen had been buried in the Valley, but Davis didn't understand what he had found. He thought he had uncovered reburied plunder from Tutankhamen's robbed tomb. Actually these were the remains of the meal eaten by the family and close friends of Tutankhamen on the day of his burial, along with leftovers from the materials used at his mummification. When Davis found a small unfinished tomb in 1909 containing ushabti figures, and some gold foil with the name of Tutankhamen, he concluded that he had found the plundered tomb of Tutankhamen.

Each year, Davis published his finds in a series of sumptuous books. At the end of each book was a catalog of the objects found, written by a professional Egyptologist. Some of these books incorporated watercolor illustrations by Howard Carter, who was then unemployed and grateful for the work. In the preface Davis gave his opinions, unhindered by facts or advice from Egyptologists. In the preface to the volume on the Tutankhamen findings, Davis concluded, "I fear the Valley is now exhausted."[7] He would soon give up his concession to excavate in the Valley, opening the door for Carter.

During the period that Davis worked in the Valley of the Kings, George Edward Stanhope Molyneux Herbert, Fifth Earl of Carnarvon, began his own series of excavations just outside the Valley. Carnarvon, a wealthy aristocrat and collector, had a passion for breeding racehorses and racing automobiles, and had the unfortunate distinction of being in the world's first near-fatal automobile crash in 1903. Advised to travel to Egypt to recover from his injuries, he developed a keen interest in archaeology and, like Davis, thought he would enjoy the diversion of excavating. His accident had injured his lungs and left him frail, so he could never actively participate, but he wanted to have some role. One excavation artist noted Carnarvon's true love of Egyptology:

> The unhealthy color of his complexion was made more conspicuous by the fact that his face was pitted from smallpox. But when he discussed Egyptology, his pale lusterless eyes lit up with enthusiasm."[8]

When Carnarvon applied to Maspero for permission to excavate, Maspero saw a chance to help the impoverished Carter. He suggested that Carnarvon employ Carter. In 1907 he and Carter formed a partnership: Carnarvon would finance a series of excavations and Carter would direct the work.

They were an odd couple. Lord Carnarvon had grown up with immense wealth, had great personal charm, and exhibited all the social graces; he was a man very much at ease with himself and, as was the fashion of the wealthy, he dabbled in the occult. He gave and attended parties where mediums gazed into crystal balls, held seances, and generally enjoyed himself.

Carter, on the other hand, came from a hardworking middle-class family where he developed a no-nonsense attitude toward life, viewing issues as either black or white—right or wrong. He was a sincere, hardworking man who had few social skills and little personal charm, a bachelor, and very much a loner. They were an unlikely team, but a lasting friendship developed. The relationship was always that of the lord and his servant, but they cared for and protected each other.

The year that Carter and Carnarvon formed their partnership, the Davis-Ayrton team found yet another tomb containing a royal coffin and a mummy. Before the excavation dust had settled, Davis would declare it was the mummy of Queen Tiye, Tutankhamen's grandmother. Arthur Weigall, the new Chief Inspector of Antiquities for Luxor, declared it Akhenaten, and George Daressy, the French Egyptologist working in the Egyptian Museum, announced that the mummy was Tutankhamen. In the end they were all proved wrong; Tutankhamen's brother, Smenkare, had been discovered.

TOMB 55

Of all the royal mummies discovered, none has caused more controversy than the one found in Tomb 55 in the Valley of the Kings. Situated near the tomb of Ramses IX, this tomb received the new number 55, and is known as KV55 (King's Valley 55). As Davis and Ayrton cleared the debris, a flight of steps appeared that had been cut into the bedrock. Clearing it revealed a doorway leading to a second set of steps that descended into a tomb, at the bottom of which stood a dry wall built of large limestone chips. Not traditional tomb architecture, the wall had obviously resealed a tomb that had been opened in ancient times. Removing the blocking wall revealed a descending corridor nearly filled to the ceiling with limestone chips to deter tomb robbers. An open space near the ceiling suggested that it hadn't worked; the tomb had been plundered.

The crowd present for the opening of the tomb included Gaston

Maspero; Arthur Weigall, the Inspector of Antiquities for Upper Egypt; Joseph Lindon Smith, an artist who had worked for several Egyptologists; and Smith's wife; Corinna. Nearly all of those present have left accounts of what happened on that clear January day in 1907. None of them agree with the others.

First to enter the tomb was Joseph Lindon Smith, whom Maspero selected because his slight build allowed him to squeeze through the narrow passage. As Smith inched forward on top of the chips, he encountered a large gilded wooden door. Quickly sketching the inscriptions, he returned to show them to Maspero, who read the name of Queen Tiye, wife of Amenhotep III and mother of Akhenaten. The door was so fragile that when, for the first time in 3,000 years, a gentle breeze entered the tomb, the gold leaf flaked off and floated to the ground. As the door was too fragile to be moved, Smith carefully crept alongside it and continued downward into the tomb.

The tomb was unfinished. What served as the burial chamber was an unpainted, roughly hewn room about eighteen square feet. More wooden panels lay on the floor and against a wall. In a niche cut into one wall, Smith could see four beautiful alabaster canopic jars with finely sculpted lids in the form of a woman's head (fig. 3). What drew Smith's attention among the jumble, however, was a badly damaged but beautiful coffin lying with its lid ajar near one wall. The coffin, like the rest of the contents of the room, had suffered water damage from rain dripping through a crack in the ceiling. The coffin had once rested on a wooden funerary bier that had collapsed, causing even more damage to the coffin. Still worse, at some time in antiquity, a rock had crashed onto it from the ceiling.

Thousands of inlays of paste and semiprecious stones formed the protective wings of a falcon encircling the coffin. More impressive than the coffin itself was the fact that inside lay a body—obviously undisturbed—for on its head remained a golden vulture, symbol of the pharaoh's power.

No one recorded how long Smith remained in the tomb, but it must have seemed like an eternity to the group waiting outside for his report. When he finally emerged, he described things as best he could. Maspero asked a few questions and sent him back to look for water damage and to sketch the objects. Smith sketched the coffin, then returned to make a second report. Everyone was impatient to enter the tomb, but they had to wait for workmen to clear a passage, and to put down boards to accommodate Maspero's ample weight.

Davis's butler was sent to bring a picnic hamper from his large houseboat on the Nile. Over lunch the group discussed the discovery. Davis was delighted, convinced that they had discovered the tomb and mummy of Queen Tiye. After lunch they were at last able to enter the tomb.

All but two of the wood panels have since disintegrated, but from what was observed in the tomb in 1907, it is clear that they were the remains of a gilded shrine that had once enclosed the coffin of Queen Tiye. Her shrine was apparently made for her by her son, Akhenaten, and shows him with his mother worshipping the Aten. Some time after the burial, someone had hacked out Akhenaten's image from the shrine, but the figure of Queen Tiye was untouched. And, nestling in a rectangular niche carved into the wall were the four canopic jars, meant to hold the mummy's internal organs, with lids in the shape of a woman's head.

Because of the fragile condition of the coffin lid they had to wait for a conservator to strengthen it so it could be removed. In the meantime, each object had to be photographed *in situ* before it could be moved from the tomb to the daylight. Several days passed before a conservator and a photographer arrived from Cairo. On the day they unwrapped the mummy everyone present had a sense of the event's historical importance. They would be the first people in more than 3,000 years to look upon the face of this famous queen of Egypt. Maspero, Weigall, Ayrton, Joseph Lindon Smith and his wife, Corinna, and Theodore Davis and his companion Mrs. Andrews all filed into the room. Also present was Harold Jones, an artist who worked for Davis; Arthur Quibell of the Antiquities Service arrived later. After the group gathered solemnly around the coffin, the lid of which had been removed by the conservator, Maspero asked Joseph Lindon Smith to do the unwrapping because he had ". . . the gentle hands of an artist."

Gold sheets the size of a piece of writing paper covered the mummy from neck to feet. Because gold does not tarnish, the ancient Egyptians associated it with eternity, encasing the mummy in gold, to ensure preservation. As Smith removed each sheet of gold, he handed it to Maspero for inspection, and Maspero pronounced each of the twelve "uninscribed." The mummy was now exposed, the left arm lay across the breast and the right arm along the side, a pose normally reserved for royal women. Three gold bracelets encircled each wrist. Davis now had even more evidence supporting his Queen Tiye theory. Maspero asked Smith to feel under the wrappings in the area of the neck and upper chest for the pectoral that should have been there. When Smith delicately began the procedure, they were confronted by a scene like something from a horror film.

> But no sooner had my hand touched the surface of the mummy than it crumbled into ashes and sifted down through the bones. So it was with the entire body until nothing remained except a pile of dust and disconnected bones with a few shreds of dried skin adhering to them. The water that had got into the tomb explained the cloth resembling the consistency of the ash of a cigar. In feeling around I found pieces of a broad necklace of gold pendants, inlaid plaques, lotus flowers of gold and numerous minute beads.[9]

It was a strange assortment of things in Tomb 55: objects belonging to Tiye, Akhenaten, Smenkare, and, many Egyptologists now believe, Kiya's canopic jars. How did all these objects of Tutankhamen's family come together there? The most likely explanation is that after the tombs of Amarna had been looted, some loyal servant gathered whatever remained, transported it to Thebes, and reburied the cache in Tomb 55. Today, most Egyptologists believe the body in Tomb 55 was Smenkare, Tutankhamen's brother. Tutankhamen was still missing.

As soon as Theodore Davis relinquished the Valley concession, Carter and Carnarvon took it over. They set out to conduct what they called "a systematic and exhaustive search" of the Valley, but work was delayed by the start of World War I until late in 1917.

Carter was convinced that the best bet for an undiscovered tomb was in a triangle formed by the tombs of Merneptah, Ramses II, and Ramses VI, the only area in the Valley that had not been fully excavated. Workmen cleared thousands of baskets of debris as Carter worked down to the base of the well-known tomb of Ramses VI. A group of ancient workmen's huts were uncovered, probably left behind from the construction of that tomb. The huts would have to be cleared to proceed further, but that would have closed access to the Ramses VI tomb, one of the most popular tourist sites. So Carter moved his work to another part of the Valley until tourism abated.

Five years went by with no success as Carter assiduously searched the Valley. Carnarvon came to agree that Davis was right, that the Valley was played out. Because of the bond that had developed between Carnarvon and Carter, it must have been difficult for Carnarvon when he invited Carter to Highclere Castle in 1922 to inform him that he had decided to end the excavation. After so many years with no results Carter could not have been surprised, but he was not ready to give up. He made a counterproposal. They would continue for one last season for which Carter would pay the expenses, though Carnarvon could keep anything they found. Carnarvon, touched by the bold gesture from the unmoneyed Carter, agreed to finance one last season.

It was not until November 1922 that Carter returned at last to the triangle he had left for later and began clearing the huts. On November 4, one of the workmen discovered a step cut into the valley floor. After another day of clearing, a stairway was exposed. At sunset on November 5, after the twelfth step, the upper part of a doorway with the royal necropolis seal still in place was uncovered. Carter knew they had discovered a king's tomb, but could not determine which king. Through a small hole near the top of the door, Carter could see that the passage behind the plastered door was filled with rubble to deter tomb robbers. The tomb might be intact. What bothered Carter was the narrow stairway, only six feet wide; the entrances to other royal tombs were considerably wider. Somehow able to keep his excitement in check, Carter filled in the stairway with sand and rubble and cabled his patron, Lord Carnarvon, in England:

"At last have made wonderful discovery in Valley; a magnificent tomb with seals intact, re-covered same for your arrival; congratulations."

Carter waited almost a month for his friend, who arrived in Egypt the last week in November. Arrangements were finally made to open the tomb. The stairway was cleared again, and this time Tutankhamen's cartouche was revealed on the lower part of the sealed door. When the door was opened, however, the excavators could see an ancient narrow path through the rubble, almost certainly made by ancient robbers. The tomb had been entered before.

An entire day was devoted to clearing the thirty-foot-long, descending passage. Strewn amongst the limestone chips were alabaster jars, pottery and workmen's tools. Finally, a second sealed door was reached. This time there was clear evidence of the door's having been breached and resealed. Carter made an opening in the upper left corner of the doorway to insert a candle for testing the air inside. At first the flame fluttered in escaping hot air, then Carter saw, "wonderful things."

The room into which Carter and Carnarvon peered was packed with all the possessions Tutankhamen would need in the next world. Chariots, statues, game boards, linens, jewelry, beds, couches, chairs, even a throne, were all piled on top of each other. The ancient robbers had apparently been caught in the act or frightened away soon, because little had been disturbed. The tomb was virtually intact.

At last it seemed that the details of the unknown pharaoh Tutankhamen would be revealed. When Carter made his discovery, two popular references on the history of ancient Egypt existed, both written by Petrie's American counterpart, James Henry Breasted. Trained as a pharmacist, Breasted soon realized that Egyptology interested him more than dispensing drugs, so he left for Germany to study hieroglyphs. The Europeans were far ahead of America in offering formal courses in Egyptology, so Breasted studied with Adolph Erman, a great philologist, and was the first American awarded a doctorate in Egyptology. Petrie was an excavator, Breasted a philologist; each was interested in completing a picture of Egyptian history, but they took different approaches. Petrie wanted to discover new material; Breasted wanted to translate it.

At the turn of the century Breasted began an incredible one-man campaign to record all the historical records of ancient Egypt. For eleven years he roamed up and down the Nile, translating inscriptions on temple and tomb walls, often risking his health. His diary entry for November 14, 1906, reads,

> We are at work at 6:00 AM, and the sun is long down before we stop. I spent yesterday on a ladder, copying from a glaring wall upon which this fierce sun was beating in full force; and I rose this morning with one eye swollen shut. Even with dark glasses, I sometimes find work on a sunlit wall impossible.[10]

After this exhaustive research Breasted published his five-volume *Ancient Records of Egypt*.[11] He had found only one monument from the reign of Tutankhamen, the tomb of Huy, Tutankhamen's viceroy to Nubia. When Breasted later wrote his 600-page *History of Egypt*[12] he devoted less than a page to Tutankhamen. There simply wasn't more to say. Carter hoped to fill in the history.

As the excavation of Tutankhamen's tomb proceeded, the information Egyptologists had been waiting for did not come to light. Spectacular objects were found, but nothing mentioned who the king's parents were or provided details or insight into what had happened during his brief reign. There was a fleeting moment of excitement when a box of "papyri" was found in the antechamber, but when examined closely it turned out to be rolls of linen, turned yellow over the centuries. Tutankhamen had eluded his discoverers.

Carter and Carnarvon, delighted with their discovery, reacted in very different ways. Carnarvon, the collector, was thrilled by the beauty of the objects. Carter, with his artist's training, could of course appreciate their beauty, but, as an archaeologist, his interest lay in discovering the hidden history of Tutankhamen. In this he was disappointed.

Carter never knew that Tutankhamen may have suffered a blow to the back of the head, nor did he suspect foul play. But even now, seventy-five years later, we can still look to the tomb for clues about what happened during Tutankhamen's brief life, and most of all for clues about his death.

THE GOLD SHRINE

The jewelry was, of course, spectacular, but for me, the most touching object found in the tomb was a small wooden shrine covered with gold that once housed a statue of Tutankhamen. Only a foot and a half high, it is actually a model of a life-sized shrine (fig. 7). When Carter opened its tiny doors, he saw two little recessed sandal prints on the floor of the shrine, where the statue, stolen by thieves in ancient times, once stood.[13] The outside of the shrine is carved with eighteen scenes of Tutankhamen doing all the things he loved—hunting marsh fowl with his bow, receiving flowers, being perfumed—and always beside him is Ankhesenamen. She brings flowers to Tutankhamen and ties a necklace around his neck. When he hunts, Ankhesenamen sits at his knee holding his next arrow. The king pours perfume on his bride's hands (fig. 8). These are not standard scenes produced from workshop patterns. This is a portrayal of a young couple devoted to each other, engrossed in each other. Their marriage took place for political reasons when they were children, but clearly a great affection grew between them. The scenes on the shrine show them constantly touching, holding hands. They were teenagers in love.

The shrine's inscriptions never mention Tutankhamen as "True of Voice," deceased, so this is no hastily fashioned funerary object commissioned for his tomb. It was probably a gift from Ankhesenamen to her husband. It is her love letter written in gold. The shrine isn't the only sign of love between Tutankhamen and Ankhesenamen. Even the royal throne shows Ankhesenamen tenderly adjusting Tutankhamen's broad collar.

The royal couple spent a great deal of time together, whiling away the hours playing games. Tutankhamen took three different sets of board games with him to the next world. One of his favorites was "Senet," something like our modern game of Monopoly (fig. 9). The Senet board consists of three rows of ten squares. Some of the squares were labeled "very good" and some were labeled "water"—the equivalent of "go to jail." The pieces were shaped like chess pawns, but in some elaborate sets they were lions' heads. We do not know the rules for the game, but it seems to have involved a race between players to avoid the pitfalls, such as "water," to reach the end of the board first. Moves were determined by throwing sticks.[14] The game was so popular that kings and queens are shown playing Senet on their tomb walls. They also played "Twenty Squares." The squares were arranged in a T. We can only surmise that the players lined their game pieces on the outer rows of the board, and, using throwing sticks to determine their moves, attempted to make their way down the center aisle.[15]

Tutankhamen was buried with nearly three dozen jars of fine wine, each holding several gallons. Egyptians were so fond of wine that they often showed the process of wine-making on their tomb walls. One nobleman from Thebes, Senefer, had the roof of his tomb left uneven so that a grape arbor painted on the ceiling would appear realistic. Another Theban nobleman, Nakht, showed the pressing of grapes, with several men in large vats trampling the grapes to release their juice. The wine in Tutankhamen's tomb was quite a treasure. The jars are labeled as to the vintner, vineyard, and year of bottling. Many of the jars are labeled from the "Estate of Tutankhamen"; most are dated to year 5, probably a vintage year. One bottle was labeled "year 31" of the pharaoh's reign, so it must have been saved from his grandfather's wine cellar. It was more than thirty years old when placed in the tomb. Of all the wine in Tut-

ankhamen's tomb, only four of the jars were labeled "sweet." Tutankhamen liked his wine dry.[16]

Tutankhamen seems to have loved hunting above all other sports.
Scenes decorating his linen chests and shrines show the king hunting
and fowling. An ostrich feather fan depicts the young king hunting ostriches with a bow and arrow from his chariot. Behind the king, a strid-
ing ankh sign holds an ostrich-feather fan that is also decorated. If one
could see the decoration on it, it would be another ostrich-feather fan, a
picture of the picture in the picture. Tutankhamen also hunted ibexes
and gazelles. Dozens of bows and hundreds of arrows were placed in his
tomb so he could continue his hunts in the next world.[17]

Objects in the tomb tell us a good deal about *what* Tutankhamen
liked, but they say precious little about *whom* he liked and his relationships with those around him. Was he fond of the members of his court?
Did he trust them? Did he welcome Aye's guidance? Tutankhamen's
tomb doesn't reveal much about his family either; there were few visible
mementos of his parents, sisters, or brother, other than Ankhesenamen.
Perhaps mention of his family was too painful a reference to Amarna.
But Howard Carter did find a great heirloom from Tutankhamen's
grandmother in the tomb. A miniature coffin that held an even smaller
gilded anthropoid coffin was inscribed for the boy king, and contained a
curious assortment of objects: a tiny painted wooden coffin, some scraps
of cloth, and a linen parcel containing a solid gold statuette of a kneeling king, identified as Tutankhamen's grandfather, Amenhotep III. An
even smaller coffin inscribed with the name and titles of Tutankhamen's
grandmother, Queen Tiye, held a lock of her hair.

Heirlooms from previous rulers or family members were often found
in royal tombs. Sometimes an unguent jar belonging to a relative, or a
scarab inscribed with a loved-one's name, was placed in a tomb as a keep-
sake. The plait of Queen Tiye's hair was the memento of a revered grandmother and it helped Egyptologists establish Tutankhamen's lineage, but
it also provided a clue that may have helped identify her mummy.

When Victor Loret discovered three unwrapped, unidentified
mummies in a side chamber in Amenhotep II's tomb, no one believed

they would ever be identified. The mummy that appeared on the left in contemporary photographs was dubbed "The Elder Lady." Photographs clearly show her right arm resting at her side and her left arm across her chest, a pose associated with royal women of the Eighteenth Dynasty. Edward Wente, a University of Chicago Egyptologist, suggested in the 1970s that the Elder Lady might be either Queen Hatshepsut or Queen Tiye.

Like fingerprints, hair is unique to each individual. If the hair found among Tutankhamen's heirlooms matched that of the Elder Lady, then she was Queen Tiye. The Egyptian Antiquities Organization is, however, extremely cautious in permitting samples from the royal mummies—even a few hairs—to be taken. They had to be convinced that the project held a good chance of identifying the Elder Lady as the venerable Queen Tiye.

As a first step toward gaining permission, Dr. James Harris, author of *X-raying the Pharaohs*, took a cephalogram of the Elder Lady in 1975, a technique that permits a precise plotting of cranial measurements. Computerized data from the Elder Lady were compared with those of the mummy of Tuya, Queen Tiye's mother, to determine if the two women were similar enough to imply a mother-daughter relationship. The test showed a remarkable similarity, increasing the chance that the elder lady was Queen Tiye. Permission was granted for hair samples to be taken from the head of the Elder Lady and the plait of Queen Tiye's hair.

Both samples were scanned by electron microprobes to chart their chemical composition. The hair found in Tutankhamen's tomb matched that from the head of the Elder Lady almost exactly. The authors of the study concluded they had found Queen Tiye.[18]

If the objects in the tomb's first room didn't reveal the king's unknown past, perhaps Tutankhamen himself would. Beyond the antechamber, in the sealed burial chamber, lay the long dead pharaoh. But Carter and Carnarvon couldn't get to him until the room was empty. Removing the objects from the antechamber took more than a year. The Metropolitan Museum of Art in New York had loaned Carter their master photographer, Harry Burton, to record the placement of each object in the tomb. This was essential because sometimes wooden objects are so fragile that they turn to dust when touched so the only record of their existence is the photograph. In a *New York Times* account, Burton told of just such an experience.

I remember, when we were clearing a series of XVIIth Dynasty tombs, which had been infested with white ants, the preliminary photographs were literally the only record of most of the wooden objects found. The coffins appeared to be in perfect condition, but when touched they collapsed into dust.

There was one very attractive small wooden statuette of a girl in one of these tombs, which appeared to be quite sound. It was standing quite alone, and after the general view of the chamber had been taken, the camera was turned on to it. I intended to expose a plate for two minutes, but after it had been exposed for one and three-quarter minutes the figure suddenly collapsed, and nothing remained but a small heap of dust. I immediately switched off the beam of light, put a cap on the camera, and went off to develop the plate. Fortunately the negative turned out to be quite good, and, although the statuette no longer existed, we had a complete record of it. This is only one of many similar cases.[19]

The Metropolitan Museum had no official connection with the Carter-Carnarvon excavation, but their team was excavating outside the Valley when the discovery was made. Realizing how many priceless objects were involved, they put their team at Carter's disposal. Even in Egypt, nothing of the magnitude of Tutankhamen's treasures had been found before; the entire archaeological community formed a support system.

Sometimes objects were so fragile that they had to be conserved in the tomb before they could be moved. Wood pieces had to be strengthened and wrapped, but Tutankhamen's clothes presented the greatest problems. Often the linen fell apart at the slightest touch, so the pattern of the thousands of beads and gold sequins had to be recorded first so that, in the event that a garment turned to dust, the decorations could later be applied to new cloth. Arthur Mace, the Metropolitan Museum's conservator, estimated that there were nearly 50,000 beads on one garment alone. He covered many of the smaller garments with wax so the beadwork would remain intact while the clothing was moved. It took Mace three weeks of intense work just to empty one chest of clothes. As Mace and Burton worked to clear the antechamber there were moments of wondering about the boy-king, who they hoped lay in the next room. Mace even pondered how he died.

> We have reason to believe that he was little more than a boy when he died, and that it was his successor, Eye, who supported his candidature to the throne and acted as his adviser during his brief reign. It was Eye, moreover, who arranged his funeral ceremonies, and it may even be that he arranged his death, judging that the time was now ripe for him to assume the reins of government himself.[20]

I know of no Egyptologist who ever commented on this suggestion, yet, as we will see, Mace was not far from the mark.

On February 16, 1923, the antechamber was finally cleared. When Carter broke through the wall into the burial chamber, he was faced with what seemed to be a wall of gold. Actually, he was looking at a gilded wood shrine that enclosed the body of Tutankhamen. The shrine was 16 feet 8 inches by 10 feet 9 inches, nearly filling the burial chamber, making it difficult for Carter to move in the narrow space between the shrine and the walls. The doors to the shrine were closed so Carter didn't know that inside were three more shrines, one inside the other, all surrounding Tutankhamen's sarcophagus. Each shrine had to be dismantled and removed from the chamber before the next could be examined, a difficult task because of the confined space. The job had been easier for the ancient workmen, who had assembled the shrines from fresh, strong timber. Carter had to deal with dry, brittle wood.

Still visible were the ancient instructions for assembling the shrines painted in black and white ink by the carpenters. On the front of the side panels was the hieroglyph 🐥 —meaning "front" and on the rear was 𓈖𓈖 —meaning "rear." These hieroglyphs matched those on the roofs of the shrines that were to be aligned accordingly—the ancient equivalent of "insert tab A into slot A." The workmen had been directed to place the shrines so the doors would open to the west, and the king could emerge into the next world, but somehow they got it backwards. Tutankhamen would have walked into this world rather than the next.

Once the shrines were dismantled and removed, the sarcophagus was at last revealed. Carved from a single block of yellow quartzite, a beautiful winged goddess on each corner protected Tutankhamen with outstretched arms. The lid was of pink granite painted to look like the yellow quartzite of the base—a precursor of faux marble. In the rush to prepare Tutankhamen's burial, something must have gone wrong and the original lid broke, so a lid of pink granite was substituted. But here, too, the stone masons had a problem: the second lid developed a crack, which they repaired with plaster and paint.

This haste with which Tutankhamen's tomb was prepared made Carter's job more difficult, as he frequently encountered the workmen's mistakes. The crack in the lid of the sarcophagus, for example, made it difficult to lift in one piece, but eventually block and tackle were brought and ropes were placed beneath the lid so that it could be hoisted. One step closer to his goal, Carter wrote:

> Many strange scenes must have happened in the valley of the tombs of the kings since it became the royal burial ground of the Theban New Empire, but one may be pardoned for thinking that the present scene was not the least interesting or dramatic. For ourselves it was the one supreme and culminating moment—a moment looked forward to ever since it became

evident that the chambers discovered in November 1922 must be the tomb of Tut Ankh Amen and not a cache of his furniture as had been claimed. None of us but felt the solemnity of the occasion, none of us but was affected by the prospect of what we were about to see—the burial custom of a king of ancient Egypt thirty-three centuries ago. How would the king be found? Such were the anticipatory speculations running in our minds during the silence maintained. The tackle for raising the lid was in position. I gave the word. Amid intense silence the huge slab, broken in two, weighing over a ton and a quarter, rose from its bed.[21]

The group working in the tomb, together with the assembled dignitaries, peered into the sarcophagus, but as if through a mist. They could not make out any details. Only after gazing into the sarcophagus for a while did they realize that they were looking at gauze-like shrouds covering the coffin inside the sarcophagus. When the shrouds were rolled back, Carter and the group were confronted with more than they could ever have hoped for, a seven-foot anthropoid coffin of unsurpassed workmanship bearing the likeness of Tutankhamen. On the forehead perched the cobra and vulture, symbols of Upper and Lower Egypt— the pharaoh's dominion. And encircling these symbols of power was a miniature funeral wreath, still perfectly preserved, a sight that so moved Carter that he became quite sentimental:

> . . . But perhaps the most touching by its simplicity was the tiny wreath of flowers . . . around these symbols, as it pleased us to think, the last farewell offering of the widowed girl queen to her husband, the youthful representative of the "two kingdoms."
>
> . . . many and disturbing were our emotions awakened by that Osiride form. Most of them voiceless. But in that silence, to listen—you could almost hear the ghostly footsteps of the departing mourners.

Our lights were lowered, once more we mounted those sixteen steps, once more we beheld the blue vault of the heavens,
where the sun is Lord, but our inner thought still lingered over
the splendor of that vanished pharaoh, with his last appeal
upon his coffin written upon our minds. "Oh Mother Nut!
Spread thy wings over me as the Imperishable Stars."[22]

The wreath had been fashioned from olive leaves, blue water-lily petals,
and cornflowers all fastened to a papyrus base. This touching memento
will provide us with a clue to the murder of Tutankhamen.

Carter and his team of excavators now believed they were within a
week or two of seeing the mummy. Inside the rectangular stone sarcophagus was the anthropoid coffin. Inside that would be two more,
then, finally, the mummy of Tutankhamen. The removal and opening of
the inner coffins would be difficult because they fit tightly inside each
other. But once the problem was overcome, they would at last gaze upon
the face of the lost king. But as Carter neared that long anticipated moment, Tutankhamen began to slip away.

Lord Carnarvon died unexpectedly in Cairo from a severely in-
fected mosquito bite. His sudden and tragic death gave rise to rumors
about a curse in the tomb. Carter and Carnarvon held thoroughly opposite views on the occult. Carter was a strong anti-spiritualist, while
Carnarvon was attracted to the occult and often visited mediums and
psychics. It was Carnarvon's personal psychic, Velma, who promoted the
idea of a curse on the tomb. After Carnarvon's death, Velma published
an account of her last sittings with Lord Carnarvon, saying that he was
the victim of "powerful occult forces." Before he was to leave for Egypt
to open the newly discovered tomb, Carnarvon asked Velma to read his
palm. At that meeting she saw a thin spot in his lifeline and she warned
Carnarvon, "I see great peril for you. Most probably—as the indications
of occult interest are so strong in your hand—it will arise from such a
source."[23]

Intrigued by what he had been told, Carnarvon returned for one
more session before his departure. This time Velma looked deep into her

crystal ball. Carnarvon also peered into the sphere, but it was cloudy and all he could make out was a temple. The skilled Velma could see far more. First, she gazed upon an ancient Egyptian funeral where an elderly official was placing a gold mask on a young man in a coffin. Then the image changed into a group of men, led by Carnarvon, working in the Valley of the Kings. Mysterious flashes emanated from the tomb. Then the old official appeared, surrounded by people who called for punishment of those who defiled the tomb. The last vision Velma saw was Carnarvon, standing alone in a storm of occult flashes.

Velma warned Carnarvon not to return to the tomb, to offer some excuse to the public for not proceeding with the excavation. But Carnarvon felt he had to go, saying, "A challenge to the psychic powers of the ages, Velma! What a challenge!" Soon after their meeting, he was dead. Velma, of course, wrote her account after Carnarvon's death, a great story that gave "the Curse of Tutankhamen" eternal life.[24]

Now Carter had to handle every crisis by himself, a job for which he was ill-suited. It was Carnarvon who possessed the social skills necessary to deal with people, whose personal charm put everyone at ease. Carter, although a fine Egyptologist, was socially ill at ease, had a rigid, quarrelsome personality, and completely lacked diplomatic skills. Carter continued the work on the tomb after the death of his friend and benefactor, but things did not go well thereafter. Almost from the day the tomb had been discovered, bad feelings existed between the Egyptian Antiquities Service and Carter and Carnarvon. One source of conflict had been how the publicity was handled. To avoid dealing with the hundreds of newspaper reporters requesting information about the tomb, Carnarvon sold the exclusive rights to the London *Times*. This allowed the busy excavators to deal with the inquiries of just one journalist. It also meant that Egyptian reporters were not permitted to interview Carter or Carnarvon. The Egyptians viewed this as British colonialism at its worst; tensions only increased as work on the tomb continued.

The sarcophagus lid was lifted on February 12, 1924. The next day

Carter invited his colleagues' wives to the opening of the outer coffin, but no wives of Egyptian officials were asked. The Egyptian Antiquities Service thereupon refused permission to the European wives. The message to Carter was clear: "This is our tomb, not yours."

They were right. Carter was a good man, but the stress of being responsible for the greatest archaeological treasure the world had ever seen was getting to him. He was behaving as if the tomb were his property. There were stories of his taking ancient objects back to the dig house to use as paperweights. He was constantly being badgered to show the tomb to important visitors but always refused, even when requests came from the Egyptian Antiquities Service. His view was that the Antiquities Service had no right to disturb him while he was working—and he was always working. The great iron door that Carter had placed at the entrance to the tomb and locked became a symbol of "Inglesi colonialism." So when the Egyptians insisted that Egyptian wives be present, Carter snapped.

He posted a notice at the Winter Palace Hotel in Luxor stating that he and his colleagues could not work under such restrictions, and that he was closing the tomb. The Egyptians responded in kind, sending police to lock Carter out of the tomb. There was little that Carter could do about this, so with the sarcophagus lid precariously suspended in midair, he departed for a lecture tour of America.

The Egyptian government knew that Carter was the only man for the job so an agreement was reached that returned Carter to work. But it was not until October of 1925 that the lid of the first of the three nesting coffins was finally set aside. Removing three coffins crammed one inside another proved a delicate task that consumed most of the 1925–1926 season. The lid of the first coffin had four silver handles, two on each side, that proved strong enough to raise it. The second, equally beautiful, six-foot-eight-inch anthropoid coffin, was now revealed, under its own shroud. It, too, bore floral wreaths. This coffin gave Carter his first inkling that the mummy might not be in the best of condition. Some of the inlays in the decoration had fallen out, indicating that there had been moisture in the coffin.

Because of the delicate condition of the second coffin, it was decided to remove the entire coffin, rather than just the lid. This was done, although no one could explain the enormous weight of the coffin they hoisted, then lowered onto planks of wood set across the stone sarcophagus.

The second coffin had no handles and fit inside the outer one with less than half an inch to spare on either side. Carter screwed strong eyelets into the outer coffin, removed the planks, and lowered it back into the sarcohapgus rather than raising its contents. This left the second coffin, still holding the innermost one, resting on the wooden platform. With room to maneuver now, the lid of the second coffin could be lifted, and the third, innermost coffin, revealed. This coffin was the reason for the unexpected weight. It was solid gold, weighing nearly 250 pounds.

The details on the gold coffin were obscured by a black coating, the remains of magical unguents that had been poured over it. The liquids had run into the bottom of the second coffin, gluing the two together, but the handles on the lid of the gold coffin allowed it to be lifted. At last the mummy of Tutankhamen was uncovered. Carter wrote:

> At such moments the emotions evade verbal expression, complex and stirring as they are. Three thousand years and more had elapsed since men's eyes had gazed into the golden coffin. Time, measured by the brevity of human life, seemed to lose its common perspectives before a spectacle so vividly recalling the solemn religious rites of vanished civilization. But it is useless to dwell on such sentiments, based as they are on feelings of awe and human piety. The emotional side is no part of archaeological research. Here at last lay all that was left of the youthful Pharaoh, hitherto little more that the shadow of a name.[25]

Like its gold coffin, the mummy had been liberally doused with unguents, which explained the evidence of moisture in the second coffin. Luckily, the famous gold mask protected the head of the pharaoh, but the rest of the body was in poor condition. An autopsy would prove difficult.

To soften the unguents, Carter took the coffins and the mummy outside into the sun, noting in his day book:

> Nov. 1st. Removed the Royal Mummy to No. 15. It took ten men to bring it out of the tomb and carry it up. Placed in the sun for a few hours . . . Heat of the sun not sufficient today to make any real impression upon the pitchlike material which has stuck fast the mummy and coffins.
>
> Nov. 2nd. Found that heat of the sun was of no avail in freeing the mummy from its coffin. In consequence, the examination of the Royal Mummy must necessarily take place as it lies.[26]

Dr. Douglas Derry, Professor of Anatomy at Cairo University, was given the responsibility of working with the body. Assisted by Dr. Saleh Bey Hamdi, Director of Sanitary Services in Alexandria, Derry began unwrapping it on November 11, 1925. Other attendees were Pierre Lacau, Director-General of the Antiquities Service, Harry Burton, the photographer loaned to Carter by the Metropolitan Museum of Art, in New York, and several Egyptian officials. No wives were present.

The unguents had caused a chemical reaction with the bandages, darkening them by a slow spontaneous combustion. Because the bandages could not be unrolled in such a state, heated wax was brushed over the outer layer so it could be cut away in a large piece. When the wax had cooled, Derry made a longitudinal incision and peeled back the first layer, to reveal amulets and jewelry incorporated within the wrappings. In all, 143 spectacular objects were removed with the bandages.

Finally, Tutankhamen was revealed, a young man with handsome, regular features (fig. 22). But when an attempt was made to remove the mummy from its coffin, it was discovered that the sacred oils had congealed, and Tutankhamen was glued to his coffin. First, Derry tried to chisel the mummy free, then he switched to heated knives, both operations causing considerable damage to the body. Finally, in desperation, he cut the mummy in half at the third lumbar vertebra so it could be removed in sections.

Derry's treatment of the mummy provides a good example of how carelessly the physical evidence that could reveal the cause of Tutankhamen's death was treated. Carter had little idea how much information could be gained by a careful investigation, so he abandoned the mummy to Derry's rough handling. If Tutankhamen's throne had been stuck in unguents, I doubt that Carter would have permitted it to be sawed in half. The unguents would have been chemically analyzed and a solvent devised to free the throne without damage. No so for poor Tutankhamen. The mummy was in poor shape when Derry started to work on it, but was in far worse condition when he finished.

The arms and legs had become disarticulated from their joints so Derry could clearly see the tops and bottoms of the long bones. This enabled him to calculate Tutankhamen's age at death. In young people, the ends of the long bones, the epiphyses, are loosely connected by cartilage that becomes bone as the person grows older. The average age at which the epiphyses join to the long bone is known, and the degree of this union is a reliable criterion of age. In the case of Tutankhamen, the kneecap could be easily lifted to examine the lower end of the femur, the longest bone in the leg. The epiphysis was separate from the shaft and movable. Tutankhamen was indeed a boy-king. Derry wrote:

> This part unites with the shaft about the age of twenty. At the upper end of the thigh bone that prominence known as the great trochanter was almost entirely soldered to the main bone, but on its inner side a definite gap showing the smooth cartilaginous surface where union was still incomplete, could be well seen. This epiphysis joins about the eighteenth year. The head of the femur was fixed to the neck of the bone, but the line of the union was clearly visible all round the articular margin. This epiphysis also unites about the eighteenth or nineteenth year. The upper end of the tibia was also united, but the lower end appeared to be quite fused. As this latter portion of the

tibia is generally found to fuse with the shaft at about age eighteen, Tut-Ankh-Amen, from the evidence of his lower limbs, would appear to have been over eighteen but below twenty years at the age of his death."[27]

Derry's estimate was accurate. Tutankhamen was about eighteen years old when he died, a handsome young man of slight build, about 5 feet 6 inches tall. Given Derry's techniques, there was little hope that he would determine the cause of death. That would have to await future generations and future technologies.

Because Tutankhamen was the only pharaoh ever found undisturbed in his tomb, the Antiquities Service decided that, rather than removing him to the Egyptian Museum in Cairo, this king should remain where he was found. The reassembled body of Tutankhamen was placed on a wooden litter filled with sand and put inside the largest outer coffin, then lowered into the sarcophagus where it remains today (fig. 23). Tourists peering into the open sarcophagus see the outer coffin, but few realize that the mummy still lies inside.

Once the burial chamber was emptied, Carter began to clear the small side room he called the "Treasury," the entrance of which had been boarded up so none of the objects would be damaged while work progressed in the burial chamber. The delicate condition of many of those objects and the precarious way they had been piled on top of each other made clearing the room extremely difficult, so it was not until 1927 that the task was completed. The Treasury was heaped with Tutankhamen's finely carved model boats with elaborate riggings, wooden statues of Anubis, the god of embalming, and a beautiful alabaster shrine holding the four miniature canopic coffins that contained Tutankhamen's internal organs.

Another simple wooden box held two miniature coffins. Inside rested the neatly wrapped mummies of Ankhesenamen's two miscarriages. One was slightly more than a foot long, the other approximately ten inches long with a tiny cartonnage (papier mâché) mask over the face. Carter removed the wrappings from the smaller of the two, revealing the five-month-old female fetus (figs. 14a and 14b). This was the first time the excavators knew of the tragedy. If either of these little girls had lived to maturity, the royal line would have continued, and Egyptian history would have been quite different.

The larger of the two fetuses was still wrapped when Dr. Derry received it for examination in 1932 at the Department of Anatomy at Kasr el Einy Hospital in Cairo (figs. 13a, 13b, and 13c). He unwrapped it, revealing the second female fetus, which he estimated to be seven months old. Four inches longer than her sister, who showed no signs of mummification, this child was developed enough to have been embalmed. Across the left side of the abdomen ran an embalmer's incision less than an inch long. The abdominal cavity was stuffed with linen, but Derry does not mention the internal organs, which are probably still inside—had they been removed, canopic jars would likely have been provided. Derry could see that despite the fetus's small size, the embalmers had removed the brain and forced linen into the cranium. Never one to worry about preserving a mummy, Derry broke through the cranium to remove the linen and there found the wire used to force the fabric into the skull. This is the only embalmer's tool ever to be found inside a mummy. Derry threw it away.

It is undeniable that Derry's handling of the three mummies in Tutankhamen's tomb was irresponsible, caused irreversible damage, and that a great deal of valuable information was irretrievably lost. But Derry was working in an era when the field of mummy studies was in its infancy and he shared the attitude of most of his predecessors who believed that mummies in themselves were of little value.[28] In the wake of Derry's destruction, could anything be learned today that would tell us how Tutankhamen died?

8

Dead Men Tell Tales:
Tutankhamen's Mummy

There is no man who does not die.

—Sayings of Ankhsheshonq
circa 300 B.C.

Today, non-destructive techniques are available for studying mummies. If Tutankhamen had just been discovered, his mummy could be examined using several high-tech processes, such as CAT scans, without the need to unwrap it. Derry focused his entire autopsy on the bones he had violently examined. He paid little attention, if any, to the body's soft tissues because no one then, least of all Derry, realized how much information is retained in the muscles and internal organs. There was no knowledge of DNA; electron microscopes and advanced chemical analysis did not exist. It was just becoming possible in Derry's day to examine tissue from mummies under a microscope, and this didn't seem to interest Derry.

Medical experts in our era employ several processes to look at both soft tissue and bone to determine the circumstances of a death. First, they autopsy the body to learn whether unusual substances were retained in organs and tissues, and what the subject had eaten and how recently. Second, they use X rays, or more advanced equivalents such as CAT scans, to view the bones. Bones can reveal not only the age of the deceased and what diseases he suffered, but also whether a trauma, such as a blow by some object, was the likely cause of death. Each of these processes contributes valuable information that the other does not.

However, ancient tissues provide a special problem for modern tests. They are so brittle that they crumble if sliced thinly enough to be put under a microscope. In a note in the *British Medical Journal* for 1909, Marc Armand Ruffer, a French physician working at the Cairo Medical School, discussed the difficulties he experienced in his first attempts to section tissue fragments of mummies.[1] Ruffer persevered and developed a technique to soften tissues by soaking them in a solution of alcohol and 5 percent carbonate of soda, a process that permitted sectioning and microscopic examination. Ruffer was a pathologist, trained to study diseases and causes of death, while Derry was an anatomist, unfamiliar with microscopes and chemical analysis. Had they joined forces, a great deal more would have been learned about Tutankhamen and the fetuses. Were the little girls healthy when aborted? Was Ankhesenamen suffering from a disease when she miscarried? Most important, was there any evidence of disease in Tutankhamen's body at the time of his death?

Anyone interested in answering these questions would have to reexamine all the evidence, but surprisingly some of it had disappeared. In 1971 F. Filce Leek, an English dentist, was given permission by the Egyptian Department of Antiquities to examine and X-ray Tutankhamen's fetuses, but when he opened their coffins in the Egyptian Museum, the mummies were not there.[2]

This, too, was Derry's fault. Throughout his long career, he had been given numerous mummies and fragments of mummies to take away for examination but he rarely returned them. They simply accumulated in a storage room at Kasr El Einy Hospital where he worked. After his death the mummies remained in storage, forgotten. Then, in

June 1992, newspapers reported the discovery of 528 mummies and parts of mummies in the hospital storeroom—Derry's cache had been found. There, along with King Zoser's foot, were the two fetuses. Prior to this announcement only a few people had known about the hoard, one of whom was R. G. Harrison who had X-rayed Tutankhamen in 1978.[3] He went to the storeroom and found and X-rayed the larger of the two fetuses, finding that there was an abnormally high right clavicle, and other indications of scoliosis and spina bifida.

Derry had said of the smaller fetus, "There is no abdominal incision and no indication as to how the body was preserved." I wondered about this. Why would one fetus be mummified but not the other? Both had similar wrappings, both were placed in coffins. Perhaps the smaller fetus was too tiny for the royal embalmers to work with. In the hope of examining the smaller fetus to settle this question, I contacted Dr. Fawzi Gabella, Head of the Anatomy Department of Kasr El Einy Hospital to see if he could locate the mummy. The hospital had recently received a grant from an American anthropologist to catalogue and properly store the mummies in their collection, so everything had been recently inventoried, boxed and labeled. Without hesitation, Dr. Gabella told me he had the mummy. I was invited to come to the hospital to examine it.

When I arrived at Kasr El Einy Hospital I found two Dr. Gabellas. His wife, also an anatomist teaching at the hospital, greeted me. Both she and her husband were eager to see what we could learn about the fetuses. They ushered me into a storage room piled high with small wooden boxes with intriguing labels—"Middle Kingdom princess?" "Old Kingdom, head only." I have worked with mummies for years, but had never seen anything like this. My fantasy was to be locked in that storage room for a few years so I could examine each box carefully, but I would be allowed to order in meals from the great chicken restaurant down the street.

Dr. Fawzi Gabella located two small wood boxes slightly larger than shoe boxes. When the lids were removed, I was face to face with Tutankhamen and Ankhesenamen's children. For more than a year, I had been trying to piece together Tutankhamen's fragmented life. To me, these fetuses were more than examples of mummification; they reflected a family's tragedy. Since Tutankhamen probably will remain sealed in his sarcophagus for quite some time, this was probably as close as I would ever get to him.

I had brought Harry Burton's photographs of the fetuses, taken when they were first discovered. In the seventy years since the photographs, the fetuses had deteriorated somewhat, but because of this deterioration I was able to answer my question. The cranial bones of the smaller fetus had disarticulated, allowing us to see that, just as with the larger fetus, linen had been packed in the skull, and the skin on the abdomen was cracked, revealing a bit of linen protruding from the abdominal cavity. The smaller fetus had, indeed, been embalmed. Remembering how much Derry had damaged the mummy of Tutankhamen, I didn't even want to touch the fetuses; I just looked (fig. 15).

Now, it was time for me to reexamine Derry's work with Tutankhamen. When he performed the autopsy on Tutankhamen's mummy in 1925, little except the boy-king's age at the time of death was determined. This opened the door to all kinds of speculation about the cause of his death. Because of his slender build, and because he died young, tuberculosis was suggested, but there was no way at the time to test for this. Additional direct investigation of the mummy had been prevented by the Antiquities Services' decision to leave Tutankhamen in his tomb. Had the body been moved to Cairo, it could have been X-rayed.[4]

To Derry it might have seemed pointless to X-ray the already-exposed bones of Tutankhamen, but X-rays reveal bone density that tells us a great deal about diet and illnesses during a person's life. For example, if there is a serious illness prior to maturity, the long bones stop growing, which shows on an X-ray as a white line across the bone. An X ray of Tutankhamen's mummy could have told him a great deal, but in 1925 there were no portable X-ray machines in Egypt that could have been brought into the Valley of the Kings. The most famous king in history had to wait forty years for his X rays.

It wasn't until the 1960s that science really woke up to the value of mummies. With new techniques for analyzing tissue samples, physicians and health scientists realized that mummies often held just the information they needed to understand modern diseases. The field of paleopathology was born. The term was first coined in 1892 by R.W. Schufeldt, a German physician, from two Greek roots (παλιος, "ancient," and παθος, "suffering"). It means the study of diseases, or pathological conditions, in ancient people.

To understand a modern infectious disease and predict its course, it is necessary to study its development through history. By analyzing Egyptian mummies and comparing the frequency of their pathological conditions with those of modern man, we glean insights into whether modern modes of living are the cause of specific diseases, or if the diseases have been around for centuries. For example, arterial disease is frequently attributed, along with our high-fat diets, to the stresses and strains of contemporary life. If ancient Egyptians also suffered from arterial disease, such theories would be placed in doubt.

By the 1960s, with scientific knowledge increasing at a fantastic rate, specialization had become essential. No one physician could read the literature in every field; the general practitioner became outmoded; teams of specialists became the rule. A similar trend overtook the study of mummies. No single physician commands all the skills required to autopsy a mummy and analyze the various tissue samples, or possesses the expert knowledge of botany, chemistry, and biology necessary to extract all the information the body offers. Paleopathologists now treat mummies like patients, doing as little harm as possible and bringing in specialists as needed to study specific problems—hematologists for blood, dentists for teeth, etc. Working virtually alone, Derry didn't have a chance to collect all the information that Tutankhamen's mummy offered.

The field of paleopathology had blossomed by the 1960s, leading R. G. Harrison, a University of Liverpool anatomist, to believe that studying the Egyptian royal mummies would shed new light on old questions. His first subject was the mystery mummy from Tomb 55, whom we now know was Smenkare, Tutankhamen's brother. Harrison examined, measured, and X-rayed the bones to determine its age at the time of death. The sternum or breastbone is a good indicator. As we grow older the costal notches, where the ribs attach, ossify, causing us to become less flexible. X rays showed that the fourth and fifth ribs of the Tomb 55 mummy had recently joined, although the facets of the fourth still showed a cleft. This indicated death at an age of nineteen or twenty, just like Tutankhamen's. A similar process of ossification occurs in the vertebrae, but is completed at about twenty-four years of age. The thorax and vertebrae were not completely ossified in the Tomb 55 mummy, indicating that Smenkare was certainly less than twenty-four years old when he died.

R.G. Harrison's X rays and measurements of the mummy revealed important information. He ended his report with the plea that "a reappraisal of the anatomical and radiological features of Tutankhamun is urgently necessary, and it is to be hoped that such an investigation may be made possible in the not-too-distant future."[5] In 1969 Harrison got his chance.

He was given permission by the Egyptian Antiquities Organization to bring a portable X-ray machine into the tomb of Tutankhamen. This would be the first time since Carter and Derry had replaced Tutankhamen in his coffin that anyone had seen the young king. Aware that a team approach was necessary, Harrison, the anatomist, brought radiologists, dentists, physicians, and Egyptologists. They were only permitted to work during daylight hours, and the tomb had not been closed to tourists, so surprised visitors looked on as they worked. There would be several surprises for Harrison as well.

For one thing, the mummy was in far worse condition than anyone had expected. Neither Carter nor Derry had published the fact that they had sawed Tutankhamen in half to free him from the inner coffin, so X-raying Tutankhamen was a piecemeal process. The head was carried to the machine and X-rayed, then the limbs, and so on, until a complete set of films was produced. The team had permission to work for only two days. On the first day they made a set of test exposures, which they developed that same evening in the bathroom of their hotel. Fortunately, they stayed at the Winter Palace, a grand old hotel in Luxor, with commodious bathrooms. They developed their X rays in one sink, fixed them in another, then washed them in the bathtub.[6] They came out fine.

The X ray of the torso provided the first surprise. Tutankhamen was missing his sternum and part of his ribs! Derry had not noticed this because of the black resin that covered the chest. Perhaps Tutankhamen was handled roughly in the embalmer's workshop and the damage was concealed by a coat of resin. Others suggested that the missing parts were the result of an accident or of intentional violence that caused Tutankhamen's death.[7] Part of Smenkare's sternum was also missing, but I have no explanation for this curious similarity other than perhaps embalmers used some special technique on both of these mummies. An argument against my view is that Smenkare died at Amarna and probably would have been embalmed there. Tutankhamen almost certainly was embalmed at a different embalmer's shop located in Thebes or Memphis. Harrison offered no hypothesis on the question. He moved on to other matters, such as determining Tutankhamen's age.

Using the same criteria he had applied to Smenkare's mummy, Harrison determined that Tutankhamen was about nineteen years old at the time of death, just as Derry had suggested almost half a century earlier. X rays of the spine dispelled any notion that Tutankhamen died of tuberculosis. Tuberculosis generally damages the epiphysial plates between the vertebrae; Tutankhamen's were perfect.

Then came the X ray of the skull, the X ray that first led me to suspect that Tutankhamen might have been murdered. On the later BBC documentary about his findings, Harrison simply pointed to a density on the X ray at the base of the skull and said,

> This is within the normal limits, but in fact, it could have been caused by a hemorrhage under the membranes overlaying the brain in this region. And this could have been caused by a blow to the back of the head and this in turn could have been responsible for death.

Harrison was cautious, never mentioning murder, merely a possible blow to the back of the head.

One reason the possibility of the murder of Tutankhamen has not received detailed attention is that Harrison never published a full scientific report of his X-raying of Tutankhamen, merely popular accounts.[8] His ominous words presented in the television documentary were never clarified by a complete written report and consequently the X ray was misunderstood by the experts.

We must remember we are not dealing with a normal X ray, but one of a mummified skull. Careful reading of the film is necessary, along with knowledge of the embalming process. The X ray clearly shows what appears to be an abnormal thickening of the interior of the skull in two places—at the top and at the back of the head (fig. 25). But what we are seeing is not bone, but resin introduced into the cranium during Tutankhamen's mummification. After Tutankhamen's brain was removed through the nasal passages, hot resin was poured into the skull to cauterize the interior, in case any of the brain remained. Once the resin was inside the skull, it hardened to become radiopaque, like bone. What Tutankhamen's skull shows is two fluid levels of the resin as it was poured in and then hardened. This means that resin must have been poured into the skull at two different times, with the mummy in a different position each time. Let's reconstruct what happened 3,300 years ago in the embalmer's shop.

Imagine the body of Tutankhamen flat on its back lying on the embalmer's table. A hook is inserted in his nose, breaking the ethmoid bone behind the nasal passages. The hook enters the cranium and is rotated to break down the brain so it becomes semi-liquid. Then Tutankhamen is turned on his stomach, with his head hanging over the table, so his brain, pulled by gravity, runs out the nose. The cranium is now ready for resin. Once again the body is placed on its back and a ceramic bowl with two small tubular spouts is filled with hot resin. The pipettes are placed in the nostrils and the bowl tilted so the resin runs through the nose and into the cranium. Gravity controls where it goes. Since Tutankhamen is lying on his back, the resin forms a pool at the back of the skull. When it cools it creates the first of two fluid levels. This resin burned out any bits of brain tissue that may have remained at the back of the skull. Next, the body of Tutankhamen is positioned on the table so the head hangs over the end, with his chin pointing to the sky. Once again resin is poured in to form a pool at the lowest point, this time the top of the head. This burns out bits of brain from the front of his skull and creates the second fluid level on the X ray. The X ray lets us understand a specific event that took place thirty-three centuries ago.

But the skull X ray shows something that seems far more relevant to the question of the cause of death. A bone fragment is clearly visible inside Tutankhamen's skull. Could this fragment have been the effect of a violent blow struck at the pharaoh's head with evil intent, a blow that killed Tutankhamen?

Actually, this little piece of bone is the red herring in the case. It has caused nothing but confusion and led researchers away from the trail of murder. Because Harrison never published his theory in a scientific journal, and most researchers had only heard that he mentioned a blow to the head, they assumed Harrison was talking about this fragment as having been violently dislodged by a blow. Harrison never said anything of the kind. As a matter of fact, he suggested that the fragment was a piece of the ethmoid bone broken off when the embalmers forced the hooked instrument into the cranium to remove the brain. But this explanation can't be right. Ethmoid means "sieve" in Greek. Because that bone is porous, it splinters when broken, and the bone fragment in the skull is substantial, not a splinter, so the fragment inside the skull cannot be a piece of the ethmoid. It must be a piece of another bone.

Which other bone almost doesn't matter. Harrison was still correct in his view that the bone was broken off *after* death. It could not have *caused* the death. For the sake of argument, let us assume that the fragment was dislodged by a blow to the head while Tutankhamen was alive, and he subsequently died. Now imagine the embalming process once again. The brain is removed but the fragment remains loose in the skull. Now comes the time to pour resin into the skull while Tutankhamen's body is lying on its back on the table. The bone fragment would now have fallen to the lowest point inside the skull—the back of the head. When the resin cools, the fragment would be embedded in the resin. If by some chance, the bone was adhering to another part of the skull, and the resin missed it, then the second application of resin to the top of the skull—when Tutankhamen's head hung over the embalmer's table—would almost certainly have enveloped the bone fragment within the resin. So, if the bone fragment had been dislodged when Tutankhamen was killed, it would have been embedded in radiopaque resin during the embalming process and would never appear on the X ray. This, of course, is not the case. The bone fragment is clearly visible on top of the resin. The only possible conclusion is that the bone was dislodged after death. In fact, the bone must have been loosened, not only after death, but after the introduction of the resin into the skull.

There were plenty of opportunities for the fragment to have been broken off after the resin was poured into the skull. The body remained in the embalmer's shop for more than a month while dehydrating in natron, plenty of time for damage to occur. Mummies were frequently damaged while they were in the embalmer's shops. Roy Moodie's pioneering X-ray studies in 1926 at Chicago's Field Museum of Natural History was one of the first to reveal such careless work. One X ray showed that in order to fit the mummy of a seven-year-old boy into a coffin that was much too small, the embalmer had removed the boy's arms, broken the legs at mid-thigh, and thrown away the lower halves of his legs.[9] My favorite example of embalmer skullduggery is that of the Lady Teshat in the Minneapolis Institute of Arts. Although the title "Lady" suggests that she was an adult, Teshat died as a teenager. A CAT scan of her mummy showed that her cadaver was roughly handled, resulting in several broken bones. It also revealed that between her legs lay a second adult skull! No one is sure why it is there, but it is quite possible that the head of another mummy became detached in the embalming house and was temporarily misplaced. Then, after that mummy was bandaged without its head and returned to its unknowing relatives, the head turned up. Not knowing what to do with an excess head, the embalmers bound it up with Lady Teshat.

While a mummy with two heads is unusual, mummies missing body parts are common. Sir Marc Armand Ruffer, the former president of the Sanitary Council of Egypt, unwrapped two mummies dating from the Persian period. After describing the wrappings (one bandage was more than eighteen feet long), he discusses the sorry state of the mummies.[10] When a body is mummified, it becomes so brittle that, with rough handing, it can break. In the case of one of Ruffer's mummies, the embalmers had broken her back and run a stick through the body to restore its rigidity. When this was insufficient, heated resin was poured inside and outside the mummy to obscure the defect. (This technique for hiding their mistakes under a coating of resin may be exactly what Tutankhamen's embalmers did to hide the damage to his rib cage.) The second mummy Ruffer examined showed just how bad embalmers could be. It looked like the first mummy, but the foot bones were found in the abdominal region and the arm bones were where the thighs should have been. The atlas vertebra (so named because it is on top of the spinal column supporting the head) had been pierced by a stick that went through the foramen magnum and into the skull. So while the wrappings indicated a whole body, inside lay a disarticulated pile of bones. With mummies receiving this kind of treatment from embalmers, it is not difficult to imagine a fragment of Tutankhamen's skull being dislodged in the embalmer's workshop. And we know this wasn't the only rough handling Tutankhamen's mummy received.

The violence done to the body by Derry and Carter in their attempt to free Tutankhamen from his coffin is documented. Although neither Carter nor Derry published details of what they did to Tutankhamen's mummy, their manuscript notes are revealing. Carter's diary for November 16, 1925, states:

> The whole of today's work was concentrated upon the head of the mummy. It was found like the body of the King. The back of the head was stuck (in the case) to the mask—so firmly that it would require a hammer and chisel to free it. Eventually we used hot knives for the purpose with success.[11]

Hammering and chiseling certainly could loosen a bone fragment. Thus it seems extremely likely that, one way or another, the piece of bone is post mortem, having nothing to do with Tutankhamen's death. This, I believe, is further confirmed by a second X ray taken ten years after Harrison's X ray of Tutankhamen's skull. Dr. James Harris, a professor of orthodontics at the University of Michigan, was given permission to X-ray the skull of Tutankhamen. Harris already had carried out pioneering work on X-raying the royal mummies in the Egyptian Museum in Cairo.[12]

He was using X rays to determine relationships between the mummies by noting similarities in facial features—family traits. Because he was a dentist, Harris was especially interested in dentition. When he saw Harrison's X ray of Tutankhamen's skull he was disappointed because the teeth were not as clear as he would have liked. After his work on the Egyptian Museum mummies, he was granted permission to open Tutankhamen's coffin and X-ray the skull. His X ray seems to confirm that the now famous bone is indeed loose and not embedded in the resin, because the bone appears in a different place on his X ray than on Harrison's. At least I think it does. Harris never published the details of how he took the X ray, nor does he even state *that* he took the X ray. In the index to his book *An X-Ray Atlas of the Royal Mummies,*[13] Harris refers to the X rays of Tutankhamen, but they are not on page 378 as stated. The only place the X ray appears is on a microfiche card in the back pocket of the book (second card, row A, Number 2). The card is difficult to read, and when I asked Dr. Harris for a copy of the X ray, he was unable to supply it, so my reading of the microfiche must remain tentative.

The reason experts have overlooked the possibility that Tutankhamen was murdered is that when Egyptologists and paleopathologists looked at the Tutankhamen X ray they saw the bone fragment in the skull and mistakenly thought that this was the supposed evidence for a blow to the back of the head. They correctly deduced that it had been dislodged postmortem. Then, they concluded the fragment provided no evidence for a blow to the back of the head. In all the excitement about the bone fragment, they neglected to look further for what Harrison had seen, the dark spot on the X ray at the base of the skull.

When I hosted a television documentary on the murder theory, I never mentioned the bone fragment, because it was not relevant to the real evidence for a blow to the back of the head. The *Los Angeles Times* wrote an article on the documentary and asked Dr. James Harris for his opinion. Here again, the bone fragment was confused with the evidence for a blow to the back of the head. The article states: "He [Harris] confirms that there is a bone sliver but notes that it could have been produced during mummification. . . ."[14] Again referring to the bone fragment, Dr. Nicholas Reeves, a leading Tutankhamen scholar commented, "Sadly Harrison (the anatomist) did not live to publish his thoughts on this feature, and it is not clear whether he believed the damage to have been sustained before death, accidentally, or intentionally."[15]

In addition to Harrison and Harris there was a third person who could have addressed the issue of the blow to the back of the head, but he too made a curious omission. F. Filce Leek, the dentist on Harrison's X-ray team, wrote an entire book titled *The Human Remains from the Tomb of Tutankhamen*, yet he only briefly mentions that he was a member of the team.[16] Incredibly, he never discusses the results of the X rays. For his analysis of the mummy of Tutankhamen, he relies almost entirely on Derry's autopsy from half a century before!

Because there has been no scientific publication of the two sets of X rays of Tutankhamen, there has been considerable misunderstanding about the evidence for a blow to the back of the head, especially among researchers outside the medical field who have no experience reading X rays. One surprising example comes from a leading British scholar of the Amarna period, Cyril Aldred. Aldred says, "the recent reexamination of (Tutankhamen's) mummy has shown that he sustained a wound. Probably by an arrow, which penetrated his skull in the region of the left ear."[17] It is not clear what Aldred's evidence for the arrow is, for this is one of the rare times he does not give his source.

Given the omissions and confusions surrounding Tutankhamen's X rays, it was clear that a careful reexamination of the material relating to Tutankhamen's death was necessary. My first step was to get a copy of Harrison's X ray, but he had died in 1979. His colleague R.C. Connolly was still at the University of Liverpool and he kindly sent me prints of the X ray along with a friendly note that was far from encouraging.

> I am afraid there is really nothing beyond our original publications on the subject which I can add about these radiographs ... Apart from the obvious features referred to in previous publications they really do not contribute anything particularly significant either to the procedures for mummification in the Eighteenth Dynasty or more important, to the cause of death.[18]

Connolly is a senior lecturer in physical anthropology who knew anatomy far better than I, but I had to see it for myself. When the X ray arrived, I took it to my university's Radiological Technology Department to see what they would say. They were fascinated by the X ray but suggested that my only hope of getting any new information was to show the X ray to our medical advisor, Dr. Gerald Irwin, head of radiology at Winthrop University Hospital. Dr. Irwin has considerable experience in reading the X rays of head trauma patients. My hope was that his combined radiology and trauma expertise might allow him to see something new.

First, I showed him the BBC video of Harrison's explanation of the X ray. Then he studied the X-ray print of Tutankhamen's skull. He agreed with Harrison. There could indeed have been a blow to the back of the head; the X ray was evidence for a hematoma, an accumulation of blood beneath the skin. But then Dr. Irwin noticed something else. Inside the skull, near the location of the possible blood clot, an area of increased density showed. This is what would be expected from a calcified membrane formed over a blood clot. Physicians call it a chronic subdural hematoma—a phenomenon that takes considerable time to develop.

Dr. Irwin also observed that the area of the skull where the alleged blow occurred is unusual for trauma—at the back of the head, right at the point where the neck joins the skull. This is a well-protected spot. Tutankhamen would have had to have been struck from behind, perhaps while he was sleeping on his side or back, to cause a trauma there (fig. 26).

What does this all mean? First of all, let me make clear that Tutankhamen's X ray does not prove he was murdered. No X ray by itself can ever do so. An X ray can show that a patient received a blow to the head, even that the blow probably killed him, but not that the blow was stuck by someone with evil intent. There will always be other possibilities that the X ray by itself will not eliminate. Further, interpreting X rays is an art, which is why some are experts in reading these films and others are not. X rays show some clear white areas—bone—and other cloudy areas whose interpretation calls for special skill. Even among experts, some will see a cloudy area as a growth of a certain sort, others will see a mere blur in the film.

In Tutankhamen's case, two renowned experts saw evidence of a hematoma in his skull. Did Tutankhamen trip and hit his head? Given the location of this hematoma, that is unlikely. By itself, evidence of a fatal blow to the back of the skull in a place where an accident is unlikely would never convince a jury to convict. But it would certainly be enough to cause a thorough investigation by the police to see if they could turn up additional evidence. They would label the X ray "indication of suspicious circumstances."

That much is clear. What is less certain is whether calcification formed over the hematoma. Dr. Irwin was quick to point out that the X ray does not unambiguously establish that, because the cloudy area is simply too faint to know for sure. It raises the possibility, however, that Tutankhamen did not die suddenly which, in turn, raises some difficult questions. If Tutankhamen lingered for the minimum two months required for calcium formation, what was his state of consciousness? Remember, this is before IV feeding and there is no evidence the Egyptians used feeding tubes. An unconscious Tutankhamen could not have been kept alive for two months. If there was a thickening, then Tutankhamen must have remained conscious at least long enough to be fed, perhaps drifting in and out of consciousness. He would have lingered until the pressure on the brain built up by the hematoma became too great, and then lapsed into a coma and died from dehydration or pneumonia.[19]

The suggestion that Tutankhamen may have lingered is very tentative, but it in no way affects the murder thesis. I mention it merely because it is part of the puzzle that may become important at some later time. In fact, physical evidence by itself never proves murder. A bullet in the brain does not show intent to kill, motive, means, etc. The X ray of Tutankhamen's skull suggests a blow to the back of the head. That is all it can do. To support a case for murder an investigation of the circumstantial evidence is crucial. Can we show that someone had the opportunity and the motive? It is here that the case will be made or not.

9

A Widow's Plea

Do not concern yourself with him,
The Asiatic is a crocodile on its shore.
He snatches from a lonely road,
He cannot seize from a populous town.

—*King Khety Nebkaure*
circa 2150 B.C.

In most murders, events surrounding the death raise the first suspicion of a crime. The sinister events that followed Tutankhamen's death would prompt any modern detective to think of foul play. They begin with a letter Tutankhamen's widow addressed to the king of the Hittites, the ancient Hatti—a traditional enemy of Egypt who pressed hard against Egypt for possession of her territories.

We learn about this letter because the Hittites were great record keepers. Excavations in Turkey have yielded thousands of clay tablets from their archives, recording everything from land deeds to military exploits. At the beginning of this century a dig at the ancient capital of Bogazköy found archives dealing with a variety of matters. One group of these tablets chronicled the reign of King Suppiluliuma, written by the king's son, Mursilis II. The composition is known today by the uncatchy title "The Deeds of Suppiluliuma as told by his son Mursilis II." Of the dozens of fragments that constitute the texts, the one that recounts Ankhesenamen's frantic letter is the "Seventh Tablet."[1]

The letter is extraordinary. The queen of Egypt writes to Egypt's traditional enemy, the Hittites, and says that she is afraid and wants to marry a Hittite prince and make him king of Egypt. Nothing like this had ever happened in Egypt. We must examine this letter very carefully.

While my father was down in the country of Carchemish, he sent Lupakki and Tarhunta [?]—zalma forth into the country of Amka. So they went to attack Amka and brought deportees, cattle and sheep back before my father. But when the people of Egypt heard of the attack on Amka, they were afraid and since, in addition, their lord Nibhuruiya had died, therefore the queen of Egypt, who was Dahamunzu [?] sent a messenger to my father and wrote to him thus: "my husband died. A son I have not. But to thee, they say, the sons are many. If thou wouldst give me one son of thine, he would become my husband. Never shall I pick out a servant of mine and make him my husband! . . . I am afraid!"[2]

The queen of Egypt who wrote the letter is called Dahamunzu, and her husband ("their lord") is called Nibhuruiya. Who were these royals? Their names are transliterations of Egyptian names into the Hittite language; an attempt not to translate, but merely to convey the phonetic sounds. There can be little doubt that the king was Tutankhamen, whose prenomen (one of his two given names inscribed in a cartouche) is Neb-kheperu-re.[3] The Hittites transliterated these sounds into "Nibhuruiya." If the king is Tutankhamen, then the widowed queen must be Ankhesenamen, his only wife. Yet, the name Dahamunzu does not look or sound anything like Ankhesenamen. What was probably transliterated was the Egyptian phrase *Ta Hemet Nesewt*— "The King's Wife"— the way she signed her letter.[4]

Ominously, Ankhesenamen says she is afraid. What frightened the queen of Egypt? Her country was safe and stable at the time, thanks to Horemheb's strong army. The administrators Aye and Maya had returned Egypt to prosperity. After the death of her husband, Ankhesenamen's position should have been that of the most royal, most powerful person in the land. But was it? The Hittites imply that they caused her fright by attacking neighboring Amka, which, although far from Egypt's borders, made the queen fear for her safety. This explanation seems improbable given Egypt's strength. Rather than pointing to a real concern that would agitate Ankhesenamen, their explanation seems a conceit, a boast Hittites would like to believe.

The truth is that the death of Tutankhamen left Ankhesenamen alone. Her life before had been full of change and turmoil, but at least her husband had been there to share the burdens and decisions. Without him beside her, there was a more sinister reason for Ankhesenamen's fear. The sequence of facts that leads up to her expression of fear culminates in a most unusual statement: "Never shall I pick out a servant of mine and make him my husband!" Of course, it was inconceivable for an Egyptian queen to marry a servant. What could have pressured Ankhesenamen into marrying the wrong man, a force so strong that it frightened her?

Ankhesenamen must have written the letter soon after Tutankhamen's death, for Egypt could not remain without a king for long. But the line of succession was not clear: she and Tutankhamen had no children and Ankhesenamen was the last member of the royal family. In such circumstances, whoever married her would become Egypt's king. Ankhesenamen's letter indicates that she was being forced to marry someone, a commoner—"servant." What an extraordinary act of desperation to write to an enemy requesting marriage to one of its princes, yet it must have seemed the lesser of two great evils. Never in the history of Egypt had a queen requested marriage to a foreigner to make him king of Egypt.

The walls of the tomb of Horemheb, Tutankhamen's general of the army, show just how remarkable Ankhesenamen's plea was. Horemheb delighted in covering his tomb with scenes of the Hittite captives he had vanquished. Egypt's generals fought and herded manacled Hittite prisoners before Tutankhamen.[5] What circumstances could have caused Ankhesenamen to beg a husband from these people?

Imagine her anxiety as she composed her letter to the Hittite king. Scribes in the Egyptian court could write in Akkadian, the international language of the day, but a letter written by a court scribe would be placed in official archives and become general information in the palace. Ankhesenamen would not have wanted that. Surely Aye, who was Tutankhamen's counselor, would never condone a foreigner's rule over Egypt. If nothing else it would jeopardize his position in the court, for a Hittite king would appoint his own officials. General Horemheb, who had risked his life battling the Hitittes, certainly would not approve of such a letter—he would never serve under a mortal enemy. So Ankhesenamen's letter could not be an official communication between two powerful nations. It was a personal plea written to the only person, in her mind, powerful enough to help her—the Hittite king. Ankhesenamen probably wrote the letter herself in hieroglyphs on a papyrus scroll—it could be translated later by scribes in the Hititte palace—all she required was one person she could trust who could deliver her plea.

Her decision lends insight into Ankhesenamen's character—she was frightened and naive. Growing up in peaceful Amarna, she had never heard the horrors of battles with the Hittites nor listened to stories of their atrocities. She must have believed an army was the only force powerful enough to save her. She must have convinced herself that if she made their prince the King of Egypt, a Hititte force would ride to her rescue. Who in Egypt was so powerful that she believed only a mighty army could sway him from his course?

So incredible was Ankhesenamen's request that even the Hittite king didn't believe it.

When my father heard this, he called forth the Great Ones for council [saying]: "Such a thing has never happened to me in my whole life!" So it happened that my father sent forth to Egypt Hattusa-ziti, the chamberlain, [with this order]: "Go and bring thou the true word back to me! Maybe they deceive me! Maybe [in fact] they do have a son of their lord! Bring thou the true word back to me!"[6]

The chamberlain's journey was a lengthy one—through the Taurus Mountains, then eastward to the plain of Aleppo in Syria where he crossed the Orontes River near Kadesh, and continued south to the Egyptian border. He was undoubtedly met at the border, but by whom? There were obviously at least two opposing factions in the Egyptian court—Ankhesenamen who wanted to marry the prince, and those forcing her to marry the unnamed "servant." Unfortunately, the Hittites do not tell us what Hattusaziti, their chamberlain, learned in Egypt. We do know, however, that when he returned to his country, he was not alone.

> But when it became spring, Hattusaziti [came back] from Egypt, and the messenger of Egypt, Lord Hani, came with him.[7]

The Hittites mention that it was spring when their ambassador returned from Egypt. Does this match what we know about Tutankhamen's death? Blossoms on his funerary wreaths tell us in which season Tutankhamen died. One wreath was woven from cornflowers that bloom in Egypt from mid-March to the end of April. One of Tutankhamen's floral pectorals included mandrake and woody nightshade, both of which ripen and bloom in March and April.[8] Thus, Tutankhamen was buried between the middle of March and the end of April, which, given seventy days for proper mummification before his burial, places his time of death in the preceding December or January.[9] If Ankhesenamen wrote her letter in January, it would have reached the Hittite capital in February. The chamberlain's (Hattusaziti) round trip would have taken a little under two months. Traveling quickly, for there must have been a sense of urgency, Hattusaziti would have returned by April, the spring, as the archive indicates. All the evidence is consistent, so this indeed is an ancient record of actual events.

While negotiations with the Hittites were proceeding, Tutankh-amen's body was being mummified, his coffin finished, his tomb furnishings prepared for the day of the burial, which drew nearer and nearer. How long could Egypt go without a king? How long could Ankhesenamen hold out?

When word reached her that a Hittite had arrived in response to her letter, she must have believed he was the prince she had sought. How disappointing to discover it was only an aged chamberlain come to verify her strange request. We have no details about Hattusaziti's stay in the Egyptian court, but we can imagine a desperate queen aware that time was running out. Perhaps it was not too late. She sent a second letter.

Why didst thou say "they deceive me," in that way? Had I a son, would I have written about my own and my country's shame to a foreign land? Thou didst not believe me and hast even spoken thus to me! He who was my husband has died. A son I have not! Never shall I take a servant of mine and make him my husband! I have written to no other country, only to thee have I written! They say thy sons are many: so give me one son of thine! To me he will be husband, but in Egypt he will be king." So, since my father was kindhearted, he complied with the word of the woman and concerned himself with the matter of a son.[10]

The Egyptian envoy, Hani, must have confirmed what Ankhesena-men's letters claimed. Suppiluliuma spoke to Hani, expressing his fear that if a prince were sent to Egypt he would be held hostage, rather than anointed king. We can imagine the desperation in Hani's voice as he pleaded with Suppiluliuma that all would be well if he sent a son to Ankhesenamen.

Oh my lord! This [is . . .] our country's shame! If we had [a son of the king] at all, would we have come to a foreign country and kept asking for a lord for ourselves? Nib-hururiya, who was our lord, died; a son he has not. Our lord's wife is solitary. We are seeking a son of our lord for the kingship in Egypt, and for the woman, our lady, we seek him as her husband! Furthermore, we went to no other country, only here did we come! Now, oh our Lord, give us a son of thine![11]

This is the Hittite account of Hani's speech on behalf of his patron. Suppiluliuma asked that an old peace treaty between Egypt and Hatti be brought from the archives and read aloud, then he declared:

Of old, Hattusa and Egypt were friendly with each other, and now this, too, on our behalf, has taken place between t[hem]! Thus Hatti and Egypt will continuously be friendly with each other![12]

Some ninety days after Ankhesenamen's first letter, Suppiluliuma sent a son to Egypt to become Ankhesenamen's husband and king. By now all seventy days of mummification and ritual prior to Tutankhamen's burial had passed and his body had been resting in the tomb with all its treasures for nearly a month. Only then did the Hittite prince begin his journey to Egypt to claim his bride. The archive tablets break off at this point, but the end of the drama is continued in another Hittite text, "The Plague Prayers of Mursilis."

But when my father gave them one of his sons, they killed him as they led him there. My father let his anger run away with him, he went to war against Egypt and attacked Egypt. He smote the foot soldiers and the charioteers of the country of Egypt. But when they brought back to the Hatti land the prisoners which they had taken, a plague broke out among the prisoners and they began to die. When they moved the prisoners to the Hatti land, the prisoners carried the plague into Hatti land. From that day on people have been dying in the Hatti land.[13]

The prince of the Hatti was murdered on the border of Egypt. By whom? Certainly the prince traveled with an entourage of guards, servants, and gifts. In addition, there should have been a delegation of Egyptian officials to greet and then escort the prince to Ankhesenamen. It is unlikely that so many people could have been massacred by a band of outlaws. The Hittites, who were about to forge a tie with Egypt, had nothing to gain by assassinating their own prince. Suspicion points to some Egyptian with the authority to order a troop of cavalry to murder a foreign emissary traveling under a flag of truce. The one who had the most to lose if the prince and Ankhesenamen married, was, of course, "the servant," the one whose chance for Egypt's throne would vanish. To find the murderer of the Hittite prince, and the suspect implicated in Tutankhamen's death, we must uncover who "the servant" was.

The first clue is found on the walls of Tutankhamen's tomb.

THE FIGURE ON THE WALL

As we know, nonroyal Egyptians decorated their tombs with paintings of daily life to show the gods how they wanted to live in the next world. Sometimes even their preparations for burial are shown, with carpenters and craftsmen preparing the coffin and shrine for canopic jars. Once in a while we even see the funeral itself. In the tomb of Ramose, the mayor of Thebes during Tutankhamen's father's time, the entire funerary procession is displayed, complete with all the objects brought to the tomb—Ramose's headrest, sandals, clothes—everything he needed for the next world. Professional mourners, all paid to wail Ramose's mummy into the tomb, cry and throw dirt on their heads. The tombs of royalty were quite different because they were covered with religious texts inscribed on the walls— *The Book of the Dead, The Book of Gates, The Book of What Was in the Next World*—instead of the charming daily life scenes of nobles' tombs. The walls of Tutankhamen's tomb do portray one realistic scene from life—the pharaoh's burial.

In modern times, the interest in Tutankhamen's tomb has focused on the treasures, furniture and the mummy, with the wall paintings receiving relatively little attention. Even now, despite their dissimilarity to all other royal tomb paintings, they have not been completely studied. Royal tombs are large, complex affairs, virtually every wall of which is beautifully decorated with religious scenes and texts intended to ensure the pharaoh's immortality. The same magical principle guides most of the texts—"the word is the deed." If you say it, write it, or depict it, it will happen. Thus, if you say, "The pharaoh is welcomed by the gods," it will happen. If you show the deceased king greeted in the next world by Osiris, the god of the dead, it will happen. Egyptians seem almost insatiable when it comes to magical spells. The more texts and scenes, the better.

This is where Tutankhamen's tomb is unusual. Only one room, the burial chamber, is painted—almost certainly because there was so little time to prepare the tomb after his unexpected death. In that one painted room, twelve baboons—the guardians of the twelve hours of the night—are depicted sitting patiently on one wall, waiting to assist Tutankhamen. They will ensure that Tutankhamen, like the sun, makes the successful journey through the night before rebirth in the next world. The partition wall that closed the burial chamber, after Tutankhamen was placed in his coffins and the shrines assembled around him, also conveys purely religious significance. That wall shows Tutankhamen given life by Hathor, goddess of the West. Behind him stands Anubis, the jackal-headed god of embalming, who has successfully completed his job and holds an ankh, the sign of life, in his hands. These two walls tell us little about Tutankhamen. It is the other two walls that present actual records of what took place and hold the clues to Tutankhamen's murderer.

On the east wall, a funeral procession is shown that brings Tutankhamen's mummy to the tomb. The mummy rests inside a shrine, mounted on a sled. Twelve pallbearers, wearing white linen headbands, pull their king's mummy to the tomb; two of them with shaven heads, wearing the robes of high officials, are Pentu and Usermont, the chief officials of Upper and Lower Egypt.[14]

Not much insight there. The last wall, the north wall, is seen by all tourists who visit Tutankhamen's tomb and has been widely reproduced in books. Little do most people realize that it contains a substantial clue to Tutankhamen's death.

The nobles of Thebes often included the opening-of-the-mouth ceremony on their tomb walls, but, until the discovery of Tutankhamen's tomb, a royal depiction of this ceremony had never been seen. It is strange that the king who returned Egypt to its traditional religion should so breach custom in his own tomb. Whoever was overseeing the decoration of Tutankhamen's tomb was moved by some reason to change the traditional iconography.

The north wall shows Tutankhamen standing upright in the form of the mummified Osiris. Hieroglyphs above his head make it clear that the figure is Tutankhamen, king of Upper and Lower Egypt, not Osiris. He stands in front of a low table on which a ceremonial feather has been placed along with an offering, the leg of a calf. On the other side of the table a man stands, a figure we can identify as the high priest because he wears the leopard skin of that office. The priest raises the opening-of-the-mouth instrument toward Tutankhamen's mouth, an act that will give him breath and life in the next world. If the priest were only wearing the leopard skin, it would look like the traditional ceremony, but one feature makes this scene unique in all the annals of Egyptian history. The high priest wears a pharaoh's crown. Tutankhamen's successor is performing the ritual. The inscription above his head reveals his identity. It is the old vizier, Aye (fig. 17).

If we reconstruct the events immediately following Tutankhamen's death, it seems obvious that Aye was responsible for including a picture of himself on Tutankhamen's tomb wall, and that he was "the servant" Ankhesenamen desperately tried to avoid marrying.

1. As soon as Tutankhamen died, preparations for his burial and the decoration of his tomb began, not before his death. Certainly Aye, the vizier, looked after these details. So Aye himself ordered that he be shown as pharaoh on the wall.

2. As the scene of Aye as pharaoh was being painted, Ankhesena-men was writing to the Hittite King requesting that he send a son to marry so she will not be forced to marry a "servant."

3. The prince, traveling to marry Ankhesenamen, is murdered on the border of Egypt, a deed probably initiated by someone who had much to lose if the prince married Ankhesenamen.

4. Aye becomes king of Egypt.

The tomb painting and chronology of events all point to Aye as a prime suspect in the murder of the Hittite prince, and, I believe, the murder of Tutankhamen as well. Aye controlled the government. Between the time of Tutankhamen's death and the crowning of his successor, Aye, as vizier, was the most powerful man in the country, above even the widow of the recently departed king. With his control of the palace guard, even of the army, he could indeed force Ankhesenamen to marry him. If, as the X rays suggest, foul play may have caused Tutankhamen's death, we have to ask who would gain from killing the king. The answer is clear. The death of Tutankhamen allowed Aye to seize the throne.

The tomb scene of Aye as king leaves two large questions dangling. How did Aye, a commoner, become king of Egypt, and what happened to Ankhesenamen?

THE NEWBERRY RING

The explanation of how Aye became pharaoh was found in a Cairo antiquity shop in the spring of 1931. It was common practice at that time for Egyptologists to visit antiquities dealers to learn what had turned up on the market and to look for interesting inscriptions and scenes of historical importance. Egyptologist Percy Newberry, who had written a catalogue describing the thousands of scarabs in the Egyptian Museum in Cairo early in his career,[15] often visited the dealers looking for new scarabs, the small amulets carved in the shape of a beetle.[16] In the spring of 1931, while examining a box of these amulets at Robert Blanchard's shop, Newberry found a blue faience finger ring among them, consisting of two cartouches—those of Aye and Ankhesenamen. Such a combination of cartouches on the same ring could only mean one thing. Aye had married the widowed Ankhesenamen. They were king and queen.

Newberry immediately wrote to Howard Carter:

> Maison Mitarchi
> Sharia Bayuni
> Zamalek
> Gezira
> Cairo

My Dear Carter,

It will interest you to know that I have just seen a finger-ring at Blanchard's which has on it the cartouche of Ankhesena-men along side the prenomen of King Ay. This can only be interpreted as meaning that King Ay has married Ankhesena-men the widow of Tutankhamen. The ring is of blue glaze and was found somewhere in the Eastern Delta. . . .[17]

Newberry's publication of an article about the ring[18] answered the first question. Aye became pharaoh by marrying Ankhesenamen, but as in any good murder mystery, there was a problem—the ring disappeared. Newberry had seen and copied the ring in Blanchard's shop, but didn't buy it. Later, it probably was sold to a tourist unaware of its historical significance and so it disappeared. As the decades passed, some Egyptologists began to doubt that the "Newberry Ring" truly existed. Fortunately, in the early 1970s a ring almost identical to Newberry's was purchased by the Ägyptisches Museum in Berlin. The ring had never been placed on display so I wanted to confirm its significance with my own eyes. I called the museum and spoke with a curator who told me she had never heard of such a ring! After my initial shock, we both realized what had happened. Berlin's two Egyptian collections—East and

West Berlin—had recently been combined, and curators were not yet completely familiar with each other's collections. The ring was indeed located, and a month later I held the fragile bit of evidence in my hand.[19]

Its hieroglyphs were exactly as Newberry had copied them in 1931, although I don't think this was the ring he had seen. Newberry describes it as consisting of a "blue glaze," while the ring in my hand was white. I could see small traces of an original blue, but most of the color had faded away; it was, after all, commissioned to celebrate a wedding 3,000 years ago. Undoubtedly several copies of the ring were produced at that time, and this was a second one. Without doubt, Aye had married Ankhesenamen.

In the Ägyptisches Museum in Berlin I came face to face with the prime suspect. Staring out at me from a Plexiglas vitrine was a life-sized plaster mask of Aye, prepared as an intermediate step before sculpting some bust in stone. It is the face of a mature man with a strong jaw and muscular neck, identified as Ay because of a resemblance to the portraits in his tomb at Amarna[20] (fig. 10). As I looked at the decidedly sinister face of Aye in the vitrine, I noticed that there was a streak of red paint on his upper lip. I couldn't help but think of blood. Perhaps it was what I knew about him that gave this man such an ominous appearance, but I think the casual passerby would not invite someone who looked like this to dinner. If Ankhesenamen was indeed married to him, what was her fate?

In his letter to Howard Carter (fig. 18), Newberry also wondered about this and suggested a way to trace her:

> Is there any chance of your going out to the Western Valley to see the tomb of Ay? If you do go out there, there is a point that would be extremely interesting to settle. On one of the walls of the sarcophagus chamber there was a figure of King Ay with the Queen Tiy behind him. . . .
>
> Is there any trace at all of a figure behind Queen Tiy? And is the cartouche big enough for the name of Ankhesenamen? My notes on the tomb made some years ago do not help me on

this point and it would be very interesting to settle it. If you have time do go out there: it wouldn't take long to do it. Had I the time to run up to Luxor myself I would do so but I shall not be free till the end of May. When are you coming down to Cairo? With our love to you and all good wishes.

Yours sincerely,
Percy E. Newberry

We don't know if Carter ever went to the Western Valley to look at Aye's tomb as Newberry suggested. Few people do because of its out-of-the-way location. As soon as Aye became pharaoh, he appropriated the remote tomb originally begun by Tutankhamen. Aye was entitled, as pharaoh, to a tomb in the Valley of the Kings, but chose an unorthodox Western Valley site. Aye not only took Tutankhamen's throne and wife, he took his tomb.

Because the Western Valley was so isolated, it had been overlooked by early travelers to Egypt. The scientists who accompanied Napoleon's Egyptian expedition in 1798 explored the Western Valley, discovering the nearby tomb of Amenhotep III. Aye's tomb must have been covered by debris at that time, for it remained undiscovered until 1818 when Belzoni, searching for treasure, happened upon it.

It was in the western valley that one of the French savants discovered a large tomb, which he found open, but was quite unknown before his time. I went to visit the tomb, and found it very extensive and in pretty good preservation. My curiosity did not end here. I went farther on in the valley, and in one of the most remote spots saw a heap of stones, which appeared to me detached from the rubbish. I happened to have a stick with me, and on thrusting it into the holes among the stones, I found it penetrated very deep. I returned immediately to Gournou, and procured a few men to open the place. Unfortunately, both

Mrs. Belzoni and myself had been much afflicted for some time with the opthalmus, which was so severe upon me at this time, that I could scarcely see anything before me.

I took the men into the same valley the next morning; but in consequence of my eyes being so bad, it was some time before I could find the spot again. On removing a few stones, we perceived that the sand ran inwards; and in fact, we were so near the entrance, that in less than two hours all the stones were taken away. I had caused some candles to be brought, and I went in, followed by the Arabs. I cannot boast of having made a great discovery in the tomb, though it contained several curious and singular painted figures on the wall, and from its extent, and part of a sarcophagus remaining in the center of a large chamber, having reason to suppose that it was the burial-place of some person of distinction.[21]

Belzoni didn't know it, but he had uncovered the tomb of King Aye. Plundered in ancient times, there was little to interest Belzoni, but Newberry, with his knowledge of the aftermath of Tutankhamen's death, realized that its tomb paintings could provide part of the answer to Ankhesenamen's fate.

The traditional scenes of the pharaoh greeted by the gods of the next world are carefully reproduced in Aye's tomb, but one wall is a complete surprise. Aye included an exact copy of a scene from Tutankhamen's tomb—the twelve guardian baboons of the hours of the night. For reasons of his own, Aye associated himself with his dead predecessor. On another wall, Aye hunts in the marshes. Standing beside him is his wife, the queen.

Pharaohs often included portraits of their queens in their tombs so their spouses would accompany them through eternity. We would expect the same for Tutankhamen—especially since Ankhesenamen was both childhood friend and devoted wife. I have probably lectured inside Tutankhamen's tomb two dozen times to my students, explaining the significance of the wall paintings, but until I started to think about the murder theory, I never noticed who wasn't there—Ankhesenamen. Given their devotion to each other, and the fact that Ankhesenamen was alive when the walls were decorated, this was an egregious omission. Only when we remember that Aye was overseeing Tutankhamen's funerary preparations, including the painting of the walls, does the absence of Tutankhamen's wife from his tomb begin to make sense. Even so shortly after Tutankhamen's death, Aye had planned to marry Ankhesenamen. He did not want her to spend eternity with her first husband.

If Aye omitted Ankhesenamen from Tutankhamen's tomb, she should appear on the walls of his own sepulcher. Under normal circumstances she would be there. If Aye became king by virtue of marrying her, then she was the queen of Egypt, "the Great Wife."

We have no record of Carter or of anyone else looking for Ankhesenamen on the walls of her second husband's tomb. Like Newberry and others interested in the tangled affairs of the late Eighteenth Dynasty, I wondered about her fate. So I made the trek to Aye's tomb.

Walking up the desolate wadi that formed the Western Valley, I couldn't help but hope I would see some trace of the young queen. When I entered the tomb, I quickly found the scene where Aye is shown with his queen. She stands regally behind Aye, as hieroglyphs proclaim her "The King's Great Wife." But who is this queen? The name in the cartouche has been hacked out. There are only two reasonable possibilities for the identity of this queen: 1) Tey, Aye's first wife who was with him at Amarna, and 2) Ankhesenamen, who was already queen of Egypt when he married her. Which one is pictured is clear, despite the erasure. The cartouche is far too short to hold the long name "Ankhesenamen," but is just right for "Tey." No second queen stands behind Tey. Ankhesenamen has disappeared from history. Tey was a powerful woman in her own right, the only woman at Amarna ever awarded a gold collar by Akhenaten. She was the "nurse," or confidant, of Nefertiti, and she knew Ankhesenamen well, perhaps even serving the young queen in Thebes. Once Aye became king, Tey rose to even higher status, but she could never be "the King's Great Wife"—not while Ankhesenamen lived.

THE MISSING WITNESS

The last word from Ankhesenamen is her second desperate letter to the Hittite king, reaffirming that she is telling the truth, that she desperately wants a Hittite prince to marry. The Berlin Museum's ring indicates she lived after that—at least long enough to marry Aye—then she vanishes without a trace. It is not just 3,000 years that have obliterated Ankhesenamen. She should have been depicted on the walls of Tutankhamen's tomb, accompanying him throughout eternity, and, even if she died soon after her marriage to Aye, there should be some mention of her in his tomb. And where, after all, is her tomb?

No tomb for Ankhesenamen has been found. Even if it existed and was robbed clean in antiquity, there should be traces. If Ankhesenamen was buried as a queen of Egypt, her tomb would have contained furniture, clothing, jewelry, and a coffin. Tomb robbers in ancient Egypt took anything of value, breaking the furniture, stripping it of gold leaf, melting down the jewelry, leaving the tomb in a shambles, but what remained would still show there had once been a burial of Ankhesenamen. There would be broken canopic jars, fragments of wood boxes for clothing and toilet objects, objects worthless to any thief, but some would have carried the name of Ankhesenamen. Along with the queen's name, there would be an indication that she was dead, that these were objects from her tomb. Following her name would have been the hieroglyphs for "True of Voice."

Egyptians used many euphemisms for the dead, such as "he went west," and was "a westerner"—not unlike our "dearly departed." Another phrase they used was "true of voice." They believed that the deceased would appear in the Hall of the Double Truth in front of forty-two gods. Here he would present his case, telling why he should be admitted to the next world. Chapter 125 of the *Book of the Dead* told him what to say—that he had harmed no one, didn't divert the irrigation ditch from his neighbor's field, etc. At the end of his plea, his heart would be weighed on a balance scale against the feather of truth—the origins of our scales of justice. If the scale balanced, the deceased was declared "True of Voice" and admitted into the next world. If the scales did not, then the deceased's heart was eaten by the "Devourer of Hearts" and he went out of existence. "True of Voice" became a synonym for "deceased." The objects that should have been in Ankhesenamen's tomb would have had "true of voice" after her name.

Even a badly plundered tomb leaves traces of the occupant; objects appear on the antiquities market; excavators thoroughly mapping and clearing a robbed tomb find fragments; but of Ankhesenamen, married to two kings of Egypt, there is no clue. Either her tomb is yet to be discovered or she was never properly buried, and her name was erased from history. While I hope her tomb may be discovered some day, I fear that the latter might have been her end.

ROUND UP THE SUSPECTS

At this point, the clues include: X rays of Tutankhamen's skull indicating "a blow to the back of the head"; Ankhesenamen writing of her fear and refusing to marry a servant; the Hittite prince being murdered; and finally, Ankhesenamen marrying a commoner (servant), then immediately disappearing from history. All raise suspicions of foul play. We started with one death—Tutankhamen's. Then we found a murdered Hittite prince, followed by the suspicious disappearance of the royal heiress. The three deaths may be connected. If so, who are the principal suspects? As in any murder case, their subsequent actions have to be closely watched for missteps that reveal their guilt.

Aye

Immediately after Tutankhamen's death Aye had his image painted prominently on the tomb of the young king he served. While we might think that, if he was the murderer, he would do everything possible to distance himself from his victim, quite the opposite occurred. There is a reason, however, why even as Tutankhamen's killer, Aye would want to show himself as a king administering the last rites to the previous monarch. This was a way to legitimize his own claim to the throne, his continuity in the succession. It is significant that, although he had himself portrayed on the tomb wall, he omitted Ankhesenamen, Tutankhamen's wife, as if he had other plans for her. Aye then appropriated the tomb in the Western Valley begun by Tutankhamen and copied decorations from Tutankhamen's tomb, again associating himself with the former pharaoh. To associate himself even more closely with Tutankhamen, Aye added his title of "the God's Father" as part of his new pharaonic name.

Aye ascended the throne in his sixties. He lived for less than four years after becoming king, leaving posterity even fewer traces of his reign than Tutankhamen did. Aye's tomb was badly damaged by tomb robbers, but not until after an official desecration—his name was erased wherever it appeared on his tomb walls.[22] This attempt at *Damnatio Memoriae* was not unusual in ancient Egypt. Names held such great magical significance that Egyptians often said, "To say the name of the dead is to make him live again." If a person's name was erased from his monuments, he no longer existed; with the last trace erased, he was damned forever. This attempt at ensuring that Aye would not enjoy the pleasures of the next world extended beyond erasing his name. Even his ushabtis, his servant statues, were destroyed. Being of no monetary value, ushabtis were usually left by tomb robbers, but, in Aye's tomb, the destruction was so thorough that not one of him as king has ever been found.[23] Someone was making very sure that Aye would not fare well in the netherworld.[24]

Horemheb

Since General Horemheb succeeded Aye as pharaoh, he was in the best position to order the desecration of Aye's tomb. To understand why Horemheb would want this, we have to study his career. Horemheb may have begun his military service during the reign of Tutankhamen's father, but he did not join the religious migration to Amarna.[25] Instead, he rose to prominence under the next pharaoh, Tutankhamen, becoming "Great Commander of the Army," "King's Deputy," and "Overseer of the King's Works," and earning a dozen other titles.[26] Apparently born of humble origins, Horemheb rose quickly in the service of the young pharaoh. One of his rewards, his monumental tomb at Saqqara, is the largest of any of Tutankhamen's officials. No private individual on his own could afford to send an expedition to quarry the stones and employ the hundreds of skilled craftsmen to carve and decorate the blocks of such a tomb, unless it were a gift from the pharaoh. Horemheb showed scenes of his military campaigns in Nubia, Libya, and Syria all over his tomb walls, for it was he who regained control over Egypt's foreign territories that had been lost by Akhenaten.

We can imagine the anger of a warrior toward Akhenaten, the pacifist pharaoh, but even stronger must have been his reaction to Ankhesenamen's letter to the Hittite King. Horemheb had risked his life fighting Hittites; now the queen wanted to marry one of them and make him lord of Egypt—Horemheb's king! It would, therefore, not be surprising if Horemheb had a hand in murdering the Hittite prince. The curator of the Egyptian Department of the Louvre, in Paris, Mme. Desroches-Noblecourt, has no compunction indicting Horemheb for the murder of the Hittite prince.

> Prince Zannanza of the Hittites duly set out with his escort, but Horemheb's police, "the men and the horses of Egypt," murdered him on the way.[27]

Could anyone have ordered a military intercession against a Hittite prince without at least the acquiescence of the commander of the armed forces?

Horemheb continued as commander in chief of the armed forces throughout the reign of Aye, but when the aged Aye died, Horemheb, with the force of the military behind him, proclaimed himself king. Now that he was the top dog, Horemheb's true character revealed itself.

Horemheb eradicated all traces of Tutankhamen, even though this pharaoh was responsible for his rise to prominence. The first target was the colonnade at Luxor Temple, the one Tutankhamen had completed for his grandfather, Amenhotep III. Scenes of the Opet festival were left intact, but Tutankhamen's name was hacked out wherever it appeared and replaced by Horemheb's name.[28] When the gods looked down upon the walls of Luxor Temple, Horemheb would receive the credit (fig. 21). Even Tutankhamen's mortuary temple, where pious priests made offerings for his soul, was desecrated. The colossal statues that once stood in front of that temple no longer bear the name of Tutankhamen. Close examination reveals that the cartouches are carved deeper than the other hieroglyphs, because the statues were first usurped by Aye, then his name was replaced by Horemheb's (fig. 20). Nothing remains of Tutankhamen except his youthful face.

The restoration stela erected by Tutankhamen in Karnak Temple, proclaiming a return to the traditional ways, no longer bears his name. The few visitors who stop to look at it in the Egyptian Museum in Cairo see the name of Horemheb, carved a bit deeper than the rest of the hieroglyphs. Horemheb did such a thorough job of erasing all traces of Tutankhamen that it has been difficult to piece together a picture of Tutankhamen's life. As is characteristic of military people, his attention to detail and ability to command others ensured a thorough job.

Does this wanton erasure betray an anger against Tutankhamen that could have erupted in murder? One fact seems to answer "no." Horemheb's assault on Tutankhamen's name doesn't seem to have been personal because he left the young king's tomb intact and may even have been the one who resealed it after it was partially robbed. The eradication of Tutankhamen's memory was part of a broader rewriting of history, erasing all traces of the Amarna period and those connected with it, which included Tutankhamen and Aye.

When Horemheb took office, Akhenaten's temples to the Aten at Karnak probably still stood. By the time his reign ended, the Aten's temples had vanished. Horemheb ordered the temples dismantled, and he reused the blocks for fill in a great gateway he built in his own honor at Karnak Temple. To complete the systematic destruction of all evidence that the Amarna period existed, he sent teams of workers to Akhenaten's city in the desert to demolish every structure in the town down to its foundation.

Intent on blotting out the memory of Akhenaten, Tutankhamen, and Aye, Horemheb began counting the years of his own reign from the death of Amenhotep III. Horemheb, as Aye's successor, should have begun his reign with year one, but instead began with year 30. It was as if Horemheb had been crowned king immediately after the death of Amenhotep III, so the twenty-nine years of Akhenaten, Smenkare, Tutankhamen, and Aye never existed. Then Horemheb sent stone carvers to his own tomb at Saqqara, where he was depicted as a commoner, a mere general of the army. The workmen carved the cobra, the sign of royalty, on Horemheb's forehead so he would be remembered only as a pharaoh.

All indications show that Horemheb's rewriting of history was no personal vendetta, it was government policy. The Amarna heresy and those connected with it had to be wiped away. To an amazing degree the fiction worked. On the official lists of kings, like the one at Abydos, Horemheb's name appears immediately after the name of Amenhotep III.

However, one exception to Horemheb's destruction of anything and anyone related to Amarna was allowed to remain. The tomb of Tutankhamen went unviolated. Not so with Aye's tomb and Akhenaten's. The reason may have been simple sentiment. Horemheb had risen to greatness under Tutankhamen and may have felt affection for the one who had awarded him power and wealth. Out of sight, the tomb was not an obvious reminder of the heresy, so the young pharaoh could slumber peacefully in his tomb even if he no longer existed officially above ground.

Today, we would call Horemheb a law-and-order pharaoh. He reorganized the courts, installing "men of good character," telling them not to accept bribes. "What will [people think] of men in your office . . . who violate justice?" he asked. As an ex-military man he exacted strict punishments for criminals. Those guilty of extortion had their noses cut off and were exiled. Anyone caught stealing received one hundred blows.[29] Throughout his twenty-seven-year reign, Horemheb strived to restore Egypt to its former position of greatness. He built temples and shrines to the gods, and sent military expeditions far and wide. When at last he lay in his tomb in the Valley of the Kings, Egypt was in far better shape than when he took over the kingship. Of course, that does not mean he was innocent of murder.

THE INDICTMENT

After Tutankhamen's suspicious death, one other murder certainly occurred (of the Hittite prince) and another may well have (of Ankhesenamen). Were all three deaths connected, was a single murderer at work? Given all the evidence, two likely suspects stand out—Aye and Horemheb. Let's consider each one.

The strongest evidence for a crime comes from the Hittite archives, which make a specific charge—the murder of their prince. Clearly, the Hittites viewed that event as an official Egyptian act of aggression, for they declared war on Egypt. They believed that officials at the highest level of Egyptian government were involved. Both Horemheb and Aye must be considered possible culprits in this death. Each had a strong motive. Horemheb, the career military man, had battled the Hittites all his life, and saw one of them about to become his king. Doing away with the Hittite prince would force the powers in charge to pick an Egyptian king. Aye's motive would have been more personal. He wanted to be king. At the moment Ankhesenamen was writing to the Hittites, he was having himself painted as pharaoh on the wall of Tutankhamen's tomb. It was clear to everyone in power but Ankhesenamen that Hittites were enemies, not to be trusted. The Hittite prince could never be allowed to reach Egypt.

Both Aye and Horemheb had the means. Aye as vizier of Egypt controlled the government. When he learned of Ankhesenamen's plans to marry a foreigner, it would have been a simple matter to alert the border patrol of a possible "Hittite invasion" under the cover of a flag of truce.

For Horemheb, too, it would have been easy to direct a chariot division to meet and destroy the prince and his entourage. Egyptian soldiers hearing that a Hittite was on his way to rule Egypt would have been willing to risk their lives to prevent this distasteful event.

Horemheb and Aye each had a motive, and each had the means. It could even be that they connived together. Wanting to ascend to the throne, Aye contacts Horemheb who abhors the idea of serving a Hittite king. The commander in chief of the army, for his own reasons, agrees to do Aye's dirty work—not an unlikely scenario.

If these events took place today, Horemheb and Aye would be questioned separately, and each offered a chance to plea-bargain in exchange for informing on the other. The most likely outcome would be an indictment of both for the murder of the Hittite prince.

What about the other two suspicious deaths, of Ankhesenamen and Tutankhamen? Today, we would look to see who had the motive and the means, then bring in an indictment against that person.

If Tutankhamen was murdered, the evidence points to Aye more than Horemheb. Although both had strong motives, Aye alone had the means. The situation is spelled out on the walls of the tomb of Rekmire, a vizier who held office more than a century before Aye. The tomb is decorated with two motifs—hieroglyphic texts and daily-life scenes—both proclaiming the power of the vizier in ancient Egypt. He had access to every luxury in the land, hosted elaborate banquets where the finest food was served. Musicians and dancers entertained, while a multitude of servants attended to the desires of his guests. Rekmire was so proud of his exalted status that he described his responsibilities as vizier. One line of hieroglyphs on the tomb wall tells it all, "Let no one enter or leave the royal residence without the vizier's knowledge"; he alone was responsible for who went in and came out of the palace. Aye could easily arrange for someone to dispatch Tutankhamen with a blow to the back of the head while the young king slept. He could orchestrate a perfect assassination in which no one would see a stranger enter, then leave Tutankhamen's room. Aye did not have to commit the crime with his own hands. He was an older man who, given his position of power, would have scores of fawning followers willing to do his bidding.

Did Aye have a motive that would drive him to such extreme measures? As Tutankhamen grew to manhood, he must have felt more and more capable of making his own decisions, becoming increasingly difficult to control. Aye would see his own power and influence slipping away. If Ankhesenamen were to have a son—and she was young enough to have every hope of doing so—it would end any hope that Aye would ever be pharaoh. He may have sensed his time was running out. Further, Aye was an intimate in the palace who had watched one pharaoh almost ruin a great country before another took the throne who was, in Aye's eyes, a child. How could Aye, who commanded all the machinery of the country, not feel that his abilities to rule overwhelmed their accidents of birth? He deserved to be pharaoh.

For Aye to become pharaoh, there had to be two deaths in a short period of time, and one of them was clearly murder. When we add the forced marriage of Ankhesenamen and her subsequent death, there is good reason to believe a string of murders occurred.

ANKHESENAMEN

Lacking any record of Ankhesenamen's death, and her tomb and body, the weakest case is the one for her murder. We know only that she was afraid, that she did not want to marry a servant, then she married Aye and disappeared from the historical record. Here, all we can cite are possible motives for murder. When Aye married Ankhesenamen, he became the king of Egypt, gaining the title and the power. Although he no longer needed her, why would he dispatch his new wife? Perhaps Ankhesenamen suspected her new husband of complicity in Tutankhamen's death and was making accusations. After all, she told even the Hittite king she was afraid.

Then, too, we must consider Aye's wife of forty years, Tey, who agreed on one matter with the twenty-year-old Ankhesenamen. Neither wanted Aye to replace his old wife with a young queen. Tey, as we noted earlier, was a woman of considerable social standing, so it is doubtful that she would happily take second place to another wife. Tey may have supported or even suggested the murder of Ankhesenamen. After all, Aye's tomb is decorated with paintings of his faithful wife Tey as the "great wife," the queen of Egypt, where not a trace of Ankhesenamen is seen.

General Horemheb also had a motive. Aye was an elderly pharaoh with no heirs. When he died, the throne of Egypt would again come up for grabs, and Horemheb, with the military at his back, would have a good chance at that prize. Ankhesenamen was a potential obstacle in his path to the throne. Horemheb would have known about her two miscarriages, which showed that she was capable of conceiving. If she had a child with Aye and it was a male, Horemheb's quest for the throne would end. It is even possible, although we have no evidence of it of course, that Ankhesenamen was carrying Tutankhamen's child at the time of his murder.

Where do these possible motives lead? My guess, speculative though it must be, is that Aye murdered not one but probably two and possibly even three people—Ankhesenamen, the Hittite prince, and Tutankhamen, though Horemheb was his accomplice in the death of the Hittite. I believe that Horemheb was not unhappy to see Tutankhamen dead, for his aged successor would be a commoner who opened the door for another commoner—himself—before long. That does not mean he killed him. He had not the ready means. Of course, a determined assassin, if willing to die in the attempt, can get to anyone. But if Horemheb had ordered the deed, he would have to deal afterward with the powerful Aye. His path to the throne could only be over that second, very powerful, body. Yet, Horemeheb had no reason to battle Aye; he was young enough to wait a few years for his turn. Nor did Horemheb have a compelling need to kill Ankhesenamen, not with Aye already at an age when the birth of a son was unlikely to even a young wife.

Aye had everything to gain from the death of Tutankhamen at an unnaturally early age. He had the means to pull off the murder of the pharaoh and not be caught. Aye had all the same reasons to prevent the Hittite prince from reaching Egypt. Poor Ankhesenamen, his obviously unwilling bride, was the one powerful person in Egypt who could accuse Aye of complicity in Tutankhamen's death. Aye, who had murdered two people to get his throne, would not find one more murder very difficult to ensure that he kept his throne.

NILEGATE

If Aye really murdered Tutankhamen, how did he get away with it? There are several answers, each one adequate in itself. During Tutankhamen's time the population did not rise up against their ruler when they were outraged by something he had done. There was no sense of accountability. Two parallel tracks—one for royalty and one for the common people—ran through the society which never intersected, allowing no mechanism by which the people interacted with their pharaoh. The people of ancient Egypt would never rise up against Aye.

At the time of his coronation a pharaoh became divine, a god on earth, the son of the sun god Re. He was so far removed from the people of Egypt they wouldn't dream of interacting with him. In our modern world, with television, radio, and newspapers, it is hard to imagine a country where most of the population lived and died without ever having seen their ruler. The people knew that Tutankhamen was dead, and little more. No news bulletins broadcast his illness or cause of death, nor would anyone wonder. One god had been replaced by another, it was their affair.

The second reason Aye could get away with murder is that no mechanism existed to accuse him, let alone bring him to justice. We are so accustomed to a system of checks and balances that it is difficult to imagine anyone being truly beyond the law, but, with the pharaoh dead, no one occupied a higher office than the vizier. The situation was like our Watergate. The President, our highest official, may have been guilty of crimes, but the highest law officer in the land, the attorney general, was also involved in his criminal conduct. How, under such circumstances, could the President be indicted, let alone convicted? In Watergate, the congress and senate made enough noise to ensure that something was done. Ancient Egypt had neither a congress nor a senate; there was absolutely no way Aye could have been subjected to legal process. Aye's immunity from prosecution is another reason marking him the more likely culprit than Horemheb.

Proof that Aye could get away with murder is found in a single sentence written in the vizier Romose's tomb: "Let no man punish the vizier in his office." The vizier was the highest law official in Egypt; he was the Supreme Court. With Tutankhamen dead, no one alive could punish Aye. He didn't even have to commit the perfect crime because he was beyond the reach of the law.

It was, indeed, possible to kill a king and get away with it. Afterward, this murder, if ever recorded, was methodically eradicated. When Horemheb became king, he erased every trace of anyone involved in the Amarna Heresy, including all the files on Akhenaten, Tutankhamen, and Aye. Everything was destroyed, including, I suspect, valuable information about Tutankhamen, his reign, relationships with his advisors, and even possible clues to his murder.

THE DEFENSE

When I began discussing the murder theory with colleagues, lively discussions ensued. Some agreed, some didn't, but the debates were always interesting and rational. Things changed, however, when The Learning Channel television documentary I had been working on presented the murder theory publicly.

A documentary has to tell a story in a simple and straightforward manner. The audience may be unfamiliar with ancient Egypt and they may be distracted, so it is important to make points clear and easy to understand. The show received good reviews and high ratings, but this has little to do with the probability of the theory being correct. Shows about alien encounters receive good ratings, too. Soon after the program aired, several close colleagues acted strangely distant. It was then that I discovered I wasn't the only one with strong feelings about Tutankhamen. One said to me, "Oh Bob, didn't you know it was Horemheb?" Another felt that I had slandered Aye, whom she viewed as a grandfather figure for Tutankhamen. Lengthy discussions and letters followed, until it became clear to me that the other side had never been presented. I had been acting as a prosecutor, presenting the case against Aye. What would Aye's attorney say? I am glad to have the chance here to present the other side's view.

The defense might begin by defending Aye's character, pointing out that he was a family man, devotedly married for forty years or more, a member of the royal court, loyal to both Tutankhamen and his father. A religious man following the Aten, he had inscribed the most complete version extant of the *Hymn to the Aten* on his tomb wall at Amarna. Further, he attended to the burial of Tutankhamen with loving care. Heirlooms, prized possessions, beautiful funerary equipment, a solid gold coffin, all were placed in the tomb. Clearly Aye loved Tutankhamen. He was a loyal servant of the royal family, not some traitor who would murder the king as he slept.

The burial of Tutankhamen's brother, Smenkare, in Tomb 55 is further evidence of Aye's loyalty to the royal family. The coffin, mummy, and the funerary equipment in the tomb all point to someone who realized that the burials at Amarna would be further desecrated, and had the coffin and mummy moved to Thebes so they would be preserved. This too was a loving act, which, given the times, was also a courageous one. Almost certainly Aye made these arrangements. What emerges is the profile of a devoted family confidant and guardian, not a serial killer.

If we examine how religious movements characteristically develop we will see Aye's actions as those of a sincere servant of the royal family. The vision of Akhenaten was fresh, ·exciting, positive when his ideas were first presented at Thebes. As always, the majority clung to the traditional religion, but some among the younger people became true believers. Liberated from centuries of dogma, they followed their charismatic pharaoh to build a new city in the desert. We can easily imagine Aye among these first converts of Akhenaten, although he was no youngster at the time. Aye rose to the highest position in Amarna, all the while devoutly practicing the new religion, but being more mature, Aye was the first to return to his senses. When he realized things were amiss, Aye led the way back to the old gods, guiding young Tutankhamen. He engineered the migration and return to traditional values. This was not a case of someone following the expedient path for his own gain; he was a cult member who had regained his senses.

With Aye's character and good intentions established, his defense might now show that Horemheb is a far more likely suspect in the murder of the Hittite prince. The ambush had to have the acquiescence if not the blessing of the General Horemheb. It was Horemheb, not Aye, who fought and hated the Hittites. If we must choose a prime suspect, surely it is Horemheb, a military leader trained to take quick and forceful action when needed.

With regard to the alleged murder of Ankhesenamen, it must be pointed out that there is no body. A young queen's husband died; would it be unusual for a woman at such a time to be distraught? Afraid? It is the most natural thing in the world. It would be natural, too, that Aye, who had guided the young couple and the country for a decade, continued ruling Egypt. There is nothing sinister in his *pro forma* marriage to Ankhesenamen. He remained her adviser, saved her from whoever the unnamed servant was, and assumed control of Egypt.

It is true that there were three deaths in just a few short months, but why view this as sinister when a far more reasonable explanation is provided by the Hittite archives? At the end of the Hittite tablet that describes the retaliatory strike against Egypt is the statement that the Egyptian prisoners taken to Hatti brought the plague. So there was a plague in Egypt. Would it be suspicious, given that circumstance, that two people in close contact die within a short period? The common cause for the deaths of Tutankhamen and Ankhesenamen was not Aye; it was the plague. The defense rests.

These are strong arguments, serious objections to the theory that Aye is a murderer. Let us examine each one.

THE PROSECUTION RESTS

Aye did, indeed, inscribe the long version of the Hymn to the Aten on the wall of his tomb at Amarna, but this was the most politically correct tomb decoration one could possibly have at that time. What better way to curry favor with Akhenaten? When Aye decorated his second tomb in the Valley of the Kings, he showed only the traditional gods, not a single reference to the Aten. Does this show religious devotion to the traditional gods? It seems rather to suggest that Aye believes in the god(s) expedient at the moment. Aye had no firm religious convictions, which is why he orchestrated the move of the royal court back to Thebes.

Aye indeed buried Tutankhamen with care, which is exactly what we would expect any murderer in his place to do—try to show that he loved and cared for the deceased. He even includes a picture of himself in Tutankhamen's tomb. Other signs also demonstrate Aye's close association with Tutankhamen. After the young king's death, Aye completed a small temple as a memorial to him.[30] All this attention to Tutankhamen was designed, I maintain, both to throw suspicion elsewhere and also to establish Aye's legitimacy as his successor. After all, Aye's sole claim to the throne was that he was married to Tutankhamen's widow. The possibility that a kindly old Aye saved Ankhesenamen from some other, unnamed, "servant" is a red herring. Aye was the power in Egypt; no one could frighten him. If he wanted to remove someone who frightened Ankhesenamen, he had only to say the word—unless it was him that she feared.

The discovery of Tomb 55 raised many questions, not the least of which is who was responsible for the reburial of Smenkare and objects from Amarna. Given Aye's position of power in Thebes, I think he had to be the one, but not necessarily as a loving family servant. Perhaps Tutankhamen, longing for his family, ordered whatever remained of his family's burial be brought to Thebes. It seems that once Tutankhamen died, Tomb 55 was opened, under Aye's orders, so Smenkare's miniature canopic coffins could be appropriated for Tutankhamen's burial—not exactly respecting the family burial vault.

I do agree that Horemheb was the one who killed the poor Hittite prince. Military force was necessary for that act and Horemheb would have provided it to avoid serving a Hittite king. Yes, Horemheb was responsible for the death of the Hittite prince, but does that release Aye from coresponsibility? Surely the vizier of Egypt would have had to authorize such an action. It is far easier to imagine Aye and Horemheb acting in concert than to think of either as a lone assassin in this event. Aye would not have the ability to attack without military agreement, and Horemheb would not have the authority without government approval.

As to the murder of Ankhesenamen, the defense makes a good case. There is no physical evidence for violence here, as there was with Tutankhamen, nor is there the report of a murder, as with the Hititte prince. All we have is circumstantial evidence. A young woman who is afraid disappears. True, she says she will never marry a servant and then marries Aye, a commoner, but even if she were forced into the marriage, it does not mean that she was subsequently murdered. In a modern court of law, we would never get an indictment against Aye for the murder of Ankhesenamen.

The claim that both Tutankhamen and Ankhesenamen were killed by a plague is interesting, but is not supported by the Egyptian records. We have no evidence of a plague in Egypt at this time, though records exist of plagues in other times. It is not surprising that the Hittites would attribute their suffering to their enemy, whether that was the cause or not, much as syphilis was called "the French Disease" by the Germans and "the German Disease" by the French.

However, we must remember that we are not in a court of law. We cannot call witnesses who have been dead for thirty-two centuries. What we must look for is not a conviction, but simply the most reasonable explanation for all the facts. The case against Aye rests on a combination of facts—an X ray suggesting a blow to the back of the head, a widow's letter expressing her fear of being forced to marry a servant, the murder of her Hittite fiancé, the ring showing she married Aye, the painting of Aye on Tutankhamen's tomb wall, and the complete disappearance of the widow afterward. Any single fact by itself does not prove the case, but taken together they indicate not one but two, and possibly three, murders. The dominant thread throughout is Aye. It is he who benefited most from Tutankhamen's death, and he who had the greatest opportunity. Given the evidence, the most reasonable explanation is that Aye is guilty of the murder of Tutankhamen, King of Upper and Lower Egypt, and Lord of the Two Lands.

Epilogue

Crime never lands its wares;
In the end it is justice that lasts.

—*Ptahotep*
circa 2275 B.C.

Soon after Tutankhamen was buried and the funeral party departed and his tomb was sealed, robbers broke into the tomb. They broke off the arrowheads from Tutankhamen's arrows (bronze was valuable), fine linens from chests and unguents from jars were taken, as were other valuable items that would not be traceable to the dead king's tomb. The robbers must have acted hastily, fearing detection. Working in near darkness, they grabbed gleaming golden furniture, only to discard it on the staircase when it became clear that it was gilded wood. The next day when the robbery was detected, officials, perhaps supervised by Maya who in addition to his role as treasurer was Overseer of the Works of the Royal Necropolis, resealed the tomb and blocked the entrance passage with tons of limestone chips in the hope of avoiding further robberies.

However, these efforts were not successful. The tomb was once again entered by robbers, who tunneled through the top of the stone chips and into the tomb. Estimates of the work involved suggest a period of seven or eight hours to tunnel through the mass of limestone chips.[1] So, starting under cover of darkness, the thieves would have finally entered the tomb near daybreak. Fearful of the light of day, they hurriedly searched small chests and grabbed whatever jewelry came to hand. It is possible the thieves were caught in the act, or nearly caught, since a twisted scarf containing eight solid gold rings was abandoned near the entrance. If any of the culprits were captured, their punishment would have been impalement on a sharp stick until death released them from their pain.

The tomb was resealed once again, until Howard Carter discovered it 3,000 years later. Two hundred years after the robberies, Ramses VI began construction on his tomb near the site of Tutankhamen's. His workmen dumped tons of limestone chips dug from the new tomb on top of the entrance to Tutankhamen's older one, obliterating all traces for more than thirty centuries. Tutankhamen finally rested well.

Aye did not survive long after the death of Tutankhamen. His reign of less than four years left little to remember, especially since his monuments were destroyed by Horemheb. Even at Aye's mortuary temple, his name was replaced with Horemheb's cartouches; his tomb in the west spur of the Valley of the Kings, once intended for Tutankhamen, suffered the erasure of his name. Aye appears on none of the Kings Lists of ancient Egypt. He is remembered today only because of his association with Tutankhamen.

When Horemheb succeeded Aye as pharaoh, he attempted to erase all traces of his three predecessors– the kings associated with the Amarna heresy. So it is Horemheb whose name appears on the Kings Lists as the successor to Amenhotep III, as if the kings in between had never existed. This fiction was not due to Horemheb alone. He did, indeed, date his reign from the death of Amenhotep III, but later kings were all too happy to leap over Akhenaten, Tutankhamen, and Aye to skip to Horemheb and count him as one of their own. The irony is that the obliterated Akhenaten and Tutankhamen were legitimate kings, blood descendants of the kings of the Eighteenth Dynasty. Horemheb had not a drop of royal blood, but he did have the army behind him, and in troubled times power resides with the army.

Horemheb ruled for twenty-seven prosperous years. He erected his own version of Tutankhamen's restoration stela at Karnak Temple, claiming that it was he who restored the temples, ended corruption, and reestablished divine order throughout the land. However exaggerated, Horemheb did in fact take firm administrative control of Egypt. Ruling from Memphis, he placed the army under the command of two generals, one for the south and one for the north. He replaced the high priests with men drawn from the army whom he could trust. Courts of law were established in all the major cities of Egypt, with judges reporting directly to Horemheb. Corruption was dealt with severely and justice was promised to all. Horemheb built extensively at Karnak and also constructed a large tomb for himself in the Valley of the Kings, far grander than Tutankhamen's little pit. When he died, in very old age, he left a well-administered, orderly country, but no children.

The country then faced a situation similar to the morass after Tutankhamen's death. There were no heirs at all, not even a female who could elevate someone to the throne by marrying him. But precedents had been set by the murders and machinations in the aftermath of Tutankhamen's death. Egypt had now experienced two pharaohs who were commoners, so a third became more possible than ever before. Like Aye before him, the vizier of Egypt took on the pharaohcy after Horemheb. This vizier had been an army comrade of Horemheb and served as commander in chief before Horemheb selected him to serve as vizier. He was as common as the commonest soldier; his father was a mere captain in the army. He was probably selected to succeed Horemheb because he had a son and grandson. When he died, there would be no doubt about succession. This man founded a great dynasty of long duration.

His name was Ramses, the first of many pharaohs of that name. I like to think that his dynasty, the nineteenth, was the consequence of the sad events discussed in this book. If so, the ending was not without its glory. Ramses I, a contemporary of the aged Horemheb, lasted less than two years as pharaoh, but his son, Seti I, was vigorously middle-aged and enjoyed a reign of fifteen solid years. He started the country in a new direction, away from the intense concentration of energies on Thebes and its god Amun. He called his reign the "Repetition of Birth," the Egyptian version of the Renaissance, and constructed one of the greatest temples in Egypt, not in Thebes but some distance north at Abydos, the birthplace of Osiris. It was to be a truly national temple with a chapel dedicated to Osiris, of course, but others for Isis, Horus, Ptah of Memphis, Re-Harakhti of Heliopolis as well as Amun of Thebes. And, beginning a practice that would become monomaniacal with his son, installed one chapel to himself. This was a man in the old mold, who saw his country's greatness as inseparable from its pharaoh's accomplishments. Appropriately, he had the largest, most magnificent tomb in the Valley of the Kings constructed for his eternal glory.

Seti's son bore a name no less familiar to us than Tutankhamen's—Ramses, known as "the Great." As a young pharaoh he led Egypt's armies as the great fighting pharaohs of the Eighteenth Dynasty had done before. As a mature pharaoh he built great monuments rivaling those of earlier kings. Ramses had more children than any other pharaoh, boastfully listing one hundred progeny. After a reign of sixty-seven years Ramses, old and wizened, met the fate that lies in store for us all. His legacy was a country as strong as ever before, a country covered through its length and breadth with temples and statues proudly bearing the name of Ramses. In a sense, he was Tutankhamen's legacy.

Whatever the impact of Tutankhamen's life on his country or its future course, his name resounds today throughout the world. The names of Aye and Horemheb are recognized only by specialists. If the ancient Egyptian adage, "To say the name of the dead is to make him live again," has any truth, Tutankhamen still lives, but not those who may have caused his death.

History is not just facts and cold stones. It consists of people motivated by fears, hopes, and desires just like ours. The objects they leave behind are not impersonal; they carry the marks of their owners' lives, accomplishments, and dreams. The artifacts discussed in this book still exist. It is still possible to stand in front of the floral collar worn by Ankhesenamen, Aye, or Horemheb at the funerary banquet held when Tutankhamen was laid to rest. It resides in New York's Metropolitan Museum of Art along with a statue of the young Tutankhamen, probably carved for his coronation at Thebes, and a magnificent statue of Horemheb with its law-and-order inscription. One can still visit Tutankhamen's tomb in the Valley of the Kings and see Aye, frozen in time, performing the Opening of the Mouth ceremony eternally on the boy-king he may have murdered. In the Egyptian Museum in Cairo, Tutankhamen's restoration stela stands in a quiet corner on the first floor. Look closely at the deep carving of the cartouches, where Horemheb replaced Tutankhamen's name with his own. This is real history.

Appendix

TESTABLE THEORIES

In chapter 8 we discussed the speculation that Tutankhamen may have lingered before dying. As we mentioned, this is far from certain, but it had to be stated because it is a real possibility and part of the overall picture. Although this is merely a theory, it is important to note that it is a *testable* theory that future research can either refute or confirm. There are methods of determining if Tutankhamen had been ill for a long time and whether he died of dehydration. The proof lies in the contents of four miniature gold coffins in the Egyptian Museum in Cairo.

When Tutankhamen was mummified, his internal organs were removed, dehydrated, wrapped in linen, and placed in four small gold coffins about twelve inches long that had originally been prepared for his brother, Smenkare. The lid of each coffin is inscribed with a prayer for Tutankhamen by one of the four sons of Horus—gods who were to protect the mummy's internal organs. Imseti guarded the liver; Hapi, the lungs; Duamutef, the stomach; and Qebhsenuf, the intestines. When Tutankhamen was buried, the coffins were placed in an alabaster shrine, described by Howard Carter as one of the most beautiful objects in the tomb.[1] They were then anointed with the same black unguents that had been poured on the mummy.

Carter commented that the miniature coffins were tiny replicas of the second of the three coffins in which Tutankhamen was buried, but he never discussed their contents. As far as I know, the organs haven't been seen since the 1920s when they were photographed by Harry Burton from the Metropolitan Museum of Art. The museum kindly sent me a set of Burton's photographs, and the photos show that the internal organs were not damaged by the oils, their linen wrapping had not turned black. A further series of Burton's photographs shows one of the organs unwrapped and in good condition. These organs, still in the Egyptian Museum in Cairo, could hold important clues to Tutankhamen's death.

If Tutankhamen died in a coma, then the intestines and stomach should be empty, and analysis of the liver could show what nutrients he absorbed during his last days. Carter never realized just how much information is contained in a mummy—or part of a mummy. With modern forensic technologies ancient murders can be solved. It is important to understand that the theories we are discussing about Tutankhamen's death are not mere speculation. They are empirically verifiable, and can be tested.

In an experiment performed in 1993, Ronald Wade, director of Maryland's State Anatomy Board, and I mummified a human cadaver in the ancient Egyptian style.[2] Using replicas of ancient tools and natron from the Wadi Natrun in Egypt, we hoped to answer questions about Egyptian mummification techniques. When the experiment was completed we had an Egyptian-style mummy. We sent small samples of tissue from the mummified organs to Dr. Michael Zimmerman, Head of Pathology at Maimonides Medical Center in Brooklyn. Zimmerman's passion is paleopathology. Besides having his M.D., he earned a Ph.D. in physical anthropology, so he is uniquely qualified to solve ancient medical mysteries. Wade and I had the full medical history of our modern mummy, but didn't reveal it to Zimmerman. After his analysis of the tissues, Zimmerman was able to give us a remarkable description of the last days of our subject's life right down to the amount of fluid in his lungs. The tissue samples sent to Zimmerman had been mummified, so it is quite possible that similar analyses could reveal how Tutankhamen spent his last days.

If Dr. Irwin's theory about Tutankhamen's lingering is correct and there was a significant hematoma that remained for some time after the injury, then there should be a buildup of hemosiderin (concentrated blood matter) and elemental iron on the bone in the area.[3] This might be detectable with a high-powered CAT scan. If and when the mummy of Tutankhamen is examined again, this should rank high on the list of procedures to be performed.

The organs of Tutankhamen raise interesting questions. There are four miniature coffins, but there are more than four internal organs. What happened to the other organs? Which ones were actually placed in the miniature coffins? If we wanted to reassemble poor Tutankhamen, it seems several parts would be missing. The lungs, liver, stomach, and intestines are the organs mentioned in connection with the four sons of Horus. What about the kidneys, spleen, pancreas, and gall bladder? In spite of all the mummifications performed, the ancient Egyptians had only a rudimentary knowledge of anatomy. There isn't even a hieroglyph for the pancreas,[4] but this is understandable if we look at how the embalmer worked.

The internal organs were removed through a small incision made on the left side of the abdomen. The embalmer inserted his hand into the incision, cut an organ free, and pulled it out through the incision. The embalmer was working blind, unable to see the relative positions of the organs, or even how many organs there were. Within the mass of intestines, the pancreas or other organs could easily be overlooked. The kidneys, located behind the peritoneum, were often left in place, for they are difficult to reach from the side. In truth, we really don't know which of Tutankhamen's organs were placed in the small coffins. What is certain is that they are not all there, and some may be partial, but still they are important clues.

When Wade and I performed the modern mummification, one of the most difficult procedures was removing the liver, the largest organ in the human body, through the small incision. We were using replicas of ancient ceramic jars to hold the organs, and even after dehydration in natron we were unable to fit the whole liver in our replica of an ancient Egyptian canopic jar. I had to section it. There is no way the liver from a nineteen-year-old male the size of Tutankhamen could have fit in one of the miniature canopic coffins. I suspect that the embalmers cut off as much as would fit in one of the miniature coffins, wrapped it, and placed it in the coffin. The rest must have been discarded along with any other organs not preserved.

Still, whatever organs or parts of organs remain from Tutankhamen, they have not yet been examined by anyone with experience in paleo-pathology. They will certainly provide invaluable information about Tutankhamen's last days.

Notes

INTRODUCTION

1. Christopher Frayling, *The Face of Tutankhamen* (London: BBC Television, 1992).

2. Karin L. Sandnass, "Dietary Analysis of Prehistoric Lower and Middle Osmore Drainage Populations of Southern Peru Using Stable Isotopes (Delta C-13 and Delta N-15)" (Paper presented at the Second World Congress on Mummy Studies, Cartagena, Colombia, February 6–10, 1995).

CHAPTER 1: THE KING MUST DIE

1. James Henry Breasted, *The Edwin Smith Surgical Papyrus* (Chicago: University of Chicago Press, 1930).

2. William J. Darby et al., *Food the Gift of Osiris* (London: Academic Press, 1977), vol. 1, p. 331.

3. Nicholas Reeves, *The Complete Tutankhamen* (London: Thames & Hudson, 1990), pp. 136–39.

4. Geoffrey Martin, *The Hidden Tombs of Memphis* (London: Thames & Hudson, 1991), pp. 148–49.

5. T. J. C. Baly, "Notes on the Ritual of Opening the Mouth," *Journal of Egyptian Archaeology* 16 (1930): 173–86.

6. E. A. Wallis Budge, *The Book of the Opening of the Mouth* (New York: B. Blom, 1972), vol. 1, pp. 184–86.

7. Thomas George Allen, *The Book of the Dead* (Chicago: University of Chicago Press, 1974), p. 34.

CHAPTER 2: EGYPT BEFORE TUTANKHAMEN

1. Trevor Watkins, "The Beginning of Warfare," in *Warfare in the Ancient World*, ed. Sir John Hackett (New York: Facts on File, 1989), pp. 15–19.

2. Yigel Yadin, *The Art of Warfare in Biblical Lands* (New York: Mcgraw-Hill, 1963), vol. 1, p. 53.

CHAPTER 3: TUTANKHAMEN'S ANCESTORS

1. James Henry Breasted, *Ancient Records of Egypt* (London: Histories & Mysteries of Man, 1988, reprint), vol. 2, pp. 43–44.

2. Arielle P. Kozloff and Betsy M. Bryan, *Egypt's Dazzling Sun* (Cleveland: Cleveland Museum of Art, 1992), p. 59.

3. Elizabeth Riefstahl, *Thebes in the Time of Amenhotep III* (Norman, OK: University of Oklahoma Press, 1964), p. 5.

4. John Romer, *Valley of the Kings* (New York: William Morrow, 1981), p. 161.

5. Ibid., pp. 161–62.

6. Loret prepared the mummies for shipment to Cairo—but, just before loading them on the boat, he received an order from the Ministry of Public Works to replace the mummies in the tomb and seal it. Many Egyptians viewed archaeologists as foreigners robbing their heritage. They believed their kings should lie undisturbed where they were found. Politics had superseded archaeology.

7. G. Elliot Smith, *The Royal Mummies* (Cairo: l'Institut Français, 1912), pp. 46–51.

8. Guido Majno, *The Healing Hand* (Cambridge, MA: Harvard University Press, 1977), p. 109.

9. Ray Winfield Smith, "Computer Helps Scholars Recreate an Egyptian Temple," *National Geographic* (November 1970): 634–55; Ray Winfield Smith and

Donald B. Redford, *The Akhenaten Temple Project* (Westminster: Aris & Phillips, 1978).

10. Donald Redford, the excavator of Akhenaten's temples at Karnak, shares my view of Akhenaten's sed-festival as extraordinary, but recently another scholar, Jocelyn Gohary, has suggested that Akhenaten was trying to stay as close to traditional ritual as possible. Jocelyn Gohary, *Akhenaten's Sed-Festival at Karnak* (London: Kegan Paul, 1992), p. 167.

11. Reed E. Pyeritz and Cheryll Gasner, *The Marfan Syndrome* (Port Washington, NY: National Marfan Foundation, 1994), pp. 8–9.

12. Victor A. McKusick, "The Defect in Marfan Syndrome," *Nature* 352 (July 25, 1991): pp. 279–80.

13. Many thanks to Dr. Jessica Davis, New York Hospital, for her most helpful discussions of Akhenaten as a Marfan's syndrome patient.

CHAPTER 4: AMARNA—THE HOLY CITY

1. Barry J. Kemp, "The Window of Appearances at El-Amarna, and the Basic Structure of the City," *Journal of Egyptian Archaeology* vol. 62 (1976): pp. 81–99.

2. Gardiner Wilkinson, *Modern Egypt and Thebes* (London: John Murray, 1843), vol. 2, p. 76.

3. Margaret S. Drawer, *Flinders Petrie: A Life in Archaeology* (Madison, WI: University of Wisconsin Press, 1995), p. 208.

4. William Flinders Petrie, *Tell el Amarna* (Westminster: Aris & Phillips, 1974, reprint), pp. 41–42.

5. Ibid., p. 6.

6. William J. Murnane and Charles C. Van Siclen III, *The Boundary Stelae of Akhenaten* (London: Kegan Paul, 1993), pp. 36–37 (based on their translation and transcription).

7. Ibid, pp. 36–37.

8. Cyril Aldred, *Akhenaten* (London: Thames & Hudson, 1988), p. 48.

9. Miriam Lichtheim, *Ancient Egyptian Literature* (Berkeley: University of California Press, 1976), vol. 2, pp. 96–99.

10. Cyril Aldred, *Akhenaten King of Egypt* (New York: Thames & Hudson, 1988), p. 48.

11. Donald B. Redford, *Akhenaten, The Heretic King* (Princeton: Princeton University Press, 1984), p. 234.

12. Barry J. Kemp, "The Window of Appearances at El-Amarna, and the Basic Structure of the City," *Journal of Egyptian Archaeology* 62 (1976): 81–99.

CHAPTER 5: TUTANKHAMEN'S PARENTS

1. Cyril Aldred, *Akhenaten and Nefertiti* (New York: Brooklyn Museum, 1973), p. 220.

2. Aidan Dodson, *The Canopic Equipment of the Kings of Egypt* (London: Kegan Paul, 1994), p. 55.

3. Williman C. Hayes, *The Scepter of Egypt* (New York: Metropolitan Museum of Art, 1959), vol. 2, p. 294.

4. H. W. Fairman, "Once Again the So-Called Coffin of Akhenaten," *Journal of Egyptian Archaeology* 47 (1961): 29–30.

5. This possible friction between the two wives is hinted at in the title of an article about Kiya. See Angela P. Thomas, "The Other Woman at Akhetaten," in *Amarna Letters III* (San Francisco: KMT, 1994), pp. 73–80.

6. Barry J. Kemp, "Outlying Temples of Amarna," in *Amarna Reports VI* (London: Egypt Exploration Society, 1995), pp. 411–62.

7. Urbaine Bouriant, *Monuments Pour Servir a l'Étude du Culte d'Atonou en Egypte* (Cairo: Mission Français d'Archaeologie Orientale du Caire, 1903).

8. Geoffrey Thorndike Martin, *The Royal Tomb of Amarna* (London: Egypt Exploration Society, 1989), p. 40.

9. Samuel A. B. Mercer, *The Tel Amarna Tablets* (Toronto: Macmillan, 1939), vol. 1, pp. 267–69.

10. Ibid., pp. 271–73.

11. Ibid., pp. 275–77.

12. Ibid., p. 291.

13. Norman de Garis Davies, *The Rock Tombs of Amarna—Part I: The Tomb of Meryra* (London: Egypt Exploration Fund, 1903), p. 15.

14. W. M. Flinders Petrie, *Tell El Amarna* (London: Methuen & Co., 1894), p. 33. In his excavations, Petrie found a pottery fragment with this inscription: *year 16 good wine . . . The great seer of the Aten Ra-Mery.* So Merire was alive at this time.

15. Norman de Garis Davis, *The Rock Cut Tombs of Amarna—Part II: The Tombs of Panehesy and Meryra II* (London: Egypt Exploration Fund, 1905), p. 29.

16. Ibid., plate 10.

17. Norman de Garis Davis, *The Rock Cut Tombs of Amarna—Part V: The Tomb of Ay* (London: Egypt Exploration Fund, 1912).

18. Donald Redford, *Akhenaten: The Heretic King* (Princeton: Princeton University Press, 1984), p. 216; Rosalie and Anthony E. David, *A Biographical Dictonary of Ancient Egypt* (London: Seaby, 1981), p. 26.

CHAPTER 6: THE RETURN TO THEBES

1. John Bennett, "The Restoration Inscription of Tutankhamen," *Journal of Egyptian Archaeology* 25 (1939): 8–15.

2. Geoffrey T. Martin, *The Hidden Tombs of Memphis* (London: Thames & Hudson, 1991), pp. 171–72.

3. Ibid., p. 147.

4. Theodore M. Davis, *The Tombs of Harmhabi and Touatankhamanou* (London: Constable, 1912), p. 128.

5. Miriam Lichtheim, *Ancient Egyptian Literature* (Berkeley: University of California Press, 1976), vol. 2, p. 101.

6. The Epigraphic Survey, *The Festival Procession of Opet in the Colonnade Hall* (Chicago: The University of Chicago Oriental Institute Publications, 1994), 1:xix.

7. Nicholas Reeves and Richard H. Wilkinson, *The Complete Valley of the Kings* (London: Thames and Hudson, 1996), pp. 116–17.

8. Hans Goericke, *The Report About the Dispute of a Man with His Ba* (Baltimore: Johns Hopkins Press, 1970).

CHAPTER 7: THE MOST FAMOUS TOMB IN HISTORY

1. Diodorus Siculus, *Library of History,* book 1, vol. 46 (Cambridge: Harvard University Press, 1968), p. 165.

2. Richard Pococke, *A Description of the East* (London: W. Boyer, 1843), vol. 1, p. 98.

3. *Description de l'Egypte* (Paris: L'Imprimerie Impériale, 1812), vol. 2, plate 77.

4. The mummies and coffins arrived safely at the Egyptian Museum in Boulaq. Brugsch unwrapped only one of the mummies, that of Tuthmosis III, the greatest of the warrior pharaohs. The mummy had been buried in the Valley of the Kings, plundered, rewrapped by the Twenty-first Dynasty embalmers, and reburied in the Deir el Bahri tomb.

When Brugsch unwrapped the Egyptian king, he and his colleagues became the first in modern times to see the mummy of one of the greatest pharaohs of ancient Egypt. What they saw was shocking. The king's body was in a horrible state, the head separated from the body, the legs and arms disarticulated, and the feet broken at the ankles. Brugsch performed a crude, quick autopsy that yielded little information. He did not continue with the other mummies, perhaps fearful that he would find them in a similar condition.

5. W. M. Flinders Petrie, *Seventy Years of Archaeology* (New York: Holt, 1932), p. 152.

6. Howard Carter, *Annales du Service des Antiquitiés de l'Egypte* (1902) 3: 115–21.

7. Theodore M. Davis, *The Tombs of Harmhabi and Touatankhamanou* (London: Constable, 1912), p. 3.

8. Joseph Lindon Smith, quoted in *The Complete Valley of the Kings,* by Nicholas Reeves and Richard H. Wilkinson (London: Thames & Hudson, 1996), p. 6.

9. Ibid, p. 64.

10. Charles Breasted, *Pioneer to the Past: The Story of James H. Breasted* (New York: Scribner's, 1943), p. 181.

11. James Henry Breasted, *Records of Ancient Egypt* (Chicago: University of Chicago Press, 1906–1907).

12. James Henry Breasted, *History of Egypt* (New York: Scribner's, 1924), pp. 133–34.

13. There is also a theory that the shrine never had a statue. See M. Eaton-Krauss and E. Graefe, *The Small Golden Shrine from the Tomb of Tutankhamen* (Oxford: Griffith Institute, 1985), pp. 5–6.

14. Edward Falkener, *Games Ancient and Oriental and How to Play Them* (New York: Dover, 1961).

15. Grahme Davis, "Reconstructing Rules for the Ancient Egyptian Game of Twenty Squares," *KMT* (summer 1993): 83–85.

16. Leonard H. Lesko, *King Tut's Wine Cellar* (Berkeley: B. C. Scribe Publications, 1977).

17. W. M. McLeod, *Composition Bows from the Tomb of Tut'ankhamun* (Oxford: Griffith Institute, 1970); W. M. McLeod, *Self Bows and other Archery Tackle from the Tomb of Tut'ankhamun* (Oxford: Griffith Institute, 1982).

18. J. E. Harris et al., "The Mummy of the 'Elder Lady' in the Tomb of Amenhotep II: Egyptian Museum Catalogue Number 61070," *Science,* June 9, 1978, p. 1199; recent research, however, has suggested that in spite of the close match of hair samples, the mummy of the Elder Lady is not Queen Tiye. Dr. Renate Germer compared the dried blood of the mummy of the Elder Lady with that of Tiye's parents, Yuya and Tuya, and found it highly unlikely that the Elder Lady could be their daughter. Tutankhamen's grandmother may still be missing.

19. Harry Burton, *New York Times,* February 15, 1923.

20. Arthur C. Mace, *Bulletin of the Metropolitan Museum of Art,* The Egyptian Expedition, 1922–1923, p. 6.

21. Howard Carter, *The Tomb of Tutankhamen* (New York: Cooper Square, 1963), vol. 2, p. 51.

22. Ibid., pp. 52–53.

23. Velma, "The Fatal Curse from the Tomb," in Christopher Frayling, *The Face of Tutankhamen* (London: Faber and Faber, 1992), p. 244.

24. Velma wasn't the only one talking about a curse. Two weeks before Lord Carnarvon's death, the novelist Marie Corelli had predicted disaster for those at the site. In more recent times the curse flames have been fanned by Philip Vandenberg in his book *The Curse of the Pharaohs.* He says, "however, the scholars especially were less euphoric. In fact, they became increasingly nervous. The reason for their concern was an ordinary clay tablet Carter had found in the antechamber. He had it catalogued, as he did the other objects. Then, a few days later, Alan Gardiner decoded the hieroglyphics on it. The inscription read: *Death will slay with his wings whoever disturbs the peace of the pharaoh.* Neither Carter nor Gardiner nor any of the other scholars present feared the curse then or took it seriously. But they worried that the Egyptians laborers would, and since they were dependent on native helpers, mention of the clay tablet was

wiped from the written record of the tomb's discovery. Even the tablet itself disappeared from the artifact collection—but not from the memory of those who read it. (The tablet and the curse on it are cited everywhere, but it was never photographed and is considered lost.)" (p. 20)

The tablet never existed, there are no reliable references to such a curse, and it is certainly un-Egyptian to speak of death as being with wings. Over the next few decades, whenever anyone who worked on the excavation died, the curse was invoked. In his book (p. 103), Vandenberg says: "Tutankhamen's autopsy at the Anatomical Institute of Cairo University on November 11, 1925, had tragic consequences: Alfred Lucand died soon after from a heart attack, and a little later Professor Derry died of circulatory collapse." This is nonsense. There was never an autopsy of Tutankhamen in Cairo. The mummy is still in the tomb where it was found. Lucas died of a heart attack in 1945, twenty years later, not soon after the autopsy. Professor Derry did not die "a little later," but in 1969 at the age of 87, more than forty years after he autopsied the boy-king in his tomb. Although the evidence is slim, the idea of the "curse of Tutankhamen" continues to intrigue people.

It was Velma's account of the curse that established a precedent for psychics of her day to claim that they also had warned Carnarvon of a curse on the tomb. Chiero, the famous palm reader, published his account of the curse on the tomb. By far the most elaborate of the curse stories, it involves a mummy's hand, a long-dead Egyptian princess, and a curse on those who would remove objects from Tutankhamen's tomb.

Chiero published his account more than a decade after Carnarvon had died, but claimed he had sworn affidavits from those who witnessed the incredible events that he describes. Chiero's tale begins with a trip he made to Egypt prior to World War I to prepare wax casts of the ancient carvings. One evening his guide asked him to come to the hypostyle hall at Karnak temple. When they reached the hall, his guide produced, from beneath a broken sphinx, a mummy's hand complete with a gold finger ring. The trusty guide explained that this was the hand of Akhenaten's daughter, Meketaten. He related the tale that only she had remained true to her father's religion when everyone else had abandoned the Aten, and she had formed an army and marched on

Thebes. Meketaten was killed in the subsequent battle and her hand severed and mummified as a grim reminder to those who might stray from the true faith of Egypt. Chiero had been singled out to become the custodian of the hand to see that the prophecy associated with it was fulfilled.

The hand was to travel the world, but after a great war was fought, and the tomb of her brother-in-law Tutankhamen was discovered, the hand would be reunited with the rest of the mummy of Meketaten. Chiero says that he accepted this great responsibility and carried the hand with him wherever he went, but after World War I, strange things began to happen. The hand had been as hard as ebony, but now the skin began to soften, and then to ooze blood. For more than thirty years Chiero had carried the hand around the world, but this was too much, so he and his wife decided to cremate the hand on Halloween Eve in 1922. As the hand was consumed by flames, a beautiful and elegant princess, Meketaten, appeared, complete with both her hands. The next day Tutankhamen's tomb was discovered. (Chiero had his dates wrong, but it didn't seem to hurt his story.) The princess appeared once more to Chiero, this time with a warning for Lord Carnarvon. None of the treasures from Tutankhamen's tomb were to be removed or death would claim him while he was still in Egypt.

Chiero published this account of the curse in *Real Life Stories* in 1934. Because he was one of the most famous clairvoyants of his era, his embellishment of the curse helped to keep the myth alive.

25. Howard Carter, *The Tomb of Tutankhamen* (New York: Cooper Square, 1963, reprint), vol. 2, p. 82.

26. F. Filce Leek, *The Human Remains from the Tomb of Tut'ankhamun* (Oxford: Griffith Institute, 1972), p. 5.

27. Douglas E. Derry, "Report on the Examination of Tutankhamen's Mummy," in Howard Carter, *The Tomb of Tutankhamen*, vol. 2, pp. 158–59.

28. The Deir el Bahri cache of royal mummies found in 1881 had the potential of providing considerable data on royal mummification techniques, yet the mummies were ravaged by notable Egyptologists who did not know what to look for, nor did they take the time to make careful notes when they performed an unwrapping. Maspero was in France when the mummies were transported

from Thebes to Cairo, so it was Emile Brugsch, his assistant, who began their unwrapping. Chastising him in the official report, Maspero says, "Within the first few weeks of their arrival at Boulaq, Mr. Emile Brugsch could not resist the desire to see for the first time one of their faces, and opened, without permission, and during my absence, the mummy of Tuthmoses III" (M. Maspero, *Les momies royales de Deir el-Bahri*, Paris: Mission Archéologique Française, 1889, p. 525). Occupied with translating the coffins' inscriptions and the labels on the mummies, Maspero waited several years before unwrapping the mummies. But when he began he was in a frenzy, tearing through one mummy after another.

By order of the Khedive of Egypt, on June 1, 1886, the mummy of Ramses II was unwrapped. Attending were the Khedive, his entire council of ministers, various doctors, archaeologists, artists and others. In his report Maspero attempts to create the impression that everything was done scientifically and with caution. He explains that every measurement was taken by two of those present, then verified by two other attendants (Maspero, pp. 525–26). In truth, the proceedings were shoddy. Maspero unwrapped *three* mummies that day, two kings and a queen—the start of a good poker hand, but bad Egyptology. The next week, in a single day Maspero unwrapped the mummies of Seti I, Seqenenre Tao II, and Ahmose I. In less than one month, from June 9 to July 1, twenty-one mummies of the Deir el Bahri cache were stripped of their wrappings. One can only wonder what Maspero's hurry was. This was how mummies were treated, so Tutankhamen's rough handling should not be surprising.

Most of the royal mummies that escaped Maspero's hands were later unwrapped by Grafton Elliot Smith, a physician who had the necessary training, but who also worked too quickly. During 1905, Smith unwrapped nine mummies, including those of Tuthmosis IV, Ramses IV, Ramses V, Ramses VI, Siptah, and Seti II. Smith's account of these unrollings is almost obsessively brief, allotting each pharaoh a mere page or two (G. Elliot Smith, *The Royal Mummies*, Cairo: Institut Français d'Archéologie Orientale, 1912). His descriptions provide a few insights into royal mummification, such as position of the abdominal incision, but at times he is clearly more interested in the features of the royal visage than how the pharaohs were mummified.

CHAPTER 8: DEAD MEN TELL TALES

1. Marc Armand Ruffer, "Notes on the Histology of Egyptian Mummies," *British Medical Journal* (1909): 11.

2. F. Filce Leek, *The Human Remains from the Tomb of Tut'ankhamun* (Oxford, Griffith Institute, 1972), p. 23.

3. R. G. Harrison et al., "A Mummy Foetus from the Tomb of Tutankhamen," *Antiquity* 53 (1979): 19–21.

4. The first X ray of a wrapped mummy was published by Flinders Petrie in 1898 as the final illustration in his excavation report of Dashasheh, a site eighty miles south of Cairo. The developed film showed the leg bones of a mummy through the wrappings. Petrie realized that X rays permitted the Egyptologist to know what was beneath the mummy bandages without unwrapping, but his example was not widely imitated. When Tutankhamen's tomb was discovered in 1922, the only royal mummy to have been X-rayed was Tuthmosis IV, who was transported in a taxi from the museum by Elliot Smith and Howard Carter to a hospital in Cairo that owned an X-ray machine.

5. R. G. Harrison, "An Anatomical Examination of the Pharaonic Remains Purported to Be Akhenaten," *Journal of Egyptian Archaeology* 52 (1966): 116.

6. R. G. Harrison and A. B. Abdalla, "The Remains of Tutankhamen," *Antiquity* 46 (1972): 10.

7. Dennis Forbes, "Abusing Pharaoh," in Christopher Frayling, *The Face of Tutankhamen* (London: Faber and Faber, 1992), pp. 291–92.

8. R. G. Harrison, "Post Mortem on Two Pharaohs: Was Tutankhamen's Skull Fractured?" *Buried History* (1972): 18–24; R. G. Harrison, "Tutankhamen's Postmortem," *The Lancet* (1973): 259; R. G. Harrison, "The Remains of Tutankhamen," *Antiquity* 46 1972): 8–14.

9. Roy L. Moodie, *Roentgenologic Studies of Egyptian and Peruvian Mummies* (Chicago: Field Museum of Natural History, 1931), p. 23, plate 14.

10. Marc Armand Ruffer, "Notes on Two Egyptian Mummies Dating from the Persian Occupation of Egypt," in *Studies in the Paleopathology of Egypt* (Chicago: University of Chicago Press, 1921), pp. 127–38.

11. Quoted in F. Filce Leek, *The Human Remains from the Tomb of Tut'ankhamun* (Oxford: Griffith Institute, 1972), p. 7.

12. James E. Harris and Kent R. Weeks, *X-raying the Pharaohs* (New York: Scribner's, 1973).

13. James E. Harris and Edward F. Wente, *An X-ray Atlas of the Royal Mummies* (Chicago: University of Chicago Press, 1980), p. 378.

14. *Los Angeles Times,* January 17, 1997.

15. Nicholas Reeves, *The Complete Tutankhamen* (London: Thames & Hudson, 1990), p. 118.

16. F. Filce Leek, *op. cit.,* p. 17.

17. Cyril Aldred, *Akhenaten, King of Egypt* (London: Thames & Hudson, 1988), p. 297.

18. Letter to the author, dated April 1, 1996.

19. Thanks are due to Dr. Michael R. Zimmerman, Director of Clinical Laboratories, Maimonides Medical Center, Brooklyn, New York, for his helpful discussion on this question.

CHAPTER 9: A WIDOW'S PLEA

1. Hans Gustav Guterbock, "The Deeds of Suppiluliuma as Told by His Son Mursilis II," *Journal of Cuneiform Studies* 10 (1965): 47.

2. Ibid., p. 94.

3. Donald Redford has argued that there is a scribal error and the king named is Akhenaten, but it is not a convincing argument. For a discussion of this issue see Alan R. Schulman, "Ankhesenamen, Nofretity, and the Amka Affair," *Journal of the American Research Center in Egypt* 15 (1977): 43–48.

4. Walter Federn, "Dahamunzu (KBo V 6 iii 8)," *Journal of Cuneiform Studies* 14 (1960): 33.

5. Geoffrey Thorndike Martin, *The Hidden Tombs of Memphis* (London: Thames and Hudson, 1991), plate 41; Cyril Aldred, *The Development of Ancient Egyptian Art* (London: Tiranti, 1961), plate 144.

6. Guterbock, *op. cit.,* pp. 94–95.

7. Ibid., p. 96.

8. Nigel F. Hepper, *Pharaoh's Flowers* (London: HMSO, 1990), pp. 9–10.

9. There is an alternative theory about the time of Tutankhamen's death. Because the Hittite text says "But when the people of Egypt heard of the attack on

Amka, they were afraid. And in addition, their Lord Nephururiya had died. Therefore the Queen of Egypt . . . sent a messenger to my father . . ." Trevor R. Bryce believes that the Amka campaign and the death of Tutankhamen occurred at about the same time. This would change the season of Tutankhamen's death, because from the Hittite accounts we know the siege was in early autumn. Bryce's scenario involves Tutankhamen dying toward the end of August, the siege in October, and Ankhesenamen's first letter being sent in November. Bryce admits that the burial took place in Spring, but wants to assume that it was delayed for six months while Ankhesenamen waited for the Hittite prince. But this is based on the assumption that the Amka campaign and the death occurred at the same time. It is quite possible that the queen only learned of the Amka affair months later, or perhaps not at all. As we have said before, her fear seems to have come from the "servant." She never mentions the Amka campaign. Also there is no need to assume the burial of Tutankhamen would have been delayed. Egyptian religion demanded the body be buried seventy days after death. It seems far more likely that the funerary bouquets are the best indicator of the time of death. See Trevor R. Bryce, "The Death of Niphururiya and Its Aftermath," *The Journal of Egyptian Archaeology* 76 (1990): 99–105.

10. Ibid., pp. 96–97.

11. Ibid., pp. 97–98.

12. Ibid., p. 98.

13. Albrecht Goetze, "Palace Prayers of Mursilis," in *Ancient Near Eastern Texts,* ed. James B. Prichard (Princeton: Princeton University Press, 1955), p. 395.

14. Nicholas Reeves, *The Complete Tutankhamen* (London: Thames & Hudson, 1990), p. 72.

15. Percy E. Newberry, *Scarab-shaped Seals* (London: Constable, 1907).

16. The Egyptians were especially fond of puns, and the hieroglyphs for beetle 🪲 (pronounced *kheper*) also meant "to exist." So if you wore a scarab amulet, your continued existence was ensured. Another reason the scarab was held in special regard is that the ancient Egyptians believed the beetle bore its young without the union of male and female. This false belief arose simply because the beetles were never seen mating. Actually, after fertilization the female deposits her eggs in a piece of dung and rolls it into a ball, so that when they hatch, the newborn will be provided with food. Since this was the only part of the reproductive

cycle the Egyptians saw, they assumed the beetle was somewhat like the god Atum who begot children without a female partner.

Scarab amulets were made from a variety of materials, faience and stone being the most common. Like other amulets, holes were incorporated in their design so they could be suspended on a chain and worn. While the top was carved to resemble the beetle, the bottom was usually flat, with an inscription. Often the inscription was merely the owner's name, so that the amulet would bring him continued existence. Scarabs could also be used as seals. If the owner wanted to seal a jar of wine and be sure none of the servants sampled it, he could plaster the top of the jar and press the bottom of his scarab into the moist plaster. Then if the seal were broken, it could not be repaired undetected.

17. My thanks to Diana Magee of the Griffith Institute, Ashmolean Museum, Oxford, for supplying a photocopy of Newberry's letter.

18. Percy E. Newberry, "King Ay, the Successor to Tutankhamen," *Journal of Egyptian Archaeology* 18 (1932): 50–53.

19. My thanks to Drs. Dietrich Wildung and Hannelore Kischkewitz of the Ägyptisches Museum, Berlin, for their help in locating the ring and making it available.

20. Cyril Aldred, *Akhenaten and Nefertiti* (New York: Brooklyn Museum, 1973), p. 181.

21. Giovanni Battista Belzoni, *Narrative of the Operations and Recent Discoveries in Egypt and Nubia* (London: Murray, 1820), pp. 123–24.

22. Otto J. Schaden, "The God's Father Aye," in *Amarna Letters II* (San Francisco: KMT, 1992), p. 108.

23. An ushbati of Aye as a commoner, made during the period he served Tutankhamen, was auctioned at Sotheby's in New York on December 17, 1997. It is one of the most beautiful ushbatis ever made.

24. Otto J. Schaden, "Clearing the Tomb of King Aye," *Journal of the American Research Center in Egypt* 21 (1984): 39–64.

25. There is an Amarna tomb for the military commander Paatenemheb, and because of the similarity in the two names, some have suggested that this is Horemheb's tomb. See Christiane Desroches-Noblecourt, *Tutankhamen* (New York: New York Graphic Society, 1963), p. 284.

26. Geoffrey T. Martin, *The Hidden Tombs of Memphis* (London: Thames & Hudson, 1991), p. 52.

27. Christiane Desroches-Noblecourt, *Tutankhamen* (New York: New York Graphic Society, 1963), p. 276.

28. Epigraphic Survey, *The Festival Procession of Opet in the Colonnade Hall* (Chicago: University of Chicago Press, 1994).

29. Ronald J. Leprohon, "A Vision Collapsed, Akhenaten's Reforms Viewed Through Decrees of Later Reigns," in *Amarna Letters* (San Francisco: KMT, 1991), pp. 66–73.

30. The blocks from this temple are now scattered, but they seem to show Tutankhamen in battle scenes fighting Asiatics—the earliest known royal chariot battle scenes. See William Raymond Johnson, "An Asiatic Battle Scene of Tutankhamen from Thebes," Doctoral dissertation, University of Chicago, 1992.

EPILOGUE

1. Nicholas Reeves, *The Complete Tutankhamen* (London: Thames & Hudson, 1990), p. 96.

APPENDIX: TESTABLE THEORIES

1. Howard Carter, *The Tomb of Tut-Ankh-Amen* (New York: Cooper Square Press, 1965, reprint), vol. 3, p. 48.

2. Bob Brier and Ronald S. Wade, "The Use of Natron in Human Mummification—A Modern Experiment," *Zeitschrift für Ägyptische Sprache und Altertumskunde* 124, no. 2 (1997): pp. 89–100.

3. Dr. Michael Perry, Chief of Trauma Radiology, University of Maryland school of medicine, suggested this to me.

4. Kent Weeks, *The Anatomical Knowledge of the Ancient Egyptians and the Representation of the Human Figure in Egyptian Art* (Ann Arbor: UMI Dissertation Information Service, 1970), pp. 74–5.

Bibliography

Albright, William F. "The Egyptian Correspondence of Abimilki Prince of Tyre."
    Journal of Egyptian Archaeology 23 (1937): 190–203. Discussion of one section
    of the Amarna Letters and the difficulties in translating them.

Aldred, Cyril. *Akhenaten and Nefertiti.* New York: Brooklyn Museum, 1973. Cata-
    log to accompany the exhibition at the Brooklyn Museum. Many unusual
    illustrations with excellent descriptions.

———. *Akhenaten, King of Egypt.* London: Thames & Hudson, 1988. Although
    somewhat dated, this book was written by the foremost Akhenaten scholar
    and is still a basic work on Tutankhamen's father.

———. "The Beginning of the El-Amarna Period." *Journal of Egyptian Archaeology*
    45 (1959): 19–33. A great Akhenaten scholar describes Akhenaten's early
    years.

———. *The Development of Ancient Egyptian Art.* London: Tiranti, 1961. Discus-
    sion of the how Egyptian art developed.

———. "The End of the El-Amarna Period." *Journal of Egyptian Archaeology* 43, (1957): 30–41. A discussion of the relationship between members of the court during the last years at Amarna.

———. "The Tomb of Akhenaten at Thebes." *Journal of Egyptian Archaeology* 47 (1961): 41–65. An attempt at reconstructing the events that led to the mummy and funerary objects being placed in Tomb 55. The conclusion that the body was Akhenaten's was reached before the later autopsy of the mummy showed this to be unlikely.

———. *Tutankhamen's Egypt.* New York: Scribner's, 1972. Excellent popular account of Tutankhamen's reign.

Allen, Thomas George. *The Book of the Dead.* Chicago: University of Chicago Press, 1974. A translation of the spells necessary for immortality in ancient Egypt.

Anthes, Rudolf. *Tutankhamen Treasures.* Washington, D.C.: Smithsonian Institution, 1961. Catalog of the first exhibition of Tutankhamen objects in the United States.

A Short Description of the Objects from the Tomb of Tutankhamen. Cairo: Institut Français, 1927. One of the early catalogs of the objects from Tutankhamen's tomb displayed in the Egyptian Museum in Cairo.

Arnold, Dorothea. *The Royal Women of Amarna.* New York: Metropolitan Museum of Art, 1996. Far more than just the catalog of the Metropolitan's exhibition held in 1996–1997. The book includes important essays on various aspects of life at Amarna and makes many suggestions about the women of Amarna. Extraordinary photographs of Amarna art.

Baikie, James. *The Amarna Age.* New York: Macmillan, 1926. A good account for its time but now dated.

Baines, John. *Stone Vessels, Pottery and Sealings from the Tomb of Tut'Ankhamen.* Oxford: Griffith Institute, 1993. A valuable work that contains an especially interesting article on the seal of the necropolis used to reseal the tomb after the robberies.

Baly, T. J. C. "Notes on the Ritual of Opening of the Mouth." *Journal of Egyptian Archaeology* 16 (1930): 173–86. Details of the ritual as it was probably performed on Tutankhamen on the day of his burial.

Bibliography

Beinlich, Horst, and Mohamed Saleh. *Corpus der Hieroglyphischen Inscripten aus dem Grab des Tutankhamuns.* Oxford: Griffith Institute, 1989. Copies of all the hieroglyphic inscriptions in the tomb. No translations—for Egyptologists.

Bell, Martha R. "An Armchair Excavation of KV 55." *Journal of the American Research Center in Egypt* 28 (1990): 97–137. A fascinating attempt to reconstruct the order in which the objects were placed in the tomb. Careful detective work.

Bennett, John. "The Restoration Inscription of Tut'Ankhamen." *Journal of Egyptian Archaeology* 25 (1939): 8–15. Complete translation cf Tutankhamen's promise to restore order to Egypt.

Bille-de Mot, Eleanore. *The Age of Akhenaten.* New York: McGraw-Hill, 1906. Clear presentation of the Amarna Revolution with some unusual illustrations.

Bosse-Griffiths, Kate. "Finds from 'The tomb of Queen Tiye' in the Swansea Museum." *Journal of Egyptian Archaeology* 47 (1961): 66–70. Shows just how careless the excavators of Tomb 55 were.

Brackman, Arnold C. *The Search for the Gold of Tutankhamen.* New York: Mason/ Charter, 1976. Popular account with some unusual bits of information.

Bratton, F. Gladstone. *The Heretic Pharaoh.* London: Hale, 1962. Popular account with a biblical slant.

Breasted, James Henry. *Ancient Records of Egypt.* Vol. 2. 1905. Reprint. London: Histories and Mysteries of Man, 1988. Breasted's translations of hieroglyphic inscriptions on the monuments of Egypt show just how little was known about Tutankhamen before the discovery of his tomb.

———. *The Edwin Smith Surgical Papyrus.* Chicago: University of Chicago Press, 1930. Translation of the only medical papyrus from ancient Egypt dealing with trauma, especially to the head.

———. *A History of Egypt.* New York: Charles Scribner's Sons, 1919. Shows just how little was known about Tutankhamen before the discovery of his tomb.

Brier, Bob. *Egyptian Mummies.* New York: Morrow, 1994.

Brier, Bob, and Ronald S. Wade. "The Use of Natron in Human Mummification— A Modern Experiment." *Zeitschrift für ägyptische Sprache* 124, no. 2 (1997). Re-creation of ancient embalming techniques.

Bristone, E. S. G. *Naphuria: The History of the True Akhenaten.* London: Jenkins, 1936. Based on the *Amarna Letters,* this eccentric theory claims that Akhenaten's grandfather was the pharaoh of the Exodus.

Brothwell, Don, and A. T. Sandison. *Diseases in Antiquity.* Springfield: Charles C. Thomas, 1967. Important survey of diseases and injuries in the ancient world. A bit dated but still useful.

Bryce, Trevor R. "The Death of Niphururiya and Its Aftermath." *Journal of Egyptian Archaeology* 76 (1990): 97–105. Discussion of Ankhesenamen's letter to the Hittite king.

Budge. E. A. Wallis. *The Book of the Opening of the Mouth.* 1909. Reprint. New York: B. Blom, 1972. Detailed description of the ritual that must have been performed on Tutankhamen on the day of his burial. Somewhat dated translations.

———. *Tutankhamen, Atenism, and Egyptian Monotheism.* New York: Brill, n.d. Reprint of a work by the eccentric former Keeper of the British Museum's Egyptian and Assyrian antiquities. Dated, but the discussion of the Aten cult is still interesting.

Burridge, Alwyn L. "Akhenaten: A New Perspective." *The Society for the Study of Egyptian Antiquities Journal* 23 (1993): 63–74. The first suggestion in print that Akhenaten suffered from Marfan's syndrome. Some of the symptoms described are not quite accurate.

Carter, Howard. "Report on the Robbery of the Tomb of Amenothes II." *Annales du Service des Antiquités de l'Egypte* 3 (1902): 115–21. Carter displays his detective abilities in tracking down the modern robbers of the tomb of Amenhotep II.

Carter, Howard. *The Tomb of Tutankhamen: Statement.* Brockton, MA: John William Pye, 1997. Reprint of the 1924 document Carter privately circulated just before the Egyptian Government locked him out of Tutankhamen's tomb. A fascinating look into the archaeological politics of the times.

Carter, Howard, and A. C. Mace. *The Tomb of Tutankhamen.* 3 vols. 1923–1933. Reprint. New York: Cooper Square, 1963. Reprint of the three volumes by Carter describing his excavation of the tomb. Fascinating reading.

Carter, Michael. *Tutankhamen the Golden Monarch.* New York: McKay, 1972. Popular and slightly sensationalizing account.

Cerny, Jaroslav. *Hieratic Inscriptions from the Tomb of Tut'Ankhamun.* Oxford: Griffith Institute, 1965. Translations of the inscriptions in the cursive form of Egyptian writing. Includes the lists of objects in the various boxes in the tomb.

Christie, Agatha. *Akhenaton.* New York: Dodd, Mead, 1973. A three-act play about Akhenaten and Nefertiti.

Chubb, Mary. *Nefertiti Lived Here.* London: Bles, 1954. Delightful account of excavation life at Amarna.

Clayton, Peter A. *Chronicles of the Pharaohs.* London: Thames & Hudson, 1995. A useful reference work briefly describing each pharaoh's reign.

Collier, Joy. *The Heretic Pharaoh.* New York: John Day, 1970. A popular account focusing on the possibility of a connection between Akhenaten and Moses.

Connolly, R. C. "Microdetermination of Blood Group Substances in Ancient Human Tissue." *Nature* 224 (1869): 325. The technique used to establish the close family relationship between Tutankhamen and the mummy in Tomb 55.

Cottrell, Leonardo. *The Secrets of Tutankhamen's Tomb.* Greenwich, CT: New York Graphic Society, 1964. Young adult book.

Darby, William J., et al. *Food the Gift of Osiris.* London: Academic Press, 1977. Detailed account of food and eating habits in ancient Egypt.

David, A. Rosalie and Anthony E. *A Biographical Dictionary of Ancient Egypt.* London: Seaby, 1992. Brief biographies of some of the important figures in Tutankhamen's era.

Davies, Norman de Garis. *The Rock Tombs of Amarna.* Part 1. London: Egypt Exploration Fund, 1903. The first volume in Norman de Garis Davies's series on the tombs of Amarna. This volume records the tomb of the high priest Meri-Re.

———. *The Rock Cut Tombs of Amarna.* Part 2. London: Egypt Exploration Fund, 1905. The tombs of Pa-Nehsey and Meri-Re II are described.

———. *The Rock Cut Tombs of Amarna.* Part 3. London: Egypt Exploration Fund, 1905. The tombs of Huya, overseer of the house of Queen Tiye, and of Ahmes, another highly placed court official.

———. *The Rock Cut Tombs of Amarna.* Part 4. London: Egypt Exploration Fund, 1906. The tombs of several court officials are described.

———. *The Rock Cut Tombs of Amarna.* Part 5. London: Egypt Exploration Fund, 1907. The tomb of Aye with the great hymn to the Aten is described in detail.

————. *The Rock Cut Tombs of Amarna*. Part 6. London: Egypt Exploration Fund, 1908. The last in the series on the tombs of Amarna.

Davies, Norman de Garis, and A. H. Gardiner. *The Tomb of Huy, Viceroy of Nubia in the Reign of Tutankhamen*. London: Egypt Exploration Society, 1926. One of the few monuments from the reign of Tutankhamen is described.

Davis, Theodore M. *The Tomb of Queen Tiye*. 1910. Reprint. San Francisco: KMT, 1990. Reprint of Theodore Davis's account of the famous Tomb 55. In spite of contrary evidence, Davis published the tomb as that of Queen Tiye. The report has an excellent introduction by Nicholas Reeves, the Tutankhamen scholar.

————. *The Tombs of Harmhabi and Touatankhamanou*. London: Constable, 1912. Davis's erroneous conclusion that he had discovered Tutankhamen's tomb, which led to his statement that "the Valley of the Kings is now exhausted."

De Gans, Raymonde. *Tutankhamen*. Geneva: Fermi, 1978. General popular work on the life and times of Tutankhamen.

Description de L'Egypte. Vol. 1. Paris: L'Imprimerie Impériale, 1812. Drawing and maps by the artists who accompanied Napoleon when he invaded Egypt in 1798.

Desroches-Noblescourt, Christiane. *Tutankhamen*. New York: New York Graphic Society, 1963. Probably the most popular book ever on Tutankhamen. The author is a senior Egyptologist with the wonderful ability to make the period come alive. The book contains quite a few speculations.

Devi, Savitri. *A Son of God*. London: Philosophical Publishing, 1946. An interesting discussion of Akhenaten's religion by a modern admirer, including letters from Aldous Huxley on the Amarna religion.

————. *Son of the Sun*. San Jose, CA: Rosicrucian Library, 1956. Expanded version of the title above.

Diodorus Siculus. *Library of History*. Book I, 46. Cambridge: Harvard University Press, 1968. Accounts of an ancient traveler to Egypt.

Dobson, Jessie. "A Curator's Curiosity." *Annals of the Royal College of Surgeons of England* (1959): 331–37. Discussion of an elongated skull found in Egypt that looks similar to the shape of the heads of Akhenaten's family.

Dodson, Aidan. *The Canopic Equipment of the Kings of Egypt*. London: Kegan Paul, 1994. Includes a detailed description of the broken sarcophagus and canopic chest of Akhenaten.

Bibliography

Drower, Margaret S. *Flinders Petrie, A Life In Archaeology.* London: Victor Gollancz Ltd., 1985. A colorful description of one of the pioneers of Egyptology.

Drury, Allen. *A God Against the Gods.* New York: Doubleday, 1976. Historically based novel about Akhenaten and Nefertiti.

———. *Return to Thebes.* New York: Doubleday, 1977. Sequel to the title above, this volume covers Tutankhamen's reign.

Eaton-Krauss, M. *The Sarcophagus in the Tomb of Tutankamen.* Oxford: Griffith Institute, 1993. Detailed and important study by a major Tutankhamen scholar. Shows the sarcophagus was altered at least once before Tutankhamen's burial.

———. *The Small Golden Shrine from the Tomb of Tutankhamen.* Oxford: Griffith Institute, 1985. Wonderfully detailed analyses of the scenes of Ankhesenamen and Tutankhamen on the miniature shrine.

Edwards, I. E. S. *The Treasures of Tutankhamen.* New York: Viking, 1972. Catalog that accompanied the traveling exhibition of treasures from Tutankhamen's tomb.

Edwards, I. E. S., et al., eds. *The Cambridge Ancient History.* Vol. 2. Parts 1–2. Cambridge: Cambridge University Press, 1973–1975. A monumental reference work, these volumes deal with the Amarna age.

Edwards, Margaret Dulles. *Child of the Son.* Boston: Beacon, 1939. A book for young adults with the monotheism of Akhenaten clearly explained.

Elerick, Daniel V., and Rose A. Tyson. *Human Paleopathology and Related Subjects.* San Diego: Museum of Man, 1997. Bibliography of thousands of books and articles on disease and trauma in the ancient world.

El-Khouly, Aly, and Geoffrey Thorndike Martin. *Excavations in the Royal Necropolis at El'Amarna 1984.* Cairo: Institut Français, 1987. Examination of two tombs in the side valley near Akhenaten's tomb. One may have been prepared for Tutankhamen when he first became king at Amarna.

El-Najjar, Mahmoud, and K. Richard McWilliams. *Anthropology.* Springfield: Charles C. Thomas, 1978. What bones can tell about a long-dead person.

Epigraphic Survey. *The Festival Procession of Opet in the Colonnade Hall.* Chicago: Oriental Institute of the University of Chicago, 1994. Complete publication of the hall decorated by Tutankhamen but later usurped by Horemheb.

Fairman, H. W. "Once Again the So-Called Coffin of Akhenaten." *Journal of Egyptian Archaeology* 47 (1961): 25–40. An attempt to determine the identity of the mummy in Tomb 55 by analyzing the inscriptions on the coffin.

Bibliography

Fazzini, Richard. *Tutankhamen and the African Heritage.* New York: Metropolitan Museum of Art, 1978. Booklet discussing Egypt's relationship to Nubia during the Eighteenth Dynasty.

Federn, Walter. "Dahamunzu (KBo V 6 iii 8)." *Journal of Cuneiform Studies* 14 (1960): 33. Explains the phrase used to refer to Ankhesenamen by the Hittites.

Forbes, Dennis. "A New Take on Tut's Parents." *KMT* 8, no. 3 (1997): 85–87. Raises possibility that Smenkare and Meritaten were Tutankhamen's parents.

Ford, John. *Tutankhamen's Treasures.* Secaucus, NJ: Chartwell, 1978. Mostly pictures.

Fox, Penelope. *Tutankhamen's Treasure.* London: Oxford University Press, 1951. Good discussion of objects found in tomb.

Frankfort, H. "Preliminary Report on the Excavations at El-'Amarnah, 1918–19." *Journal of Egyptian Archaeology* 15 (1929): 143–49. Early excavation of the northern suburbs of Amarna, with diagrams of the houses.

———. "Preliminary Report on the Excavations at Tel el Amarnah, 1926–1927." *Journal of Egyptian Archaeology* 13 (1927): 209–18. Some spectacular photographs of finds at the residence of Panhesy and the Aten temple.

Frankfort. H., ed. *The Mural Painting of El-'Amarnah.* London: The Egypt Exploration Society, 1929. Beautiful reproductions of the Amarna paintings.

Frankfort, H, and J. D. S. Pendlebury. *The City of Akhenaten.* Part 2. London: Egypt Exploration Society, 1933. This reports the excavation of the city's northern suburb and includes maps and diagrams of the houses, as well as photographs of the objects found.

Frayling, Christopher. *The Face of Tutankhamen.* London: Faber & Faber, 1992. Based on the BBC's five-part television series and includes interesting material on Tutmania.

Freud, Sigmund. *Moses and Monotheism.* New York: Vintage, 1955. Freud's theory that Moses got monotheism from Akhenaten. Highly speculative—Freud knew very little about Egyptology.

Gardiner, Alan. "The So-Called Tomb of Queen Tiye." *Journal of Egyptian Archaeology* 43 (1957): 10–25. The leading translator of his era analyzes the inscriptions on the coffin in Tomb 55 and concludes that the mummy is Smenkare.

Goetze, Albrecht. "Palace Prayers of Mursilis." In *Ancient Near Eastern Texts.* Edited by James B. Prichard. Princeton: Princeton University Press, 1955. Transla-

tions of ancient texts from all over the Near East, including some relating to
the aftermath of Tutankhamen's death.

Green, L. "A 'Lost Queen' of Ancient Egypt . . ." *KMT,* winter 1990–1991,
pp. 23–67. Informative article on Ankhesenamen by an expert on women of
the Amarna period.

———. "The Origins of the Giant Lyre and Asiatic Influences of the Cult of the
Aten." *The Society for the Study of Egyptian Antiquities Journal* 23 (1993):
56–62. Two musicians playing a giant lyre, depicted in the Amarna tomb carvings, were Asiatic musicians in Akhenaten's court.

Guterbock, Hans Gustav. "The Deeds of Suppiluliuma as Told to His Son, Mursili
II." *Journal of Cuneiform Studies* 10 (1965): 75–98. The definitive study of
Ankhesenamen's letter to the Hittite king.

Harris, James E., and Edward F. Wente, eds. *An X-ray Atlas of the Royal Mummies.*
Chicago: University of Chicago Press, 1980. An attempt at answering questions about family relationships among the royal mummies by X rays. Contains two X rays of Tutankhamen's skull.

Harris, James E., and Kent R. Weeks. *X-raying the Pharaohs.* New York: Scribner's,
1973. Pioneering study of what can be learned from X-raying mummies.

Harrison, R. G. "An Anatomical Examination of the Pharaonic Remains Purported
to Be Akhenaten." *Journal of Egyptian Archaeology* 224 (1969): 325–26.
Demonstrates that the blood groups of Tutankhamen and Smenkare are so
close that they may have been brothers.

———. "Post Mortem on Two Pharaohs." *Buried History* (1972): 18–25. This is
where Harrison says in print that Tutankhamen may have died from a blow to
the back of the head by a blunt instrument.

———. "Tutankhamen's Postmortem." *The Lancet,* February 3, 1972, p. 259.
The only expert to perform a modern examination of Tutankhamen's
mummy explains that there is no evidence for pathological conditions such as
Klinefelter's syndrome or Wilson's disease, as had been suggested by some
physicians.

Harrison, R. G., et al. "A Mummified Foetus from the Tomb of Tutankhamen."
Antiquity 53 (1979): 19–21. X ray of one of the two fetuses found in the tomb
revealed the little girl would have been deformed if she had lived.

Harrison, R. G., and A. B. Abdalla. "The Remains of Tutankhamen." *Antiquity* 46 (1972): 8–14. The most detailed publication of the examination of Tutankhamen's mummy, but it is merely a preliminary report.

Hayes, William C. *The Scepter of Egypt.* Vol. 2. New York: Metropolitan Museum of Art, 1959. Catalog of the Metropolitan Museum of Art's collection. Includes detailed descriptions of the objects used at the last meal eaten outside of Tutankhamen's tomb on the day of burial.

Hepper, Nigel F. *Pharaoh's Flowers.* London: HMSO, 1990. Detailed and fascinating analysis of the botanical specimens found in the tomb of Tutankhamen. Crucial work in determining the time of year in which Tutankhamen died.

Iscan, Mehmet Yasar. *Age Markers in the Human Skeleton.* Springfield: Charles C. Thomas, 1989. How physical anthropologists determine age at time of death from bones.

James, T. G. H. *Howard Carter, The Path to Tutankhamun.* London: Kegan Paul, 1992. The definitive biography of Carter.

Janssens, Paul A. *Paleopathology.* London: John Baker, 1970. An older but still useful work on diseases and injuries in the ancient world.

Johnson, William Raymond. *An Asiatic Battle Scene of Tutankhamen from Thebes.* Ann Arbor: UMI Dissertation Services, 1992. Doctoral dissertation by an expert on carved temple blocks. Blocks from Tutankhamen's mortuary temple show Tutankhamen in battle.

Jones, Dilwyn. *Model Boats from the Tomb of Tutankhamen.* Oxford: Griffith Institute, 1990. Brief discussion of model boats and sailing in ancient Egypt.

Kemp, Barry J. "The Window of Appearances At El-Amarna, and the Basic Structure of This City." *Journal of Egyptian Archaeology* 62 (1976): 81–99. The excavator gives an overview of the city of Amarna and discusses one detail—the balcony where the royal family appeared before the people.

Kemp, Barry J., et al. *Amarna Reports.* Vol. 1. London: Egypt Exploration Society, 1984. The author is the excavator of the site, and this work begins an important series of publications of his finds at Amarna.

———. *Amarna Reports.* Vol. 2. London: Egypt Exploration Society, 1985. Reports on the workmen's village at Amarna, with detailed scientific analyses of the textiles and botanical material found.

————. *Amarna Reports.* Vol. 3. London: Egypt Exploration Society, 1986. Reports on the workmen's village, pottery finds, and the alabaster quarries.

————. *Amarna Reports.* Vol. 4. London: Egypt Exploration Society, 1987. Excavations of the workmen's village and a discussion of pottery found at the main city.

————. *Amarna Reports.* Vol. 5. London: Egypt Exploration Society, 1989. Excavation of the main city, discussion of the pottery found, and an interesting discussion of grain and bread baking.

————. *Amarna Reports.* Vol. 6. London: Egypt Exploration Society, 1995. Reports on the excavation of a private house at Amarna and also the smaller temple of the Aten called "Mansion of the Aten."

Kemp, Barry J., and Salvatore Garfi. *A Survey of the Ancient City of El-'Amarna.* London: Egypt Exploration Society, 1993. Detailed maps and plans of the city where Tutankhamen was born.

KMT: Amarna Letters. Vols. 1–3. San Francisco: KMT, 1991–1994. Written by scholars for a popular audience, these three volumes provide a wealth of readable material on all aspects of the Amarna period.

KMT: A Modern Journal of Ancient Egypt, summer 1991. This special issue of the popular magazine on Egyptology is devoted to discussions of Akhenaten.

Kolos, Daniel, and Hany Assad. *The Name of the Dead.* Ontario: Benben, 1979. Hieroglyphic inscriptions and their translations from some of the objects in Tutankhamen's tomb. Intended for the beginning student in hieroglyphs, this book contains some errors, but still it is a good way to start.

Kozloff, Arielle, and Betsy M. Bryan. *Egypt's Dazzling Sun.* Cleveland: Cleveland Museum of Art, 1992. Exhibition catalog for major show on Amenhotep III, Tutankhamen's grandfather.

Leek, F. Filce. "How Old Was Tutankhamen?" *Journal of Egyptian Archaeology* 63 (1977): 112–15. Suggests that Tutankhamen may have been as young as sixteen at the time of death.

————. *The Human Remains from the Tomb of Tut'Ankhamen.* Oxford: Griffith Institute, 1972. Description of Tutankhamen's mummy and the two fetuses found in the tomb. Much good information, especially quotes from Carter's diary. Leek, however, was unable to locate the two fetuses and relies on an earlier examination. He relies primarily on Derry's examination of Tutankhamen's mummy in 1925 and hardly mentions later important work.

Leprohon, Ronald J. "A Vision Collapsed, Akhenaten's Reforms Viewed Through Decrees of Later Reigns." *Amarna Letters.* San Francisco: KMT, 1991. A textual analysis of the aftermath of Akhenaten's revolution.

Lesko, Leonard H. *King Tut's Wine Cellar.* Berkeley: BC Scribe, 1977. A delightful discussion by a distinguished Egyptologist who has made his own version of the wine found in Tutankhamen's tomb.

Lichtheim, Miriam. *Ancient Egyptian Literature.* Vol. 2. Berkeley: University of California Press, 1976. Translations of Egyptian literature that give insights into the ancient Egypt mind.

Littauer, M. B. and J. H. Crouwell. *Chariots and Related Equipment from the Tomb of Tutankhamen.* Oxford: Griffith Institute, 1985. This discussion of the six chariots found in Tutankhamen's tomb is so detailed that you could construct one from the diagrams.

Mace, Arthur C. "The Egyptian Expedition." *Bulletin of the Metropolitan Museum of Art,* 1922–1923.

MacQuitty, William. *Tutankhamen's Last Journey.* New York: Crown, 1978. Photographs used to discuss the death and burial of Tutankhamen.

McKusick, Victor A. "The Defect in Marfan Syndrome." *Nature* 352, July 25, 1991. Scientific discussion of Marfan's syndrome.

McLeod, W. *Composite Bows from the Tomb of Tut'Ankhamun.* Oxford: Griffith Institute, 1970. The archery equipment, including arrows, quivers, etc., found in the tomb.

———. *Self Bows and Other Archery Tackle from the Tomb of Tut'Ankhamen.* Oxford: Griffith Institute, 1982. The archery equipment, including arrows, quivers, etc., found in the tomb.

Majno, Guido. *The Healing Hand.* Cambridge: Harvard University Press, 1977. Fascinating discussion of ancient medicine.

Manniche, Lise. *Musical Instruments from the Tomb of Tut'Ankhamen.* Oxford: Griffith Institute, 1976. Brief description of clappers, sistra, and trumpets from the tomb.

Martin, Geoffrey Thorndike. *A Bibliography of the Amarna Period and Its Aftermath.* London: Kegan Paul, 1991. An indispensable reference listing most articles and books on the subject.

———. "Excavations at the Memphite Tomb of Horemheb." *Journal of Egyptian Archaeology* 62–65 (1975–1979). This series of excavation reports presents each year's findings at the tomb of Tutankhamen's general.

———. *The Hidden Tombs of Memphis.* London: Thames & Hudson, 1991. Contains description of General Horemheb's tomb at Memphis and that of Maya, Tutankhamen's treasurer. Important information on the men surrounding the boy-king.

———. *The Royal Tomb at El Amarna.* Vol. 1. London: Egypt Exploration Society, 1974. Description of the objects and fragments found in Akhenaten's tomb in the remote valley outside Amarna.

———. *The Royal Tomb at El Amarna.* Vol. 2. London: Egypt Exploration Society, 1989. Detailed description of Akhenaten's tomb, including architecture and wall carvings. Martin suggests that one scene shows the birth of Tutankhamen.

———. "The Tomb of Horemheb, Commander in Chief of Tutankhamen." *Archaeology* 31 (1978): 14–23. Popular account of the tomb.

Meltzer, Edmund S. "The Parentage of Tut'Ankhamen and Smenkhkare." *Journal of Egyptian Archaeology* 64 (1978): 174–75. Explains why Akhenaten could be the father of Tutankhamen.

Mercer, Samuel A. B. *The Tell El-Amarna Tablets.* Toronto: Macmillan, 1939. Compilation, translation, and brief discussion of the *Amarna Letters.*

Merezhkovsky, Dmitri. *Akhenaton.* New York: E. P. Dutton, 1927. Early novel translated from the Russian. *Very* dated.

Montague, Jeremy. "One of Tutankhamen's Trumpets." *Journal of Egyptian Archaeology* 64 (1978): 133–34. Describes construction and use of the bronze trumpet from Tutankhamen's tomb. The silver trumpet shattered when it was played on a BBC radio broadcast in 1939.

Moodie, Roy L. *Roentgenologic Studies of Egyptian and Peruvian Mummies.* Chicago: Field Museum of Natural History, 1931. The pioneering study on the use of X rays to study mummies.

Moran, William L. *The Amarna Letters.* Baltimore: Johns Hopkins, 1982. The most recent and authoritative translation of the *Amarna Letters.*

Muller, Hans Wolfgang, et al. *Nofretete. Echnaton.* Berlin: Ägyptisches Museum, 1976. Exhibition catalog of objects from the Amarna period. Photographs of many objects not usually seen.

Murnane, William J., and Charles C. Van Siclen III. *The Boundary Stelae of Akhenaten.* London: Kegan Paul, 1993. The definitive work on the subject.

Murray, Helen, and Mary Nuttall. *A Handlist to Howard Carter's Catalogue of Objects in Tut'Ankhamen's Tomb.* Oxford: Griffith Institute, 1963. A key reference work. Carter described each item in the tomb on index cards. The cards were left to the Griffith Institute, and this work is the index for these notes.

Nahas, Bishara. *The Life and Times of Tut-Ankh-Amen.* New York: American Library Service, 1923. One of the first popular books written after the tomb's discovery. Dated and containing much from the author's imagination rather than from history.

Newberry, Percy E. "Akhenaten's Eldest Son-in-Law, 'Ankhkheprure." *Journal of Egyptian Archaeology* 14 (1928): 3–9. An early discussion of Smenkare.

———. "King Ay, The Successor of Tut'Ankhamen." *Journal of Egyptian Archaeology* 18 (1932): 50–52. First publication of the ring that indicates Aye married Tutankhamen's widow.

———. *Scarab-shaped Seals.* London: Constable, 1907. A basic study on Egyptian scarab amulets.

Paulshock, Bernadine Z. "Tutankhamen and His Brothers." *Journal of the American Medical Association* 244, no. 2 (1980): 160–64. A physician suggests that the statues of Tutankhamen with breasts indicate that he and members of his family may have had gynecomastia—feminizing of the male body.

Peet, T. Eric, and C. Leonard Wooley. *The City of Akhenaten.* Part 1. London: Egypt Exploration Society, 1923. Important detailed excavation report of the city of Amarna. Many photographs of walls now gone and of objects found at Amarna.

Pendlebury, J. D. S. *The City of Akhenaten.* Part 3. London: Egypt Exploration Society, 1951. This volume describes the central city of Amarna, including the palace, police barracks, and records office.

Petrie, William Flinders. *Seventy Years of Archaeology.* New York: Holt, 1932. Fascinating memoirs of the founder of modern Egyptology, including much on his excavations at Amarna.

—. Tel el Amarna. 1894. Reprint. London: Aris & Phillips, 1974. Account of Petrie's excavations at Amarna.

Phillips the Egyptian. *Tutankhamen's Victims in America.* Los Angeles: Egyptian Antiques, 1977. Wild and inaccurate, this book ends with several pages of reproductions for sale.

Piankoff, Alexandre. *The Shrines of Tut-Ankh-Amon.* New York: Harper, 1962. A discussion of the shrines that enclosed the sarcophagus, coffins, and mummy of Tutankhamen. A thorough and important analysis of their religious texts.

Pococke, Richard. *A Description of the East.* Vol. 1. London: W. Boyer, 1843. One of the early travel accounts, this book includes the first map of the Valley of the Kings.

Pyeritz, Reed E., and Cheryll Gasner. *The Marfan Syndrome.* Port Washington, NY: National Marfan Foundation, 1994. Publication explaining the genetic defect called Marfan's syndrome.

Reeves, C. N. *After Tut'Ankhamen.* London: Kegan Paul, 1992. Collection of research papers on the Valley of the Kings after the discovery of Tutankhamen's tomb.

—. *The Complete Tutankhamen.* London: Thames & Hudson, 1990. An indispensable reference work on all aspects of Tutankhamen, including his life, excavators, and objects in the tomb. Many photos and diagrams.

—. "A Reappraisal of Tomb 55 in the Valley of the Kings." *Journal of Egyptian Archaeology* 67 (1981): 48–55. An attempt to determine the identity of the mummy in Tomb 55. Suggests mummy may have been switched after it was sent to Cairo.

Reeves, C. N., and John H. Taylor. *Howard Carter Before Tutankhamen.* London: British Museum, 1992. Catalog of an exhibition about the life of Howard Carter before he discovered Tutankhamen's tomb. Wonderful illustrations.

Redford, Donald. *The Akhenaten Temple Project.* Vol. 3. Toronto: University of Toronto, 1994. Description of the pottery fragments found during excavations of Akhenaten's temples at east Karnak.

———. *Akhenaten, The Heretic King.* Princeton: Princeton University Press, 1984. Important work by the excavator of Akhenaten's temples at Karnak. As Redford's excavations continued, he grew to dislike Akhenaten more and more.

———. "Some Observations on 'Amarna Chronology.'" *Journal of Egyptian Archaeology* 45 (1959): 34–37. The excavator of Akhenaten's temples at Karnak discusses the confusing evidence regarding Akhenaten's reign.

Redford, Donald, et al. *The Akhenaten Temple Project.* Vol. 2. Toronto: University of Toronto, 1988. An important work by the excavator of Akhenaten's temples at Karnak; focuses on inscriptions and scenes relating to foreigners.

Redford, Susan and Donald. *The Akhenaten Temple Project.* Vol. 4. Toronto: University of Toronto, 1994. The tomb of a royal herald just before Akhenaten became king.

Riefstahl, Elizabeth. *Thebes in the Time of Amenhotep III.* Norman, OK: University of Oklahoma Press, 1964. Overview of the city of Thebes and all its glory during Amenhotep III's reign.

Robbins, G. "The Representation of Sexual Characteristics in Amarna Art." *The Society for Study of Egyptian Antiquities Journal* 23 (1993): 29–41. A discussion of the nude colossal statue of Akhenaten with no genitalia, suggesting that the feminizing of the statue indicates fecundity.

Romer, John. *Valley of the Kings.* New York: William Morrow, 1981. A lively account of the travelers and scholars who visited and worked in the Valley of the Kings, and their discoveries.

Romer, John and Elizabeth. *The Rape of Tutankhamen.* London: O'Mara, 1993. A somewhat slanted discussion of the condition of Tutankhamen's tomb and others in the Valley of the Kings.

Ruffer, Marc Armand. "Note on the Histology of Egyptian Mummies." *British Medical Journal* 1 (1909): 1005–6. An early work on soft tissues of mummies.

———. "Note on Two Egyptian Mummies Dating from the Persian Occupation of Egypt." In *Studies in the Paleopathology of Egypt.* Chicago: University of Chicago Press, 1921. pp. 127–38. A study showing just how careless ancient embalmers could be.

Saad, Ramadan, and Lise Manniche. "A Unique Offering List of Amenophis IV Recently Found at Karnak." *Journal of Egyptian Archaeology* 57 (1971): 70–72. A discussion of a block from one of Akhenaten's temples listing offerings he gave to the temple. A good example of the small clues that help Egyptologists piece together the big picture.

Sampson, Julia. "Amarna Crowns and Wigs." *Journal of Egyptian Archaeology* 59 (1973): 47–59. An example of how art historians examine stylistic details to identify and date Egyptian art.

Sandford, Mary K. *Investigations of Ancient Human Tissue.* Langhorne, PA: Gordon and Breach, 1993. Technical articles on chemical analyses of bone and tissue.

Sandnass, Karin L. "Dietary Analysis of Prehistoric Lower and Middle Osmore Drainage Populations of Southern Peru Using Stable Isotopes [Delta C-13 and Delta N-15]." Paper presented at the Second World Congress on Mummy Studies, February 6–10, 1995, Cartagena, Colombia. Discussion of state-of-the-art technology used to gain information from examination of mummies.

Sayce, A. H. "The Hittite Correspondence with Tut-Ankh-Amon's Widow." *Ancient Egypt,* part 2 (1927): 33–35. Translations of the Hittite response to Ankhesenamen's letter to the Hittite king.

———. "Texts from the Hittite Capital Relating to Egypt." *Ancient Egypt,* part 3 (1922): 65–70. Early publication of Ankhesenamen's letter to the Hittite king.

———. "What Happened After the Death of Tut'Ankhamen." *Journal of Egyptian Archaeology* 12 (1926): 168–70. Supplies a previously missing part of the Hittite response to Ankhesenamen's request to the Hittite king.

Schaden, Otto John. "Clearance of the Tomb of King Aye." *Journal of the American Research Center in Egypt* 21 (1984). The only excavation report on King Aye's tomb in the Valley of the Kings.

———. *The God's Father Ay.* Ann Arbor: UMI Dissertation Services, 1977. Doctoral dissertation on Ay, with much good material on his two tombs.

Severence, Catherine Needham. *The Last Day of Ikhnaton.* New York: Exposition Press, 1953. A romantic novel.

Shulman, Alan R. "Ankhesenamen, Nofretity, and the Amka Affair." *Journal of the American Research Center in Egypt* 15 (1978): 43–48. Discussion of Ankhesenamen's plea to the Hittite king, and the response.

Silverberg, Robert. *Akhenaten the Rebel Pharaoh.* New York: Chilton, 1964. A popular work on the life of Akhenaten.

Smith, G. Elliot. *The Royal Mummies.* Cairo: Institut Français, 1912. Catalog of the royal mummies in the Egyptian museum in Cairo. Contains an early description of the mummy from Tomb 55 that suggests it is Akhenaten.

———. *Tutankhamen.* London: Rutledge, 1923. One of the first books on the discovery of Tutankhamen's tomb. Mainly a historical curio.

Smith, Ray Winfield. "Computers Help Scholars Re-create an Egyptian Temple." *National Geographic* 139, no. 5, November 1970. Early use of a computer to reconstruct on paper Akhenaten's temples at Karnak.

Smith, Ray Winfield, and Donald Redford. *The Akhenaten Temple Project.* Warminster, England: Aris & Phillips, 1976. Detailed description of the project to reassemble on paper Akhenaten's temples at Karnak. Many important details.

Smith, Sir Sidney. *Mostly Murder.* New York: McKay, 1959. Fascinating autobiography of a famous professor of forensic medicine who applied his skills in Egypt to solve murders.

Strunsky, Simon. *King Akhenaten.* New York: Longmans, Green & Co., 1928. Early fiction stimulated by the discovery of Tutankhamen's tomb. *Very* dated.

Swales, J. D. "Tutankhamen's Breasts." *The Lancet,* January 27, 1973, p. 201. Physician's response to the suggestion that Tutankhamen's statues with breasts indicated a pathological condition.

Tabouis, G. R. *The Private Life of Tutankhamen.* New York: McBride, 1929. Description of daily life during the reign of Tutankhamen. Dated.

Tait, W. J. *Game Boxes and Accessories from the Tomb of Tut'Ankhamen.* Oxford: Griffith Institute, 1982. Excellent descriptions and discussion of the board games that Tutankhamen and Ankhesenamen played.

Taitz, L. S. "Tutankhamen's Breasts." *The Lancet,* January 20, 1973, p. 149. A physician suggests Tutankhamen's depiction with breasts is an artistic holdover from Akhenaten's reign.

Thomas, Elizabeth. "The Plan of Tomb 55 in the Valley of the Kings." *Journal of Egyptian Archaeology* 47 (1961): 24. Fifty years after the discovery of Tomb 55, there still was no published plan of the tomb. This one-page diagram is the first.

Tobin, V. A. "Akhenaten as a Tragedy of History: A Critique of the Amarna Period." *The Society for the Study of Egyptian Antiquities Journal* 23 (1993): 5–28. Discussion of the legacy of Akhenaten, with somewhat negative conclusions.

Ubelaker, Douglas, and Henry Scammell. *Bones: A Forensic Detective's Casebook.* New York: HarperCollins, 1992. A readable account of how physical anthropologists determine the cause of death from bones.

Vandenberg, Philip. *The Curse of the Pharaohs.* Philadelphia: Lippincott, 1975. Pure nonsense.

Van Den Bourn, G. P. F. *The Duties of the Vizier.* London: Kegan Paul, 1988. Gives an idea of the power held by Aye, Tutankhamen's vizier.

Velikovsky, Immanuel. *Oedipus and Akhenaten.* New York: Doubleday, 1960. A highly eccentric work that draws parallels between Akhenaten and the Greek king Oedipus. Fascinating reading, to be taken with a grain of salt.

Vergote, J. *Toutankhamon dans les Archives Hittites.* Istanbul: Nederlands Historisch-Archaeologisch Instituut, 1961. Discussion of Ankhesenamen's request for a Hittite prince to marry.

Walker, James H. *Studies in Ancient Egyptian Anatomical Terminology.* Warminster: Aris and Phillips, 1996. The latest word on the subject by a physician-Egyptologist.

Walshe, J. M. "Tutankhamen: Klinefelter's or Wilson's?" *The Lancet,* January 13, 1973, pp. 109–10. Physician's theory on why Tutankhamen's statues show him with breasts and sagging abdomen.

Watkins, Trevor. "The Beginning of Warfare in the Ancient World." In *Warfare in the Ancient World.* Edited by Sir John Hackett. New York: Facts on File, 1989, pp. 15–19. Discussion of warfare in ancient Egypt.

Weeks, Kent Ried. *The Anatomical Knowledge of the Ancient Egyptians and the Representation of the Human Figure in Egyptian Art.* Ann Arbor: UMI Dissertation Information Service, 1970.

Weigall, Arthur. "The Mummy of Akhenaten." *Journal of Egyptian Archaeology* 8 (1922): 193–200. Weigall's claim that the mummy in Tomb 55 was that of Tutankhamen's father.

———. *Tutankhamen and Other Essays.* New York: Doran, 1924. Weigall was Inspector-General of Antiquities when Tutankhamen's tomb was discovered, and his writings are full of interesting perspectives, but his imagination sometimes leads him astray.

Weller, Malcolm. "Tutankhamen: An Adrenal Tumor?" *The Lancet,* December 16, 1972, p. 1312. A physician suggests an adrenal tumor may have caused breast development in Tutankhamen.

Bibliography

Wells, Calvin. *Bones, Bodies and Disease.* New York: Praeger, 1964. Dated, but still a classic in the history of paleopathology by a master.

Wells, Evelyn. *Nefertiti.* London: Hale, 1964. A romanticizing and often inaccurate account of the Amarna period and Nefertiti.

Welsh, Frances. *Tutankhamen's Egypt.* Princes Risborough, England: Shire, 1993. A brief and useful discussion of the life and times of Tutankhamen and the objects found in his tomb.

Wente, Edward, et al. *Treasures of Tutankhamen.* New York: Metropolitan Museum of Art, 1976. Catalog to accompany the exhibition of Tutankhamen's treasures that toured the world.

Wilkinson, Gardiner. *Modern Egypt and Thebes.* Vol. 2. London: John Murray, 1843. One of the first guidebooks to Egypt; gives early impression of Amarna.

Winlock, H. E. *Materials Used at the Embalming of King Tut-'Ankh-Amun.* New York: Metropolitan Museum of Art, 1941. Not only embalming materials, but also remains of the ritual meal eaten outside the tomb on the day of burial.

Winstone, H. V. F. *Howard Carter and the Discovery of Tutankhamun.* London: Constable, 1991. Solid biography of Carter.

Wise, William. *The Two Reigns of Tutankhamen.* New York: Putnam, 1964. In addition to discussing Tutankhamen's reign at Amarna and Thebes, it includes a brief history of Egypt up to the time of Tutankhamen.

Wynne, Barry. *Behold the Mask of Tutankhamen.* New York: Taplinger, 1972. Not just another popular account, this book has interesting material not found elsewhere, especially on the possibility that Carter and Carnarvon entered the burial chamber before the official opening.

Yadin, Yigal. *The Art of Warfare in Biblical Lands.* Vol. 1. New York: McGraw-Hill, 1963. Overview of warfare in the ancient Middle East.

Index